Movie Stunts & Special Effects

Movie Stunts & Special Effects

A Comprehensive Guide to Planning and Execution

ANDREW LANE

Bloomsbury Academic
An imprint of Bloomsbury Publishing Inc

B L O O M S B U R Y
NEW YORK · LONDON · NEW DELHI · SYDNEY

Bloomsbury Academic
An imprint of Bloomsbury Publishing Inc

1385 Broadway	50 Bedford Square
New York	London
NY 10018	WC1B 3DP
USA	UK

www.bloomsbury.com

BLOOMSBURY and the Diana logo are trademarks of Bloomsbury Publishing Plc

First published 2015

Library of Congress Cataloging-in-Publication Data
Lane, Andrew, 1951-
Movie stunts & special effects : a comprehensive guide to
planning and execution / Andrew Lane.
pages cm
Includes index.
ISBN 978-1-62356-307-3 (hardback : alk. paper) –
ISBN 978-1-62356-366-0 (pbk. : alk. paper) 1. Stunt performers.
2. Stunt performers–Vocational guidance. 3. Cinematography–Special effects.
I. Title. II. Title: Movie stunts and special effects.
PN1995.9.S7L36 2014
791.4302'8–dc23
2014023603

ISBN: HB: 978-1-6235-6307-3
PB: 978-1-6235-6366-0
ePub: 978-1-6235-6274-8
ePDF: 978-1-6235-6176-5

Typeset by Integra Software Services Pvt. Ltd.
Printed and bound in the United States of America

Contents

Acknowledgments

I have a number of people to thank for helping me through this process. Thanks to Barbara Doyle for suggesting I write this book. Thanks to Gayle and Buddy Joe Hooker for their tireless enthusiasm, support, and generosity in sharing their knowledge and vast network of professional and personal relationships to meet and learn from. Thanks to Katie Gallof for seeing the usefulness of a book on this topic and her warm support and guidance through the process. Thanks to all my friends and colleagues at Chapman University and Dodge College of Film and Media Arts for their support and encouragement in ways both large and small, especially David Ward, John Badham, and Paul Seydor, who have been not only an inspiration to me, but endlessly supportive. Thanks to Wayne Crawford with whom I shared many of the adventures that found their way into this book. To everyone I interviewed, who are all busy professionals who took the time to share their knowledge and experience simply because they love what they do and want to share their passion, I say thank you from the bottom of my heart.

Preface

A getaway driver, with guns blazing, eludes a hot pursuit in rush hour traffic.... A daring secret agent scales the world's tallest building to stop a madman's catastrophic attack ... With nothing to defend himself and his wife but his fists, an unassuming English professor battles an overwhelming force of nunchaku-wielding, ninja assailants.

Movies excite our imagination. They make it possible to experience life not only as we know and live it, but also as we *dream* it. When we enter into a world that is revealed to us in a movie theater, on television, or a personal device, anything is possible.

Throughout film history, one of the fundamental fantasies portrayed on screen has been the kind of physical action few of us could ever experience in real life. The image of an "everyman" engaged in hand-to-hand, mortal combat, defending his family or even the world population against an overwhelming and malevolent force, speaks to our most primal instincts and has thus become a mainstay of movie entertainment.

In order to translate these deep-seated fantasies to the screen, filmmakers have developed special skills and crafts for over 100 years. Stunts and special effects are two main categories of "movie magic," which have allowed audiences to take part in the primal hopes and fears we all possess. This book will advise, instruct, and inspire filmmakers and visual storytellers of all sorts, to conceive, plan, and employ those who execute stunts and special effects.

The component of the filmmaking process that uses stunts and special effects is as common as it is mysterious to most filmmakers. This is easily one of the most broadly applied crafts in the industry, yet is profoundly unfamiliar to most.

With few exceptions, anyone making or hoping to make a movie should read this book!

- Professional filmmakers
- Film production students of all levels of skill and development

- Anyone planning to shoot a movie or raise the funds to make a movie, as stunts and special effects will most likely impact the budget

- Anyone responsible for the safety of the cast and crew

Movie Stunts & Special Effects is designed to inform you as to how to plan for and utilize these crafts. It will engage and empower you to better communicate with stunt and special effects practitioners, and thereby enable them to more fully realize their vision. Here's why that is so important.

Factors such as cost, time to implement, safety accommodations, and assessing the competence of those employed to plan and execute stunts and special effects are numerous and very specific. When stunts and special effects are not done well or go awry, the loss of time and money can cripple a production. If the production is not properly prepared, the potential for severe injury or even death is present as well. This book will serve to help you, the director, producer, assistant director, or cinematographer and the filmmaking generalist, to prevent those extreme consequences from occurring and to bring your story to life on the screen as you imagine it.

Stunts and special effects are tools as valuable as lenses, cameras, cranes, and remote heads. While numerous books have been published explaining camera equipment and technique, *Movie Stunts & Special Effects* will describe and illustrate the evolution of stunts and special effects through the entire process of producing stories for the screen, so that you will be well prepared to recreate *life as we dream it.*

What Is a Stunt?

We sort of specialize in creating the illusion of painful events.

DAN BRADLEY, STUNT COORDINATOR AND SECOND UNIT DIRECTOR

A stunt is a physical action described in a script that must be performed by a person other than the actor required by the story, to dramatize that moment. That moment often is the point in a story where words and rational actions no longer suffice. Something bigger must move the story forward; some kind of heightened action or energy must be applied to the situation. A trained performer and sometimes the principal cast member will be called upon to perform a dangerous or risky action. The reason another person is usually called upon to perform the action or stunt, instead of the principal actor, is for considerations of safety and skill. To actually be able to physically, safely, and repeatedly enact the potentially injury-causing action described in the script is a skill most actors do not have.

> BUDDY JOE HOOKER: *Any kind of movement or anything that would be slightly unsafe or an area where you would need somebody with a stunt expertise to either explain how to do it to the actors or teach them or just be on the set when they're doing these things has now become a stunt. The reason being is the safety, of course. The only way that safety came about was due to issues of liability. People started getting hurt. Producers had actors that couldn't work for several weeks because they had a broken nose or worse.*
> DAN BRADLEY: *It takes a great deal of training to accomplish not hurting yourself.*

A fall, a fight, a demonstration of precision driving, enduring being roasted alive, all require training and skill to "sell" an action moment dramatically and sell it safely. The audience must believe what they just witnessed on-screen happened, *really* happened. They must not be aware that if that action were to be closely examined, it might reveal that another, specially trained performer replaced the original one, that it did not take place where you believed it to take place, that the action was accomplished with the help of mechanical devices just out of view from the camera or erased from view by means of computer technology, or that an abundance of safety-related equipment is being employed, also eliminated from the view of the audience.

The concept behind the successful stunt is to create the "illusion" that something exciting just happened. Stunts are not about engaging in the actual physical event hoping to rely on training and skill to avoid injury. That would be foolhardy. The skills developed and performed in stunts are aimed toward making an action appear to be real. In most cases, if a stunt performer were to actually experience what the story is suggesting, serious injury or death would be the inevitable consequence, such as a high fall. Sometimes, stunt performers do actually reenact what the script suggests and, due to their training and fitness, will escape injury. Car crashes are an example.

> DAN BRADLEY: *It's the things that if you saw in your real life, you'd be calling 911. If you want that in front of your camera, call the stunt guy.*

Every employee has an obligation to maintain safety standards and protocols. Whether you work in an office environment, a factory, or a restaurant, there are safety protocols that must be followed. The motion picture, television, and related production industry has more than its share of safety challenges. Anyone can be injured: a stunt performer, an actor, an electrician, a camera assistant, a background talent, or a lady walking her dog next to your set who trips over an electrical cable. This means it's everyone's obligation to be vigilant in their workplace for potential danger and diligent in the performance of their job in the safest possible manner.

> MARTIN CAMPBELL: *It's often the smallest things that go wrong. On Casino Royale, when the panic of that opening sequence starts in that swimming pool and then they start running through the jungle. I had shot a stuntman chasing Bond through the heavy undergrowth. When we cut, his pinky finger was at a right angle. He hit a tree or something.*

Every workplace has potential safety risks. Dry cleaners, doctor's offices, restaurants, schools…every workplace can pose a danger, and there are federal, state, and municipal laws and regulations that require employers to take reasonable steps to make the workplace a safe environment for their employees. When discussing the demands of stunts and special effects such as pyrotechnics or atmospheric effects, the issue of safety is heightened. Because the execution of these techniques has a higher level of risk, in some cases very high risk, safety is front and center on everyone's mind connected with a stunt or special effect. It is priority number one. How good the crash is or how high the explosion is not even close, in terms of importance.

> BUDDY JOE HOOKER: *One of the big components to stunt work is safety and that's where your stunt coordinator comes in. Anytime there's any kind of action whatsoever on a film, producers...stunt performers are required. It's in the stunt portion of the Screen Actors Guild contract, that if you have stunt people working, you have to have a stunt coordinator on the set. So what that does is, it's helped producers out a lot. It helps actors out. It helps us out, because there's a lot less accidents. You get a much better product. It's golden.*

The idea is to eliminate the possibility of injury by deconstructing and recreating a physical action or series of actions that will give the audience no reason to suspect that what they are watching on-screen didn't happen exactly the way it would in real life. This is the suspension of disbelief that moviemaking relies on to draw an audience into the world storytellers have created and to make them accept its reality. While showing an action in all its naked glory may (or may not) prove very impactful, even the most modest of violent actions can cause major problems and delays on a shooting day.

> DALE GIBSON: *I was on a low-budget show where one character had to slap another one. The actress wanted to really slap the actor and he was good with that. They wanted to go for realism. I said you can't really do that because after a few takes, his face will be all red and he won't be able to continue shooting. I knew this was easy to avoid. I walked away for a few seconds. I came back just in time to see the actress slap the actor to see how it would work. His face had a huge red welt on it.*

By carefully designing shots or series of shots that, when cut together, create an illusion of dangerous action, very clever people can make us think we saw something that we in fact did not see. We think we saw a character fall five stories onto a car below, crushing the roof on impact, killing the character. In fact, we may have only seen the man begin to fall over the building's edge, soar in mid-flight, crash onto a car roof, and then bounce off onto the pavement. The filmmakers are relying on the human mind and the way it thinks, to fill in gaps in what it actually saw, by linking the event they are witnessing to the way they believe it would be happening in real life. With that strategy in mind, what we may have actually and specifically seen was only an actor move toward the edge of the roof, fall off what "appears" to be the rooftop, flail away in a midair free fall, crash on top of a car, causing the roof to appear to sag under the weight of his falling body, and then, finally, ... land on the sidewalk in a heap.

The roof edge may have been a recreation of a small section of the roof that is positioned only a safe ten or fifteen feet above the ground or enough height that the actor can vertically pass through the bottom of the frame (and land on a safety pad). This method would suggest to the audience the height of the real five-story location they have seen in previous "establishing" shots. The fall through midair can also be a safe ten to twenty feet in height, just enough for the actor to enter the frame from the top and exit the frame from the bottom (with nothing but clear sky in the background), once again relying on the mind's eye to place that moment of action in the context of the real five-story location. Then we will see the stunt actor fall onto a car roof that has been previously weakened structurally to allow a man falling just a very few feet, to collapse the roof as we imagine would actually happen if the character had fallen five stories.

So a combination of camera and editorial techniques can create a visceral, if not totally realistic, impression on-screen, that a character has fallen five stories to a terrifying and certain death. An interesting and important question someone may ask is, "who figures that stuff out?" Is it the director, the stunt coordinator, the cinematographer, the editor, ... or the actor? The answer is, there is no single answer. The collaboration between directors and their key creative team is defined by the strengths, interests, and the level of experience of each of the key creative talents on a production. But make no mistake about it. It is a collaboration.

There is no set list of qualifications for a director. And what qualifications do exist, exist on a relative scale. How good a storyteller is the director? That's a tough one to quantify. Various directors exhibit strengths and talents in at least a few important areas necessary to direct a movie. They may have a superior sense of story and pacing. Others may have a great visual sense but lack clear narrative abilities, but they make you *feel* the story, if not explain it coherently. Some directors are known for their character-based storytelling and others for their action-driven stories. A few possess both talents.

Certain directors have a knack for creating exciting action scenes. They know what the components are, how to capture them in the camera, and then piece them together. For the many directors who don't claim that innate ability, they need the stunt coordinator to shore up that area of expertise critical to telling the story through action. They may not think in terms of what a required action scene should actually look like. They may not understand their options: what is possible for their resources or what the limits of the people and machines at their disposal are. Even experienced directors may not be aware of the limitations of their resources.

> JOHN BADHAM: *The director might say, "You can do that? We can do that with these people?" "Oh, absolutely," says the stuntman. In the film I did about skydiving called* Drop Zone, *the lead actor, Wesley Snipes, is taken up in a little single-engine plane by a woman who runs a Drop Zone and he insults and demeans her two or three times and she's had enough of it. She pulls a lever which opens a trap door right below him and drops him out into space and he's got no parachute at all! She lets him fall for a little bit and then she leaps out of the plane after him to catch him. She's going to ride him all the way down. That's what's in the script. I get my stunt coordinator for skydiving in, who is a world champion skydiver, and he says, "Well, I'll tell you what will happen. She's going to go down after him and at the last second, she's going to grab him with her legs. She's going to scissor her legs around his body and hang on to him." And I said, "You can do that?" I thought he was kidding. He said, "Oh, absolutely." I said, "We're not talking about CGI? We're talking about real human beings thousands of feet off the ground?" He said, "Oh, yeah, real human beings. We'll have a skydiving double for Wesley Snipes and my wife will double for the co-star, Yancy Butler. No problem." And they demonstrated for me on the carpet of my office, which is a little different than 10,000 feet up in the air, and that's what we have on film. It was an exciting scene. What a wonderful thing to have happened. Your good storytellers whether they're editors or production designers or assistant directors can be an enormous help to directors if you'll just be open to it and not let anybody feel like they're going to get yelled at for saying an idea, even though the idea might be unbelievably stupid. You never treat it that way. You accept ideas, evaluate them, and use the good ones and ignore the poor ones.*

The director's creative talents may not lie in imagining an action event at all. To them, the right thing for a character to say or do at the right moment may be their forte, but not whether a fast-driving car sequence should include a near miss or a crash and whether the camera should be placed inside the car or shot from a helicopter.

> DAN BRADLEY: *A coordinator might've had one relationship with a previous director he worked for and a very different relationship or responsibilities with the next. He was more responsible for the*

storytelling of the action beats because the first director didn't feel confident to tell the story through action. When you're working with Steven Spielberg, you do what he tells you. You find ways to make what he's asked you exciting; you bring your more mechanical aspects of your expertise to the scene. But he's very involved with the specific storytelling. Sometimes, you work for people and they want you to create all of it. Sometimes, it's up to you, because that's the way you and the director have agreed it will best serve the story. So, it's really how the director and stunt guys want to work together.

To be clear, most stunt coordinators would prefer to work with directors who know what they want and are clear in their storytelling goals. But that isn't required by any means. It can certainly enhance action storytelling when you have experts collaborating, not only combining their expertise and creativity, but actually elevating it through their collaboration. When you have people on your team who are good at what they do, know their strengths and stretches, and pursue their responsibilities accordingly by deferring to others who may have more experience or a better idea, *that* is ideal. But the director has the prerogative to determine the dynamic between them and anyone else on the team including the stunt coordinator. This is an area that can distinguish a director. Knowing how best to utilize your resources, both human and otherwise, is a valuable attribute that pays real dividends in the form of a better movie. This dynamic is not unlike that valued in other businesses or activities. Teamwork, knowing how to use the very best team members have to offer, can be an innate gift. But I can tell you, it can certainly be learned as one gathers experience in their field. A touch of courage, even fearlessness, helps as well, as long as it's tempered by *some* common sense. You have to be willing to do the impossible.

ROY WAGNER: *To make the most of what you have, I think being able to think outside the box is important. To have some sense of what is possible, what is the right way to do it, and be able to incorporate that knowledge into what you know you have as far as the budget and time constraints go. Not having fear of failure. And knowing what is possible. And chutzpah is what carried me through many of the early times. Even to this day, I think knowing what is possible and not taking no for an answer.*

A director with no experience and or talent for designing stunts could very well say to the stunt coordinator, "I'll design the stunts. I'll decide where to put the camera and what the coverage will be, you just hire the guys, rent the 'whatever' and make it happen." In feature filmmaking, a director can conceivably operate that way. In episodic television, where the writer-producer is the ultimate authority, not so much. Directors in that form of television production are almost always experienced, because the short shooting schedules pretty much require that a director be able to make creative and technically correct choices as a condition of employment. When that happens, and I don't think it happens very often, that approach is often adjusted by an experienced and sensible producer who has the best interests of the movie in mind. In that circumstance, the producer will explain to the director why it's in *their* best interest to allow others to help, that it doesn't have to be all up to them to make every decision or invent every moment on-screen. This is a collaborative industry, by necessity. Embrace it or risk not fully realizing your vision or, worse, disaster.

Another common limitation some directors possess is, by virtue of their inexperience, they may not fully understand or appreciate their role and the roles of others on their team. Not everyone knows intimately all the moving parts of a movie production. This is where the good producer comes in to shepherd the less experienced director. The producer should edify the unschooled director in such a way as the director still maintains their authority, hands firmly on the helm. The producer should be the teacher, the guide, the mentor, and of course a creative partner. These are truly critically important roles to fulfill. In the world of stunts and special effects, an area so unfamiliar to most, the producer with experience in these areas is vital. If the producer doesn't possess that experience and knowledge, it really behooves the production to recruit someone who does. Find the producer with action credits, make them an executive producer, or offer them a shared "Produced By" credit in return for their consultation or assistance in guiding the production through the veritable minefield that a stunt- or special effects-heavy movie represents. If you can't afford to compensate them with a fee, talk them into some role that they will perform for no money. Offer them a percentage of profits with the same definition of profits as all other principal equity holders in the production have. Any help can make a real and positive impact on your final product. Moviemaking is deal-making. Promise all you possibly can to anyone who will bring expertise and experience to your movie. When you're dealing with stunts, that expertise will not only make a difference in smart allocation of budgetary resources, but also help provide the safest possible environment in which to do dangerous things like crash cars and blow big holes in the ground. It's very important for others on the crew to have stunt and special effects experience. It is by no means one person's department to make the decisions as to whom to hire and how to manage and, eventually, execute stunts and special effects. But a smart place to start is at the top, a producer with that expertise.

If you don't have the cash, don't be stingy with your equity. If you don't have the experience and know-how and are attempting sophisticated and dangerous things in your production, give all you have to give away in return for success and safety. It's a very smart investment. Holding on to 10 percent of the equity in your production is far more advantageous if the balance of the equity has been given in return for funding and expertise. You now own 10 percent of something potentially very valuable, a good movie. Holding on to 50 percent of your production is a pretty hollow victory if your movie falls short of expectations because of poorly executed "money shots" such as stunts and special effects, the kind of eye candy that can entice an audience to come see your movie, if not actually enjoy it and tell their friends. You don't want to look back on the experience of making your movie, thinking you should've been more generous, willing to share the upside of any success that may come your way with anyone who could've upgraded the quality of your product, the movie. With all my counseling about sharing the "back end" (profits) of your movie in return for services, that doesn't always fly. Among those with industry experience, it's well known that distributions of profits to equity holders in a movie are rare. So offering 1 percent or 20 percent may represent no real added value or income potential to someone you want to bring on board to help. If movies rarely profit, then most likely, no percentage of ownership has value. But I can say that understanding that reality may still provide an incentive to someone. Don't try and persuade someone as to why your movie will make money and will distribute profits, unless it's demonstrably true by virtue of financial deals that are actually in place and will ensure profitability. You may be perceived as trying to con them and assume they're naïve. But if an experienced pro likes you, likes your movie, or is any other way attracted and motivated to help you, then the size of your offer, the grand gesture, may seal the deal. If a young filmmaker offered me a few points (percentage points) of their profits to produce their movie, I'd feel underappreciated and not want to get involved. If they offered me as much or more equity than the other principals, I might say to myself, this probably will add up to nothing earned, but I feel loved and respected. I'm in. I'm not saying this is a surefire strategy, but when you have little else to offer a more experienced or valuable potential creative team member, use it. There's an old adage that I have *often* found to be very useful when making movies, "if you don't ask, you don't get." Take that one to the bank.

So once you have the best team possible assembled, you work with what you got. The best movies are often made in an environment of freely flowing creative ideas among the filmmaking team. I can assure you, many, many directors know where their strengths and weaknesses lie. Those directors set aside their healthy egos and actively solicit the assistance and collaboration of experts in the areas they lack. If for no other reason, they welcome the help because they understand it will only improve the movie by realizing the vision more successfully, and that success will inure to their benefit. So even if your desire to collaborate comes from a place of selfishness and ego, it will result in a better movie.

> DAN BRADLEY: *Knowing what you want is a very important quality of a director. But they might not know how to achieve it on-screen. There are directors I worked with who are very specific, know exactly what they want, what feeling they're looking to evoke, like David Russell. He's very, very specific about what he wants an audience to feel. But David could tell you, "I want it to feel it very frustrating," or he's like, "or scrappy." He used the word "scrappy" a lot. He didn't want a very formal fight. He wanted something that was more "scrambling." There would be an emotional quality he'd want, a feel to the fight.*

There's no one way to direct a movie or to communicate with others on the creative team. Words often fail us as filmmakers, because what we're looking for can't be described accurately or, more to the point, is open for interpretation.

The director may know how they want an audience to experience the event, but not exactly what that can look like. They can accurately convey the feeling they want a fight or stunt to have. So a stunt coordinator and or a fight choreographer will design a very specific sequence that reflects what the director wants to evoke. The director will review and possibly revise the plan, but the actual designing of the fight or stunt can be done by the coordinator or choreographer.

Others can write a very specific description of a fight or stunt and the coordinator's job is then to figure out how to execute it. A hybrid of that situation is when a coordinator can enhance a very specific scene.

> DAN BRADLEY: *The Bourne movies are unique because I wrote all the action for the Bourne movies. Tony Gilroy actually writes great action, but Tony writes in his hotel room in New York and I'm on location and I can literally see what the locations and resources we have. Tony writes great emotion in the action. The emotional stakes are always incredibly clear. I would always try do the best I could to service that. Sometimes I was able to increase the stakes through the action like in the bathroom fight in* The Bourne Supremacy.

As in any creative pursuit, there are diverse opinions as to what the role of action scenes in movies should be. As we look at some movies, particularly the "tentpole" movies that are the staple of studio releases every summer and holiday season, one could assume the function of action scenes is to thrill the audience, to have them sit back in their seats and think, "wow, that was spectacular, amazing!" Sometimes scenes or sequences that feature spectacular events, the scenes people talk about when they leave the theater, are called "set pieces." As the name implies, those scenes are separate, departures from the flow of the story. They take time out from the narrative to offer an elevated and unusual extension of the story, something that will stand out as a piece of entertainment, almost on its own. The director is saying to the audience, "Let's stop here for a bit, sit back and enjoy what you are about to see. It's going to be a great ride!"

> DAN BRADLEY: *Some stunt guys left to their own devices will show you the tricks that they've perfected in their backyards and, most of the time, when you're doing a film; you're using their ability to do actions and trying to fit them into an emotional structure. I prefer doing the reverse, finding ways to invest emotion into the action as a way of telling the story. I don't think it's that interesting to watch people do tricks.*

Different strokes for different folks. What happens in scenes can sometimes be random. The event itself isn't critical to the development of the story; its outcome may be critical, as in whether someone survives a violent event or not. Even if an action scene does meet the criteria of being an event that moves the story forward in an organic way, it may not emanate from a character. The way the character deals with a physical challenge or conflict may not feel authentic, but it does seem exciting. Creative license? Maybe. There are stunt people and directors whose style of storytelling reflects that thinking; it's the cinema's equivalent of going to a huge fireworks display. You may find that Dan Bradley's point of view of creating action from character matches your sensibilities and he would be the right guy to work on your movie. I will point out that most action directors use action to tell the story: to develop the character and to push the narrative forward. But, you may say, "I want the adrenaline to pump! I want the audience to talk about the amazing, death-defying stunts to all their friends and family! The hell with story; that can wait!" The director must decide the intentions of the movie and the use of stunts and special effects as storytelling devices. What is the basis the movie is operating under to entertain?

> BUDDY JOE HOOKER: *I start first with what I think the intention of the movie is. You can't add stuff into a story that's just stunts for stunts*

sake unless it's the kind of film that that's what's going to make it successful. You have to stay within the boundaries of what the director and the story is calling for. Different folks have different ideas of what an entertaining movie is. You don't necessarily want to start throwing out stuff that's great, but has nothing to do with the story.

It's about the vision: the thing that the director and producer use as their touchstone. The vision is what is honored above all else. It's the movie's compass, the thing that informs all choices.

GAYLE HOOKER: *I think you always start with a vision. The coordinator's job is ultimately to be safe. But, the first thing is, what is the director and producers' vision?*

BUDDY JOE HOOKER: *After you talk about the vision and we've all agreed on that part, I don't really have to talk to them much more until I need to. At that point, it's about how to create that vision. That becomes my job.*

Many, if not most, filmmakers insist that action come from character and story. Their approach to storytelling is to make an action sequence a natural progression of the story and character development: an event that reflects who the character is and/or provides an opportunity for the character to develop along a specific arc.

MARTIN CAMPBELL: *As important as all other elements, all the action has to be related to character. Action for action's sake is boring.*

DAN BRADLEY: *I call it stunt commercials. You'll be watching a movie and you'll be all into it. There will be an action sequence that has no sort of emotional resonance. So, it doesn't really help the story along. You don't learn anything about the character. You're just watching somebody do something sort of big. And frankly, many, many producers don't think about stunts beyond being this action beat.*

What is the role of action in your story? As a storyteller you might say to yourself in the construction of your story, "Our hero has really been talking too much or that scene where he meets his future wife has lulled the audience. We need to kick up the energy. We need some action!" The action should be informed by or reflect who the character involved in the action is, so that the action is an expression of character and narrative progression.

DAN BRADLEY: *We've had all this dialogue. Now, we needed action beat. And it's like the good producers and the superior directors*

understand that there are things to be learned about character, the
story can still be told, the characters can still be served and must be
served doing action. You can learn a lot more about the characters, I
think, under extraordinary circumstances than with dialogue, because
how people respond, how characters react under great stress, is very
interesting.

Maybe you agree with the following: nonstop action movies are boring. Or maybe not. But if you do come down on that side of the character-through-action approach, you may consider this.

DAN BRADLEY: *Action sequences in movies that are very noisy and*
  violent are boring, without a doubt. They forget the emotional content.
  You stop telling the story. You stop servicing the character. Suddenly,
  you're just watching all this mayhem.

DAN SPEAKER: *The most important thing for young directors to realize*
  is that the action sequences are stories. If they have this vision in their
  mind of huge explosions and cars flipping over, the thing they should
  be asking themselves is, "What is this telling the audience about my
  story?" We can put together an amazing action sequence, but it's
  almost like cutting to a dance number in a musical and then coming
  back to the story. It needs to meld. We've all seen this with even good
  directors, where the action sequences don't look like they belong in
  the same movie. The young director should really say, "What am I
  trying to say with my action?" It should be a microcosm of the whole
  story. If the young director can express that to their stunt coordinator
  or fight choreographer, then they'll have a better movie.

A Little Stunt History

The roots of the stunt business reach into the early days of organized rodeos that began sometime after the Civil War. By the early part of the twentieth century, these events had become popular forms of entertainment offering cash prizes and trophies. Traveling shows featured daredevil horsemen performing all sorts of daring maneuvers on horseback, entertaining audiences from coast to coast. In the 1910s, the rodeo was popular enough to fill major arenas around the United States. Audiences in the east, where this form of entertainment and culture was considered exotic, were particularly enthusiastic.

Sometimes referred to as Wild West shows, these spectacles presented all sorts of events in which riders demonstrated their skills and speed on horseback. The notion that the kind of characters connected to the lore of the winning of the West could be experienced in all their glory was a big draw. In fact, to capitalize on the lore of the Old West, actual legendary figures of that era such as Buffalo Bill Cody and Annie Oakley were featured in shows drawing sellout crowds around the world. They would display thrilling horsemanship and marksmanship that their legends were built on.

These shows seemed to satisfy a demand for entertainment connected with the Old West and all it had come to mean. It was natural for the newest form of mass entertainment, motion pictures, to catch that wave. Short films and eventually feature-length films in the Western genre became a staple in earlier stages of the motion picture business in America. Cowboys, *real* cowboys, became performers and star attractions in these action "quickies." Recruited from the rodeo circuit and drawing from the vast pool of skilled, daredevil riders, the motion picture business capitalized on this colorful group of men and women. As these performers perfected the new application of their talents, they got the hang of this new moving picture-making. They began to understand how their performances looked on-screen and began to appreciate the relationship between the camera and the performer. As their sophistication grew, so did their role in the making of movies. These performers were able to suggest better camera placement, better placement of the performers, and, very importantly, how to achieve the most exciting action, safely.

One of the pioneers in motion picture stunt work was Yakima Canutt, a young man who grew up on a ranch, taming horses. He brought his unique abilities with horses to the rodeo circuit, where he won numerous championships and achieved legendary status in that world. He attracted the attention of Hollywood, where he went on to star in numerous short Western movies. He quickly gained an understanding of the elements required to piece together an exciting action sequence using man, horse, and speed. He created and perfected many techniques to capture and dramatize action still employed in modern filmmaking. He developed the technique of shooting an action sequence by deconstructing, then recreating an action event by shooting brief segments or shots, the basic use of montage. The piecing together and ordering of those brief moments in time captured on film, created, if not the replication of an exciting piece of action, at least the perception that we have witnessed something exciting.

Canutt discovered that by replacing actors with experienced riders at critical and dangerous junctures of an action sequence, then resuming the scene with the principal actors, an amazing sleight of hand could be achieved. The audience would never know the principal actor had been replaced. They would fully assume the star had just performed a daring and dangerous maneuver on screen. This method became a fundamental practice of shooting action sequences. He was the most respected and sought-after expert when it came to action on the hoof or even on wheels. Canutt staged and directed countless action sequences over his long career. Among his most known and duplicated work was the stagecoach chase scene in John Ford's *Stagecoach* (1939), starring John Wayne, and the unbelievably exciting chariot race in *Ben-Hur* (1959), starring Charlton Heston. It should be pointed out that it has been reported that Canutt took five months to create that scene in which Heston and costar Stephen Boyd were trained to actually drive the chariots in the race sequence and no horses were hurt or actors seriously injured. This is in stark contrast to the 1925 version of Ben-Hur, in which it has been reported that over a hundred horses and one performer were killed in the making of that movie.

Training and Background

Stunt performers are highly trained and very experienced in a number of fields of physical action. Many are top motorcycle racers, car drivers, gymnasts, martial artists, horsemen, pilots, aerial specialists, and fight choreographers, who apply their skills to the demands of stunt work. In other words, they combine their skills and experience in their field of accomplishment with the skills demanded of doing stunt work for movies. Once trained and experienced in creating stunts for the screen, these professionals must be so expert in their fields that a reasonable person (I'm thinking of producers or directors, but they are not always associated with the term "reasonable") can expect the stunt to be successfully executed each time it is attempted, with minimal risk.

In the early days of movie production, it didn't take long for specialized performers to see the confluence of their equine skills and the demands of movie production. By repeatedly observing filmmakers and understanding how their own talents were integrated into the storytelling process, the notion of stuntmen as directors and second unit directors was born. The evolutionary path from horseman to stunt performer to director was set forever.

I must point out a very important distinction between those with highly developed skills in real-world pursuits such as motor racing, aviation, professional fighting, or gymnastics and those who have been trained to apply those same skills for purposes of being useful in a movie. All of these areas of competition demand a number of talents along with experience to attain specific and tangible results such as drive around a track faster than anyone or beat another man into submission … for real. People train to achieve those outcomes. The outcome required in recreating those events for the camera is significantly different. Remember, it's the illusion. Not the reality.

So you can't hire your Uncle Harry who won a regional Golden Gloves contest in his day. He may know many of the fine points of the "sweet science," the point of which is to hit a human target and not be hit yourself. But he doesn't know how to *not* hit a human target, but make it *seem* like he did. While those skills can definitely serve as a foundation to create safe and effective stunts, those skills are separate and apart from the kind of skills stunt work requires.

How do you create the illusion that someone is driving 100 mph, when in reality they're driving less than half that speed in order to be safe? While many stunt performers have a strong background in the worlds of racing, fighting, and other skills translatable to making movies, they must also demonstrate the additional skills of creating the illusion, not the reality.

> DAN BRADLEY: *If there's something hard to do in real life, like driving a car very fast, it becomes nearly impossible on a film set. Everything becomes increasingly difficult. So, all those things that you assume you can do in life aren't necessary if you're on a film set. Yeah, sure, they can stop. But when in movies, they're talking about a guy coming in and sliding a car and hitting a mark. He has to hit a mark. The mark isn't the size of the car either. They want the right side of the car on this little spot… right there and they need the door handle favoring the camera just so. That's far different than your ability to pull in successfully to a parking spot at the supermarket or drive around a track at high speeds.*

As stunt work became more and more a staple of the filmmaking process in Hollywood's early years, a vast amount of employment opportunities were created for the immense number of qualified stunt performers ready to work. Those who became qualified by virtue of their previous life experience in ranches, rodeos, and Wild West shows represented one major source of stunt performers. As time marched on and means of transportation, weapons, and fighting techniques evolved, experts came streaming into the motion picture and television industry that itself was diversifying in its content, to adapt their skills to the demands of movie production.

> DAN BRADLEY: *I've seen Formula One drivers and all these big names come in to do stunt driving, and they're not interesting or good, because most of these disciplines have cars that are incredibly powerful and incredibly sophisticated, and these guys' job is to keep them in perfect balance. So, they're driving very, very straight or follow a prescribed route, and it's not exciting to watch. They haven't been trained to create the illusion of what they really do with those cars.*

Some types of racing that have become popular in more recent years have proven more adaptable to the screen. Less controlled, more erratic, and less predictable styles of racing provide more visceral thrills that translate to the screen. Even for them, there is a learning curve to adapt to the necessities of moviemaking.

DAN BRADLEY: *I actually brought in drifter and rally car racers who make great stunt racers and drivers because their style is to slide sideways. They look out of control all the time. Suddenly, the quality of the driving jumps. It's very, very exciting. In fact, I have to say to those drivers, I don't want you to do anything that's more than 70% of your ability. This is not about you proving you can do it. I know you can do this all day long in your sleep. It's exciting for us. But if you have 30% to 40% cushion of your abilities and abilities of the vehicle you're driving, that means I can bring the cameras in close, that means we can all work together and be safe. I'll make it look exciting because your driving styles are already exciting.*

Another path for training is the system of apprenticeship, starting from scratch. Young aspirants often begin training in their teens, serving as assistants, interns, or kids who just hang out observing and absorbing pro stunt work. They clean, pack, and lug the myriad of equipment such as pads, mats, air compressors, tools, and hardware of an astonishing variety, in return for the opportunity to learn at the feet of skilled masters. Many stunt performers are second- and third-generation stunt people. Kids grow up watching and then actually participating in stunts under or alongside the watchful eye of their parents.

Some young apprentices actually begin their professional careers having gained enough experience and acquired enough skills, in their teens. Often there is a need for teenaged stunt performers who can more readily double for young principal cast members. You can find these fledgling professionals listed on various rosters such as the Screen Actors Guild (SAG) or various stunt associations. All applicable state labor laws that pertain to underage actors also pertain to stunt performers. They are also members of SAG and are protected, as all performers are, by the rules that apply to working conditions on movie and television sets. Those rules are not always enforceable, however. But the safety rules and working conditions for minors that are enforceable are the child labor laws of any given jurisdiction. In California, they are very specific, are very comprehensive, and are strictly enforced.

Special Effects

We recreate acts of God.

JOHN HARTIGAN, SPECIAL EFFECTS COORDINATOR

Here's the scene. It's a rainy night; sheets of rain pound against the candlelit living room. A young couple snuggles in front of a fireplace, warmly illuminated by the roaring flames. Simple, right?

Before I reveal how this may be done, it's important to understand what special effects are. In recent years, the term has come to mean images that are generated on a computer. Those images are called visual effects or VFX. The people who create those images are true wizards who recreate lifelike environments and images, once only accomplished with a wide array of methods that ranged from physical construction to the use of miniatures, models, and various camera tricks that used mirrors or manipulated perspective. The special effects I explore and explain in this book are the means by which the illusion of weather or atmospheric conditions, running water on a set, fire, explosions, blood, and bullet hits is practiced. They are also referred to as physical effects or floor effects. Weather and atmospheric conditions include wind, rain, snow, fog, and dust storms, whatever condition you can imagine. Pyrotechnics include explosions, fire, and bullet hits. Rigging has traditionally been a responsibility of special effects practitioners, but has become less exclusive to their domains as stunt people have become more responsible for that area. Rigging includes the wire supports actors and stunt performers use to prevent them from falling or to support them midair.

> JOHN HARTIGAN: *Lots of people wonder what kind of special effects I did for* Catch Me If You Can. *You don't realize that when you do the script breakdown and see what the script calls for, there's wind, rain, smoke… there's wet down streets, steam, sinks in kitchens and bathrooms, showers… If you look back at that movie, it has all of those things.*

And someone has to create those conditions. It's easier to understand how you might need to have trained people create smoke and operate wind machines.

You might not have thought that someone had to do some plumbing to have water come out of faucets, because we're often not aware that the interior location being used is, in fact, a constructed set on a sound stage. Practical or real locations such as apartments, houses, or offices are often *not* used for a variety of practical reasons, most of them logistical. In real apartment or office buildings, for instance, it's difficult to move equipment onto and off the set (small elevators that you have to wait forever for, antsy tenants, limited space), it's hard to control noise from tenants (and placate them for being inconvenienced), and it's impossible to control sunlight streaming through windows without a major technical effort; it can be expensive. Sound stages are often the answer to those problems. So if a set is built and running water is necessary (think *Psycho* or *Fatal Attraction*), your special effects team will install running water on that set. The knobs and controls to the faucets or toilets may or may not actually be operable, controlling the flow, just as light switches on sets often don't control the practical lights; off-camera technicians are controlling them.

Getting back to the cozy scene I described above, the answer to the question of how simple that scene is to create is very and not so much. To set up this shot, here's what you don't do. You don't do what you might do in real life. You don't wait to shoot this scene until the weather provides the downpour (you knew that, right?). There are no film gods to cooperate with filmmakers by providing atmospheric conditions on demand. Even if luck smiled on your production and it happened to be raining, you can't control how hard it will rain or for how long, much less, when it will rain. And even if it were really raining, this would cause significant delays in your work schedule; setting up lights in the rain, transporting equipment back and forth from the equipment truck to the set, protecting the set from water tracked in by cast and crew, insuring that all electrical cable connections are elevated off the ground and protected to avoid electrocution … you get the point. It's a huge deal. Rain causes delays in our everyday life. Imagine the complications rain can cause when dealing with heavy, expensive, and dangerous electrical and optical equipment. There are very specific issues of safety and cost that impact your production plan.

So how *do* you shoot this scene? There a few ways. If you're on a practical or real location, the cheap and easy way to sell the idea that it's raining is to position a streaming water hose above a window on the outside of the building. Place a strong light source outside and aim it through the water streaming down over the window. The exterior light source will suggest moonlight or a street light. Shoot the actors in the foreground and the wall in the background. The shadows of the water flowing down the window projected against the wall sells the rain. The addition of sound effects in postproduction that suggest rain and thunder will complement and sell a very believable scene. That's the "poor man's" rain special effect.

The more expensive, but more visually accurate way to shoot the rain can be accomplished by special effects professionals. That person will set up "rain towers" or giant water sprinklers or suspend perforated pipes just out of view of the frame. By actually recreating real-looking rain, any angle can be shot to actually show the falling water that looks on screen to be no different than the real thing. By controlling how and where the water falls, all the challenges of a real rainstorm are avoided and work can proceed efficiently. Actors can walk, talk, or even sing in the rain. The only illusion is the source of the rain.

The cinematographer will be an important collaborator in producing a convincing scene with rain. He must consult with the special effects person in planning the shots. In order for "rain" to be seen by the camera, it must be back-lit. This means a strong light source must be placed behind the pouring rain, positioning the falling water between the camera and the light source. When shooting exteriors on location, you can actually shoot in a light rain without seeing it fall, if the primary light source (maybe the sun?) is in front of the rain. The only evidence of rain will be any wetness that appears on surfaces such as the ground or on clothes. Therefore, actors and their environment will eventually appear to be wet if the rain persists ... but you may not see it falling from the sky! Sometimes managing to squeeze out a couple of badly needed takes when it begins to sprinkle is a most welcome reprieve from the costly consequences of not finishing the work planned for the day.

Let's consider the roaring fireplace. Just chuck a few logs in the hearth and light it. Right? Maybe there's a gas bar inside, the kind that is commonly used to start fires in home fireplaces. Easy. Here's what you need to consider. Keeping the fire at a constant or controllable level is important to convey many story points. Is the fire just beginning, at its height, or softly burning out? Based on what the story requires, someone who is qualified must be on set to ensure consistency and safety. If appropriate, they also should have the proper licensing. California is a very regulated state for handling explosives, flames, and other dangerous materials. Other states, maybe not as much. In California, a license ("three card") is required to light a candle or to light a fireplace on a set.

Experienced and preferably licensed special effects coordinators and technicians are the people you want on set to ensure safety, reliability, and efficiency. You don't want crew members doing double duty or being responsible for something as potentially dangerous as fire or explosions of any size. Some prop masters may know a thing or two about bullet hits or fire bars. They are not necessarily qualified to ensure safety and predictable results. Depending on the jurisdiction you're shooting in, prop people or grips may not be *legally* allowed to perform those functions on your shoot.

> JOHN HARTIGAN: *Take a movie like* 50 First Dates, *which was not a big pyro movie at all. If you are shooting in California, you need to make sure you have someone who has at least a Three Card on your crew because you're going to have campfires, candles, tiki torches; all of those things required a Class III permit. But when the company moved to Hawaii, the permit was not required, although I did hire local guys who had their own cards. But these were cards issued by the state of Hawaii, which are different than California's. So it depends on the state. All states have their own regulations.*
>
> *When it comes to pyrotechnics, certain states require that you deal with a police bomb squad or the ATF or the local fire authorities. Once you're out of the state of California, most of these other authorities haven't got a clue about what it is we do in the movie industry. That's where the state of California has always had the upper hand; the authorities are geared up for these types of shows.*

Bullet hits or squibs are little blood bags that are hidden under clothes, attached to a small explosive charge and a protective surface. They are usually set off by the person wearing them by pressing a button attached to a wire that leads to the charge or charges. If the actor is not well protected or if there's too much gunpowder in the charge, they can do damage. Hire the guys who have done it thousands of times, not a few or even a few dozen times.

> JOHN HARTIGAN: *Make sure the person you're hiring has the qualifications and the licensing to do what you're asking for. There are a lot of kids out there who don't have their One Card. In California they have what they call a Three Card. A lot of these guys only have a Three Card, which technically allows them to work with candles or a campfire. But guys will bid on jobs as if they have One Card. If they get the job, they'll come back and try to nail the production company by having them hire another guy with a One Card who the producer should've hired in the first place. That person with the One Card had the licensing and the experience to do the job right. So all the sudden you're having to add to your budget the price of the One Card or Class I operator which runs from $600-$750 a day, plus the guy you hired who can't legally do the work, at least in California. So if you have a show with a lot of pyro, you should definitely look for somebody who has that One Card. The Two Card allows you to do sparks, campfires,*

or other small flames. But you still can't do body hits, bullet hits, explosions, ground hits, or anything like that.

It takes about 10 years now to get your One Card. Now this is only for California. Other states are starting their own licensing systems. Somebody like myself, who belongs to INTERPOL, the International Bomb Society, the ATF (Alcohol, Tobacco and Firearms) are the guys you want handling dangerous materials. I am also a licensed manufacturing and storage facility. So we can make our own explosives and store it. A lot of people don't have that to offer. The insurance that goes with that is outrageous.

Safety, a word you will hear over and over…and over again in this book or in any discussion involving stunts or special effects, is paramount. Not only are efficiency and authenticity desired from your crew, but someone must be employed who is trained, licensed, and certified to deal with fire and pyrotechnics (explosives) in the jurisdiction you are shooting in. This licensed expert will make sure no materials used in constructing or decorating the set or location are potentially vulnerable to catching fire. They will also try and make sure that no flammable materials or materials that can melt such as polyester are used in wardrobe or set dressing. This is a judgment call only a trained and experienced professional can make with the kind of certainty you not only may prefer, but must insist on.

JOHN HARTIGAN: *The wardrobe has to be safe too. This goes back to our preproduction meetings with the wardrobe department. The first thing I say to them is, "absolutely no synthetic fabrics are to be used. It has to be all cotton." Also the hair and makeup department needs to know that no hairspray can be used. The wardrobe department has gotten the wrath from me a few times because we talk about it and talk about it in meetings, they'll read the script where it's obvious that there's going to be fire and then the actors show up on the set with synthetic clothes! Even with the cotton materials we use, we have certain safety products that we treat all the wardrobe including shoes socks, pants dresses…everything gets soaked in this fire blocking solution, gets dried and ironed out. We do that with all the wardrobe that's going to be in scenes where there's flame.*

Too many stories can be recounted in which lives were lost or cast or crew members were seriously injured because precautions were not taken or taken seriously enough. Making movies can be a dangerous occupation. Heavy equipment, powerful electrical sources, explosives, weapons, fast-moving vehicles, and more, all populate movie sets. They all represent serious harm if not utilized or supervised by experienced experts. Trained, experienced, licensed professionals are the only ones to be hired to handle fire or explosives, no matter how minor that "gag" might be. It's a very adult activity in every sense of the word. So if you're in a supervisory capacity, if you're the producer, you must back up your special effects and stunt teams by making sure others on the crew who are providing elements to a dangerous scene are doing their jobs properly. If you're a producer, you need to be aware of what your stunt or special effects team has requested from your various departments such as wardrobe, props, and transportation … and make sure they get it. Make sure the wardrobe has been fire-treated; make sure the brakes have been correctly adjusted or the right prop gun is ready. As a producer, that's a big part of your job: making sure everyone else is doing *their* jobs.

Another area how special effects coordinators bring valuable experience to the party is in knowing how other visual elements of a scene will integrate with what they're creating. A perfect example would be what color wardrobe will best reveal a bullet hit and/or what is the optimum lighting condition that a bullet hit should be shot under: daylight or moonlight?

JOHN HARTIGAN: *Wardrobe's a big thing, people don't realize how important it is. If you're doing a show with a lot of bullet hits, they all want to shoot those scenes at night. And often the actors are in dark clothes. If you do it that way, you're wasting your money. The blood is dark, you're not going to see it. The only way you'll see it is if you're lighting the guy like it's daylight. So in our concept meetings, when we're talking about doing pyro and putting squibs on people, we have to make sure we talk with the wardrobe department, the producers and the director. We tell them all, if they want to see this shoot out, and everyone's in dark clothes, it's a waste of time. Then you have to do it in CGI. If I come on set and notice that the wardrobe and lighting are going to hide rather than show the squibs, I'll say cancel the squibs. They should then go ahead and shoot it how they want to shoot it, indicate that visual effects are needed on the slate and put the bullet hits in during postproduction. You'll never see the actual squibs go off if it's at night and they're wearing dark clothes.*

The situation described above will be costly too. Squibs cost about $35 a piece, and the special effects people are already on the payroll anyway. If you have to CGI them in postproduction, they'll run $500 or more and you paid for special effects techs to be on set for doing nothing. Buying properly colored shirts would've been a much smarter allocation of funds. You should only consider placing digital bullet hits using CGI if it makes financial sense. One scenario that might indicate CGI bullet and blood effects makes sense is when the production is so far behind schedule, that the extra time necessary to work with squibs will cause the production to fall further behind, which can have all kinds of financial repercussions. If spending an extra hour rigging squibs causes you to incur overtime charges for your cast, go into a second meal penalty situation, or incur additional rental fees, do the math. You may want to compromise (and CGI squibs are a visual compromise) to fight again another day.

Another critical addition to the team may be required when introducing fire of any scale on a movie set. Whether the scene calls for a single-lit devotional candle or a room ablaze, a city or county fireman (fire marshal or safety officer) may be required by law to be on set to supervise and approve the how fire is created, maintained, and extinguished. In major production centers such as southern California or New York, there are strict laws that govern the use of fire and explosives in movie or television production. In jurisdictions where city or county permits are required to shoot, those permits will stipulate as to whether or not a fire marshal and or policeman will be required to be on set to ensure safety. When it comes to hiring firemen or policemen, you may have a few cost options. You may be able to hire retired firemen or cops at reduced rates. But your permit may require you to hire off-duty or even on-duty firemen or cops at considerably higher rates. That's at least three tiers of rates; retired, active but off duty, and active and on duty. If you're shooting candles or fireplaces, the retired guys will suffice. When you start getting into fire bars, off-duty active guys are usually fine, but explosives or larger fires in public places usually require the higher-priced, active, and on-duty firemen. Once again, depending on the jurisdiction.

In California, if there will be fire or explosives used on the day of shooting, the set must be deemed safe and suitable by a fire marshal. He will make sure all required city or county permits have, in fact, been obtained. He'll usually check that the safety equipment has been maintained according to regulations as well. Extinguishers may have required tags that indicate recent fire department inspections. Anyone who presents a rusty old fire extinguisher that hasn't been used or inspected for a long time will probably be told to find another, more reliable extinguisher before anything gets lit up on set. Safety officers want to make sure that the special effects team is ready for any mishap or eventuality they may be responsible for directly or indirectly. If an explosion is too big and spreads beyond the set, if untreated wardrobe catches fire or melts, or if noxious fumes are produced from something the special effects wizards set up, the fire marshal wants to feel confident those types of incidents can be quickly handled by the effects techs to prevent injury to anyone. Be familiar with your local laws and regulations that will spell out what a production's legal obligations are, if any, when using pyrotechnics on a set. Then use good judgment.

> JOHN HARTIGAN: *Firemen basically want to know what safety steps are being taken to be prepared for whatever it is we plan on doing. I'll show them my CO_2 extinguishers, water trucks, water extinguishers, fire hoses laid out… I'll show them the safety perimeter that I've established. I'll do that with the fireman without everybody around, so he knows that we're doing things right. So then if anybody from the crew comes up and says that they have a problem with my safety parameters or the way I've set things up, because they need to be positioned in a certain place to do their jobs, the marshal will step in and say, "no, this is where the effects guy says things need to be, so you can't be there." He has the authority to make the production step back from anything he thinks is too risky or not set up right.*

Let's say the soft, romantic, fireside scene I described has been revised. The director has a brilliant idea. The scene that was once a quiet celebration of intimacy will suddenly become one in which the lovers will demonstrate their need to survive against all odds. A perfect metaphor for their lives ahead! As the cozy lovers dream of a life of happiness and fulfillment, flames will erupt and spread throughout the living room. As the producer and 1st AD try and suppress their panic, the special effects team comes alive and readies their equipment.

> JOHN HARTIGAN: *For the scenes where rooms get engulfed in flames, a lot of that is still practical fire bars in the foreground and maybe a few in the background. Then CGI is usually added on top of all that later. In post, they can take the fire out and build it up with CGI, and then put the real fire back in, add smoke and more layers of flame as well. It's pretty amazing. Real fire is still the best way to go if you can stack it and line them up so that the actors are safe. They will always have their predetermined safety paths to get out and plenty of fire protection around them.*

The effects guys will designate safe paths that actors or stunt performers can easily follow to safety if, for instance, a fire gets too hot or has been placed too close to the performer. An important safety consideration is whether it'll be safe to use principal cast or it will be better to replace them with stunt doubles when the action requires they be near open flames. Your principal players should not be near real fire during a shot, and that decision should be made well before the day of shooting.

The marshal will make sure the cast and crew have been advised of those plans and all relevant safety issues before shooting begins. This happens in the safety meetings, which will be described here and in other parts of the book. The fire marshal will also go over the production's evacuation plans in case an unexpected emergency arises, such as an electrical fire, power failure, or a natural emergency like an earthquake. Special effects teams will map out safety zones where it's safe for anyone to stand during shooting if effects are in play.

JOHN HARTIGAN: *If I'm doing a big day, I'll get together with the fireman first thing in the morning and we'll walk through everything I'm going to do. I'll explain everything, telling him or showing him how I'm going to do it and where I'm going to do it. Sometimes the AD will be there, especially if there's big stuff for the day. But if they're shooting, they just carry on with their business. I've probably filled them in earlier.*

While we're prepping and getting close, we have the safety meeting on the set. The AD will run the safety meeting, which starts once he has gotten everybody on the crew together. Make sure all the crew is there. That's a hard thing to do, but everybody needs to be there to listen and see what we're planning. The AD will go over the broad strokes of the event, and then I'll step in and explain everything in more detail. If there's a stunt involved, the stunt person will step in and explain in detail what they're going to do, as well as an armorer, if there's going to be firearms used in the scene. Before everyone disperses, we go over the exact order of how it's going to work; where the cameras are and where all the camera operators' safety positions are. I make sure everyone on the crew will be properly protected if they need to be. Those are the final things I say in the meeting. When the shot is all prepped and we're ready to go, I'll address everybody once again and announce that we're "hot" and ready to go and turn it back over to the AD. The AD will then say okay let's make everything hot and then depending on what kind of shot it is, the AD will either call action or turn it over to the director. No matter who calls action, we prearrange our cues, which we may or may not initiate ourselves. That just depends on what I've worked out with the director. A lot of times I'll be in the video village next to the director, especially if specific

things have to happen. That way the director can say "now!" as my
cue for me to cue my guys.

When using fire, explosives, or any materials that are flying through the air near your actors, it's advisable to give them a preview of what to expect when the effect is initiated. To be clear, I'm suggesting a session prior to the safety meeting. The actors will attend the safety meeting if at all possible and get a good indication of what's going to take place. The actor wants to know what to expect and assess the risk they're being asked to take. They will want to know what safety measures have been implemented. You really want to make sure your actor is comfortable with what's going to happen; the special effects tech and whoever else will be a participant in the effect should walk the actor through the process. If the director is available and the producer is too, so much the better. You want to avoid a situation where questions and fears are gathering momentum in the mind of the talent and they get so nervous that they back away from doing the shot at the last minute. The whole cast and crew will be stuck in neutral, while waiting for this impasse to resolve: money pouring down the drain. The other scenario is that the actor goes ahead with the shot, their reluctance obvious to everyone, especially the camera. Then, you're either looking at reshooting a time-consuming and expensive shot or painfully seeing the results of an uncommitted actor in the editing room when it's too late to do something about it. As always, communication is the key. Show and tell the talent everything germane to the effect. Explain how the mechanics work, what precautions are built into the mechanics, what precautions the crew has taken, what the effect will sound like, what it will look like, what if anything will be airborne…Think of it this way: What would you want to know if explosive charges or shattering glass or wood were a whisper away or even on your body?! I would want to know everything so I can relax, do my job, and keep everyone around me happy. Or I'd want to know as soon as possible, if I can't agree to the plan, so satisfactory modifications can be arranged. If you're the producer or director and you're aware of some fact that might be disturbing to the actor, that's a pretty clear sign you should put on the brakes and either rethink the way the shot has been conceived and planned or ask for clarification so your doubts can be erased. Since most of us who produce or direct aren't experienced or trained in special effects or stunts, we do place a certain amount of faith in the professionals we've hired to do the job. We don't understand or have a set of experiences that help us make informed judgments as to how safe an effect or stunt is. The more experience we gather from years of production, the better position we're in to make reasonable safety assessments. It's a game of mitigation as opposed to elimination, but the steps taken to mitigate risk can be virtually foolproof in certain situations and merely acceptable in others.

> DAN BRADLEY: *Demonstrations from the special effects, the physical special effects people who are doing the explosions, like fire gags, or the atmosphere on the set, are important. All of that stuff needs to be shown in advance. I've done things where an actor is standing by a glass window and a bullet goes through the glass and we're seeing the window and the actor at the same time. And how do we do that so we don't endanger the actor? Well, the special effects guy knows how to do it and it's not quite as intuitive as you might think. It's completely safe, but it's a little unnerving when they start to talk about this to the actor whose eyes start to get kind of wide, saucer-like. The actor's going to ask, "What's going to happen while I'm standing 2 feet away from this piece of plate glass"!?*
>
> First, we'll do a test off the set for ourselves. If the actor is uncomfortable, we just take him outside and do it with the special effects guys or with me, because I know it's safe and I'll demonstrate it for the actor. That makes a big difference in terms of a nervous actor that you think will be completely safe, but she or he is way too scared and so now, you're dealing with the opposite kind of actor from the one who claims to be fearless, you're dealing with the one who's too nervous to want to do whatever this effect is, because they're afraid something will go wrong.

In larger production centers such as Los Angeles and New York, where filming is common, certain fire marshals either have undergone specialized training or, because of their past experience on film sets, are more likely to be designated for duty on productions. They know the equipment, the techniques, and the very specific needs of filmmaking. With that being said, even in Los Angeles and particularly outside of major film production cities, firemen know next to nothing about the techniques and equipment employed when special effects are created. They of course know the laws and safety procedures that apply to everyone. They know how many people in a room is safe and what to use to extinguish an electrical fire. They know a lot, but they don't know about bullet hits, smoke machines, and fire bars.

Whether fire safety officials are experienced or not, they are in theory, there, not to impede, but to facilitate the efficient and safe execution of shooting with incendiary materials. It's easy to lose sight of their critical role, complain, and get frustrated by the exhaustive safety checklist they go through. This is part of the deal. They have a lot of discretion on sets they have been assigned to and must be satisfied that your set is safe.

Do not cut corners when it comes to safety. The stakes are too high. Cast and crew members have lost their lives because someone decided making a movie was more important than someone's safety or proper precautions were inadvertently not taken. I'm certainly not painting producers or those in positions of authority as callous captains of industry who will run roughshod over workers' rights and safety to save a buck. Accidents do happen. People make mistakes in judgment or execution. Unfortunately, moviemaking is rife with shortcuts that sidestep ponderous safety protocols. These shortcuts are sometimes devised by directors or other members of a crew who are under tremendous pressure to meet deadlines, not just unscrupulous producers. The vast array of safety measures that has been developed over the years is to catch those mistakes and avoid bodily harm or worse. One thing to think about is if you hire special effects pros who really know what they're doing and have been doing it a long time, there's a better chance that your fire safety officer will interfere less, if at all. This is true, in part because the special effects team has much more experience with fire and explosives, as utilized in production, than the fire safety officers do. So if they feel confident in your special effects personnel, things should go very smoothly.

Wherever you're shooting, make yourself aware of and follow all regulations as they apply to safety, that is, police and fire issues. Here's how it works in California and Los Angeles in particular. It's good to understand how it works there, where standards are high, to at least give you an idea of how you might approach interacting with local safety authorities anywhere.

JOHN HARTIGAN: *If I'm going to blow up a car in Chinatown. I'll call the LA City Fire Department at least 72 hours in advance, tell them what I'm going to use. I'll list everything like the amount of bombs I'm going to use, the amount of gasoline I'm going to use, what kind of igniters I'm going to use, the size of the lifters... everything. And they will put all of that down on a permit and because in this particular case I'm saying I want to use bombs, they will send an officer to the set. I'm going to get an officer that may be off duty, but when he's on duty, he is a practicing fire inspector. If tomorrow I'm going to do candles on a set, I'm going to call that same office and they're going to issue me a retired fire safety officer at a special, lower rate. So from the point of view of a producer, when you're budgeting an explosion in public, I'm going to have to figure in an on-duty officer, which is probably around $750 a day for 10 hours. Plus you're going to figure in a water truck, not a fire department truck, but a water truck and the driver.*

The procedure described above reflects a few concepts. The seventy-two-hour advance notice to the city of LA is prescribed by law. From a practical perspective, this amount of advance notice allows for revisions in your special effects plan if the authorities require them. They may require that the explosion be moved further away from buildings or a smaller amount of gasoline in the bomb that will be set off. The term "bomb," as used in the world of special effects, has specific meaning. The purpose of the bomb is not to destroy and do damage, as much as it is meant to create a fireball and lift that have great visual power and *suggest* greater destruction than it actually causes. To be clear, they *are* explosions with great force and are designed to only do the amount of damage necessary to sell the story. They aren't fake, but are very controlled. Special effects bombs normally stop short of causing craters or lasting damage to the environment. When a bomb is designed and built to blow apart a car, the special effects tech should have the knowledge and experience to utilize the precise amounts of elements necessary to give the impression that the blast was powerful enough to destroy the car. That impression, like much in the world of filmmaking, is deceptive. The car can be prepped to blow apart with much less force, by loosening or partially detaching body parts and weakening the vehicle's structural integrity with torches and saws. You may need half the amount of explosives if the vehicle is well prepared and if the right explosives and accelerants are used and well placed. In any case and wherever you may be executing these types of actions, have pros on your team and work with local law enforcement and fire safety authorities.

Another interesting issue that you may have to negotiate is determining which governmental jurisdiction will have authority on your set. Most major metropolitan cities are comprised of many jurisdictions. Many large metropolitan areas are made up of incorporated cities and unincorporated areas that the county governs by default, for example, the City of Los Angeles and the County of Los Angeles. Each has its own government and public safety departments. The City of Miami is another example of a jurisdiction that coexists with and within a larger governmental authority, Miami-Dade County. This dynamic can have confusing and costly consequences.

JOHN HARTIGAN: *The State of California Fire Department oversees all production in the state when it comes to fire and explosives. If you are shooting in the City of Los Angeles for instance, the City of Los Angeles Fire Department governs any pyro on your shoot. If you're in the County of Los Angeles, in unincorporated areas, the LA County Fire Department is in charge. But they are all overseen by the California State Fire Marshal out of Sacramento. It's a matter of jurisdiction, which can get tricky.*

It can get very tricky and maddening.

JOHN HARTIGAN: *I've had this happen a few times at the beach in Venice here in Los Angeles. I'm doing a shoot by the Boardwalk (a paved path that separates the beach from residential and commercial buildings). Let's say we have a campfire on the beach for this scene and a shoot-out is going to take place inside the house just on the other side of the Boardwalk. I've had this happen at least 25 times over my years in the business; in Venice, anything on the Boardwalk and towards the buildings is within the City of Los Angeles' jurisdiction. But everything on the beach (on the other side of the Boardwalk) is under the County of Los Angeles' control. We're shooting in two jurisdictions! Sometimes we get lucky and they'll issue one fireman, but technically you can get stuck with two high-rate firemen, one from each jurisdiction. You have a County guy covering the campfire on the beach and for the shoot-out in the house, which is only 20 feet away, you have an LA fire inspector, even if we were only using a candle! So you end up using two firemen, who are doing absolutely nothing. This situation doesn't happen all the time, but it is the kind of thing that has annoyed producers so much they want to shoot in other cities.*

The Responsibility of a Safe Set

If you don't have the funds to do it right, DON'T DO IT! Rethink the scene. Do not adopt a "fingers crossed" mode of thinking in areas of safety! Do not be the one to assess the safety needs of a scene. Leave that to the experts. Do not presume that you can decide whether or not certain equipment or personnel are necessary to do the job professionally or safely. This is absolutely the wrong and irresponsible way to do your job. If you are in any position of authority, that is, producer, director, or department head, it is your solemn (I mean just that) duty to protect the people under your supervision.

In fact, the person who traditionally is given ultimate responsibility for safety on a set is the first assistant director (1st AD). In California, the 1st AD is *legally* liable for the safety of the cast and crew. If any injury or death occurs on their set, the 1st AD can be criminally or civilly liable. On union sets, the 1st AD has the authority to shut down production if they deem any aspect of the production to be unsafe.

Now, going back to the fireside scene I suggested earlier, once the plan to create the simple (or revised, not-so-simple) romantic living room fire has been devised, it must be ready to implement when the cameras roll. With on-set safety reasonably assured, your special effects person or team will most likely use their own equipment to create the fire. They will use their own fire bars or fire logs that they have maintained or built themselves and can reasonably guarantee their safety and reliability. You want this. This aspect of the process is another issue most of us would not think of. By arranging to use the equipment of the special effects company, you are, in a sense, getting an insurance policy that the equipment is properly maintained, thereby improving the chances that the "fire gag" will be safe and reliable. So don't try and cut corners by running down to Home Depot and buying stuff you hope you can return after the shoot. It's not worth the risk, and the professionals you hire will refuse to use equipment they have not had control over. Do you see prison as worth the risk for a pretty shot? I didn't think so.

I hope you can appreciate the challenges of special effects and the need to hire competent people to execute them. What should you keep in mind when looking for the right special effects coordinator, supervisor, or company for your production? Look for a person or a company that's reputable with a long list of credits, that's insured and bonded. It takes a substantial and well-established company to carry the proper insurance. It's really expensive, so it's at least *a* sign of quality and reliability that a company would be fully insured and bonded. Make sure that insurance is not charged back to your production. That is not your cost and may indicate they aren't established enough to carry insurance year round, but only take it out when they work on a job.

Don't be intimidated and think that someone is too big or established to work on your modest or even skimpy budget. I'm not referring only to special effects people. There very well may be a way to not only work with these more experienced people, but benefit from their experience in ways that save you money and enhance your special effects with freebies and deep discounts. This is not an area you want to risk employing someone or a company with limited experience or the wrong kind of experience. There are too many people eager to say they can do anything for a chance to work. Maybe you've overstated your credentials yourself and that's admirable (assuming safety wasn't at stake). But when it comes to hiring people who work with dangerous materials and operate safety equipment, you have to demand the best you can possibly afford.

Much like other businesses, we have entered an age of specialization. Make sure the guy who claims to be a special effects pro is proficient in the specific areas your script demands. Just because he can legitimately call himself a special effects technician doesn't mean he's qualified to handle explosives or fire, to rig safety lines, or to even create rain. It *may* mean he's only qualified to do one of those things. It may mean he handles wind fans like nobody else. He could legitimately be known as "the Leonardo daVinci of wind." When you want wind, call him. But don't hire him to supervise or to directly handle anything outside his zone of experience and expertise. Make sure your special effects techs have the training and experience to do what you're requiring them to do.

JOHN HARTIGAN: *Once we have been brought on to a show, we often have to hire people to fill all the positions we need. On* Charlie Wilson's War, *directed by Mike Nichols, we had 50 or 60 guys on that show. Half the guys were only good at specific tasks; they weren't really all-round, special effects guys. When I got in the business I started out at the bottom. When I hired guys who have now gotten very big in the business, I made them start out at the bottom too. They learned how to clean the floors, how to clean equipment; they learned how to fix and operate the equipment. They learned how to look ahead at what they're doing. See the big picture.*

Union members, the International Alliance of Theatrical Stage Employees, (IATSE) are not allowed to work on productions of any budget level that don't sign union contracts. Generally speaking, the experience level of a nonunion crew is pretty low. You can imagine how this can impact the jobs that carry risk, such as special effects. Stunt players are covered by the Screen Actors Guild, although many stunts rely on special effects people to rig or, in other ways, prepare a stunt. Sometimes an IATSE local will force a nonunion production to unionize. This means anyone working on the show that would fall into their jurisdiction will become a member and receive all the benefits that come with membership. That would include virtually your entire technical crew from the camera department to the grip and electric to the art department. But there is no competency exam for these inexperienced film workers. Someone who called themselves a special effects coordinator, but who could be more accurately described as the producer's nephew, who likes to play with firecrackers, could rightfully claim to now be a union special effects coordinator. He might literally have one day's (or no) experience. Now that he's in the union as a special effects technician, he can call himself a supervisor or coordinator if his uncle granted him that credit, deserved or not. His future has many more options thanks to his uncle Sid. Buyers beware.

> JOHN HARTIGAN: *A lot of people who have gotten into the industry haven't got a clue. They ended up on some low-budget movie with a lightweight job that turned union and got them into the union, but they never have done anything. I think that's a big challenge now in the industry.*

Thoroughly check out credits and what experience they specifically reflect. Upon closer examination, those credits may reveal a more complete picture of what someone wants you to believe about their experience. It's sometimes hard to read between the lines of a credit. You sometimes have to ask probing, specific questions that will either confirm or debunk someone's claims.

> JOHN HARTIGAN: *When you're talking to someone who wants a job, you should have an idea if the person you're talking to is knowledgeable in the fields your show requires. Even for me, when I'm hiring guys who have been in the business for years, I found a lot of them might be good at plumbing or might be good at standing by a fan and doing wind and that's about all they can do. They don't have that imagination or creativity to see what's coming ahead to be a coordinator. They don't have the overview.*

When you look over someone's resume, you might see many impressive credits: big movies. Someone can technically claim a special effects tech credit on a movie and have performed very simple tasks, ones that didn't require much experience and requiring no licensing or special, technical training. Probe deep when examining and assessing a resume for any job where safety is critical.

> JOHN HARTIGAN: *I would highly recommend you call everybody on their resume and check them out, unless less they are somebody big. I've been working in the business long enough so that producers call me and ask me what I think about other special effects guys. Sometimes I know them, sometimes I don't. I can pull their names up on IMDb while we're talking and I can tell sometimes from their credit that they may have only worked one day, an online movie and television data base, on my show, so the credit doesn't mean all that much.*

IMDb has become a ubiquitous and, often, helpful tool in getting a very quick look at the nature and extent of someone's career. It is however, prone to misleading or inaccurate data. I've had listed numerous credits attributed to me in fields I've never worked in. The database has either confused me with someone else with the same name or just plain gotten bad information. But it also reports directly from credits taken from released movies, which can be vague and open to interpretation and explanation in an interview.

> JOHN HARTIGAN: *I've been in a lot of meetings with producers in concept meetings and when we bring up the name of anybody whether it be possible cast or a specialty people, we can quickly look up their credits and see if they have the experience we're looking for. So they may check out on IMDb and I'll ask them to come in to discuss the job.*
> *On the other hand, I had this one guy come in and tell me he worked on this movie called* The Comebacks. *This was a sports movie and he said he did a couple of Rocky movies, which I happened to have worked on. So I said, "Really, what did you do?" He said he was the foreman on the show. I said, "Really? Our meeting's done, you can get up and leave the office." The guy said, "What are you talking about!?" "I was the coordinator on those shows and you weren't the foreman." If you look up his name on IMDb, it lists him just like he said, as the foreman. Obviously there's a way for people to create their own resumes. It's not totally accurate.*

Also beware of the guy who claims to know everything and everybody. You know, that guy who seems just a little too good to be true, whom you've never heard of? If your radar rises just a little bit, dig deeper. You won't regret it.

JOHN HARTIGAN: *There's a lot of guys out there who think they know it all. Like I was told 30 years ago, if the special effects guy comes to you and says or acts like he knows it all, you should walk away.*

Young people, the ones who obviously are still learning and working their way up, have to work, right? Otherwise, how would they get experience? The well-managed special effects companies understand this dynamic. Youth brings enthusiasm and hard work, but it's particularly important for them to be supervised, taught, and teamed with seasoned veterans.

JOHN HARTIGAN: *With a company like us, we have brought on to a show a lot of young guys, but I've always surrounded them with the old-timers. That way everybody learns. There's always things to learn. You've always got to be open and willing to learn, but at the same time, you need to know what you're doing, especially when you're blowing up stuff.*

So where do you start when interviewing candidates for your special effects coordinator position? It's a logical process. Send the script to your candidates for the job along with a shooting schedule, even one that's a work in progress. Shooting schedules, in the form of a strip board, can tell someone a lot about your production. It's a reflection of your resources and can also indicate special challenges you may have with cast availabilities that may dictate how your show must be scheduled.

JOHN HARTIGAN: *When a producer calls me, the first thing we do is strike up a conversation and go over the broad strokes of what he wants. Then, I need the script and the schedule, if they have one. When I talked to young producers, hopefully they can tell because I've been around, there's a lot I can do for them. Especially if it's a low-budget show, I own millions of dollars' worth of equipment, which gives me the flexibility to make most budgets work. We'll read it at my company and break it down and look at the schedule they have and try to work out a way they can do all the things they want to do, like bullet hits or water gags.*

When you submit your script for bids from effects or stunt companies, you expect to get not only a price but also suggestions on how to better allocate your resources in ways that improve on your current planning. That kind of creativity is a great sign of experienced and dedicated professionals; people who show interest in helping you make your production the best it can be, not just in getting the gig.

JOHN HARTIGAN: *If after looking at the schedule and I see your show has all these effects you want to do, spread out over three days in the same location, with all the same actors, and you're trying to save money, maybe it's better to do your stunts and effects in one or two days instead of over three days. That way you only pay for our company a couple days and you can afford more of what we do. More bullet hits, more explosions, rain and fire can go on screen.*

It goes without saying that anyone you employ on your production should be thoroughly vetted, as I've described throughout this book. The stakes are high. In the context of this book, which explores stunts and special effects, your employees' safety is always a real concern. It should also be clear that the financial stakes are high as well. Lots of high-priced man-hours, costly materials, and sophisticated equipment go into stunts and special effects. Mistakes can have very damaging consequences to your production. The cost of reshooting is huge. The domino effect of having to shoehorn in more shooting days and possibly returning to locations that hopefully are available is any producer's nightmare. Situations like that have obvious repercussions on the overall quality of the production. You quite possibly may have to take money away from other scenes to correct the problem scenes caused by inept or unreliable special effects companies.

JOHN HARTIGAN: *On Kill Bill, they wanted me to do the job in the beginning but then they didn't want to pay me what I wanted. So they hired another effects guy and then went through three more effects guys, before I came back on the job. I spent six months with my guys fixing all kinds of stuff the previous guys did. We had to reshoot a lot of stuff. They thought they were going to save a lot of money, yet they ended up having to redo a lot of stuff and spending more. You have to get the guys who can do the job.*

I truly believe that the business surrounding movie and television production is a reasonably honest one, but there are rotten apples to be sure. It's not all that hard to overcharge a busy show by inflating costs of materials and submitting an inaccurate list of rentals.

JOHN HARTIGAN: *There are young guys out there who are running shows who are also running games on producers. I've been in the business long enough and know enough people to hear a lot of stories. I was talking to a TV writer-producer the other day and he was telling me their effects and stunt guys weren't doing the job. What they had to do was pretty standard stuff. They were getting all kinds of money*

*on rentals, on all kinds of equipment and of course, their services. I
looked at the episode. I thought to myself, "where's all the money they
spent?" All I saw on the show was some smoke, one car gag and a
couple of bullet hits. He told me they were spending close to $100,000
per episode on stunts and effects. That's a rip-off of the producers. It's
also poor management on their part. It could be mismanagement on
both sides. They had some young production manager on the show
who didn't have a clue what these things cost.*

There are a few business points you should be aware of when making the
deal with your special effects professionals. In most cases, they will provide
all the equipment and rigging necessary to do the job. You should not expect
that equipment to be included in their rate. You should get a bid or a detailed
list of costs including day rates and/or hourly rates for labor plus the cost
of equipment and expendable supplies or materials they use for your shoot.
However, they often will not charge for the equipment they did *not* use.
After meeting and discussing what your vision is for your production with its
challenges and the resources you have, the effects company will initiate their
process of costing out your show.

JOHN HARTIGAN: *We read the script, we break it down, highlight it
and then we input it all into a computer program and start plugging in
numbers such as for rental equipment, purchases, material and labor.
We have it broken down into various categories. The categories are
broken down into shoot, labor and materials, also by job description.
Then we start coming up with a rough price. We'll break down each
scene and figure out what we need per man to do that scene. We'll
figure out all the materials, like breakaway walls, windows or doors.
We might figure out, for instance, that it will take 25 days to build
those breakaway walls. $15,000 in materials and another $6000 in
purchases. And then in pyrotechnics, we're probably going to use
a couple of thousand dollars worth of pyrotechnic supplies to blow
through the walls. Rentals for pyro might be another $5000 or $6000
on top of that.*

One half of your special effects budget is usually labor, one quarter is rentals,
and the other quarter is materials and purchases.

JOHN HARTIGAN: *After going through the whole script, we might find
that there's multiple gags on the same day. We'll adjust the labor cost
to take into account that there's already somebody on set that we*

costed out for one gag. We won't double charge to do the other gags. We'll adjust down the man-days when we're costing out the job. That's why it's important for us to get the schedule to figure everything out. If we don't have the schedule when we're doing the breakdowns, you can end up with a budget that costs say $250,000. But if we have the schedule and see that we could be more efficient by scheduling things on the same day, that same budget could be as low as $150,000. So not only does the producer get a more accurate budget, but it doesn't force us to do multiple passes on a budget, which is very time consuming.

This is especially important when you're doing low-budget shows. It's really important for the producer to send a special effects supervisor the shooting schedule, even if it's a rough schedule with at least a good idea of all the scenes and shoot days. If this schedule indicates that you've got a number of different special effects for any given day, such as you might have a sink working or a fireplace and maybe a breakaway wall, you shouldn't be charged for separate man-days for each effect. So there is a real economy in grouping these things together whenever possible.

If after all the accommodations an effects company can possibly manage and you still can't afford them, there's one more "hail Mary" card to play. I don't endorse, recommend, or have an opinion on what, if any, consequences this approach may trigger. Don't sign a union (IATSE) contract and hope that they will not pressure you to sign a union contract. Then ask your choice of special effects guy, who is in the union, if he would work in your nonunion show. He may just say yes. He may choose not to receive a credit, work under a pseudonym, or not ask for any special accommodation at all. Your show has to be of a small enough scale to justify this request. He also will not be able to bring in many other effects guys on your show as they will have to make the same decision to work nonunion. You would benefit in a few ways; you'd have a veteran on your team at reduced rates and with no fringes to pay. You might just find someone who finds the chance to work in the relatively looser environs of a nonunion production as attractive.

JOHN HARTIGAN: *I still do nonunion shows once in a while, because I get to be more creative on it. Since I own all the equipment, I can do more things. I can give them more stuff and have more freedom. On big shows, things are laid out very specifically and I have less chance to play around. A lot of times, less experienced directors and producers don't really have much of an idea about special effects. I can dazzle them for not much money. They're actually appreciative. Bigger*

*shows could really care less; it's all about the bottom line to them.
I've been on lots of shows for what amounted to be pretty much free.
Sometimes on big movies, I'll end up with a lot of pyro left over and
we can cut deals on that stuff for my lower-budget pictures. Maybe
they can only afford in their budget 25 bullet hits, but we can come
in and give them 200 squibs and they really appreciate it. Nowadays,
that's more what I care about. I like helping out people.*

Back to the fireplace scene. When the fireplace is prepared, lit, and approved by the director, shooting can proceed. The dedicated special effects person will be focused on ensuring the fire remains consistent with the story and the director's wishes. The competent special effects person will provide cuttable material take after take. You will not be grinding your teeth in the editing room trying to figure out a way around mismatched images of an erratic fire as it appears in the background, drawing the audience's attention away from the important drama of the scene. You won't be reaching for the antacids because every time you cut to another take or angle, the fire's appearance is inconsistent or mismatched.

In the culture of low-budget, independent filmmaking, being fearless or "crazy"…doing it "guerrilla style" is sometimes admired. Shooting on a location without a government issued film permit? Seems harmless and you will probably get away with it. If a cop does see you and decides to inquire as to whether or not you have a permit to shoot at that specific location and you can't produce one, he'll tell you to pack up and move out. Not the worst thing in the world (although real and serious risks lurk in this scenario as well). But taking the DIY approach to working with fire, explosives, or stunts? Dumb. What can go wrong can be a nightmare.

A recent and tragic example of this approach to going around authority and "stealing" shots can be found in the incident surrounding the death of assistant cameraperson Sarah Jones on the indie production *Midnight Rider* in Georgia. As of this writing, a full investigation has not been made, and findings are preliminary. The crew was setting up for a shot that was to take place on railroad tracks that were actively used by a railroad company. But a few facts do appear to be confirmed at this point in time. No permission was given for the crew to be shooting on or near the tracks. No representative from local, state, or federal governmental safety offices or the railroad company was present to supervise any necessary safety measures. In fact, had safety officers or representatives from the train company been there, they most likely would've prevented the production from shooting on the tracks. Whoever made the decision to proceed on this basis probably assumed there would be sufficient warning to clear everyone away to safety if a train was heard coming. They were wrong. Sarah Jones was killed, apparently by items left on the tracks by the production that the train collided with.

The higher-stakes choice to avoid stringent safety regulations is to shoot out of the country. Many lower-budget action movies choose to shoot in Eastern Europe, where labor is cheap and safety regulations are scarce. Little, if any, governmental oversight exists. Licenses and permits often aren't required. Other parts of the world offer little in the way of impediments to blow things up and execute risky stunts. There have been a number of accidents in which non-American stuntmen have died or been severely injured making American movies. There's probably a rational approach to taking advantage of less restrictive jurisdictions. If you have American stunt and special effects coordinators who abide by protocols and accepted practices used in the United States, then you can avoid higher costs of labor while not avoiding safe practices. Your special effects team can access and use all the same dangerous materials, but not be required to apply for licenses and permits or pay for supervision by local authorities. There's plenty of ways to save, but only to a point. I've heard stories of an American production shooting in Eastern Europe, using local crews and stunt and effects teams from Asia, on which a couple of stuntmen died on the job. The American producers knew they alone could determine safety protocols on the production. If someone didn't feel comfortable with their policies, they had no recourse but to quit the show. There were no authorities or unions to protect the workers. As the story goes, the American 1st AD, experienced with stunts and special effects, was uncomfortable with the precautions or lack thereof and voiced his objections. Remember, in California or on any full union shoot in the United States, the AD can shut down any set they feel is unsafe. But in this, an Eastern European, country, no such protocols exist. The producers, under pressure to stay on the already very tight schedule, dismissed their AD's concerns, so he quit. Another AD was quickly hired, one with less experience with stunts. He may not have been able to assess the level of risk on the production. Shortly thereafter, two stunt players were killed in a boating mishap during the shooting of a chase scene that had a few stunts and explosions included. Accidents happen, and maybe that's what was in play in this situation. But there's a distinct possibility that some corners were cut, some extra risks taken, and the margin for error was reduced, resulting in a fatal accident. Were the boats going faster than they needed to go? Were they being driven too close to one another? Was the plan for rescue, if something went wrong, insufficient or nonexistent? Whether this occurrence actually happened or not, things like this have happened when filmmakers were trying to skirt safety regulations or established protocols by flying under the radar. So whether you take your show to "country X" that has no regulations or oversight or to your own neighborhood, without having met requirements described in this book, legal statutes, and the literature published by industry organizations, you're risking more than mere words can describe... *if* your intention in going to those places is to avoid adhering to professionally accepted safety practices. If you're going to far-off lands in order to save on union fringes, get cheap locations, or access government subsidies, terrific. Let's see those dollars saved up on the screen.

Beyond Fire, Bullets, and Explosions

I briefly and obliquely mentioned the other activities and responsibilities special effects teams engage in. Acts of God or atmospherics such as wind, rain, snow, fog, and dust storms are among the most commonly in demand on productions. Rain towers, which are basically big sprinkler systems, huge industrial fans, foggers and hazers, which spew out fog, a fine haze, or smoke from heated chemicals such as mineral oil, and all other repurposed or especially designed machines are tools of the special effects trade. These devices can be rented to you from a special effects company, which either owns them or will procure them for your show.

These atmospheric effects can now be enhanced with CGI in postproduction to correct mistakes, fill in empty patches, or add density. When planning shots using these effects, you should discuss with your coordinator what he thinks it will look like on screen and if it could use help from visual effects. If it's decided that VFX are in order, then a meeting will take place with the VFX producer, your special effects coordinator, and appropriate members from your production team, that is, the director, producer, DP, production designer, or stunt coordinator. It depends on the scene, but everyone whose job may be affected by an atmospheric special effect (or any kind) should be communicated with and all relevant information gathered and plans made should be shared and discussed.

JOHN HARTIGAN: *Special effects cover such a wide range these days, especially with visual effects being such a huge part of the overall filmmaking process. A more recent evolution of what we do is when we have to build things on a set to help support visual effects. We did the show* Walking with Dinosaurs *on Discovery Channel. We shot the show at real locations and created footprints with dust effects coming off the ground, so they can then CGI in the dinosaurs. To further sell the idea that these CGI dinosaurs were moving over the land, we also created movement in the bushes, so it would seem like the dinosaurs were moving through them.*

First we shot these plates in practical locations [plates are shots taken that will be used as backgrounds in scenes where other visual elements like dinosaurs or people or anything are added or composited]. They need us to do all the physical effects in order to complete the visual effects. A lot of people don't realize this. They think it's all CGI, but we shot real practical locations with computerized creatures. To really get an audience to buy into the effect, we create real images such as the footprints, rising dust, and moving bushes that when placed along with the CGI created creatures looks very real. A lot of producers and directors have not been involved with that type of CGI work, it's all new to them too. They're seeing a whole new approach on how to shoot their stories.

The consensus among visual effects and special effects professionals is that the greater is the proportion of real images to computer-generated ones, the better a result you'll get. Often it's a balanced mix between real and manufactured. So while you could create footprints, dust, and moving bushes in a computer, it won't look as real as if those elements were in fact, at least originally, real. Real fire is hard to beat for authenticity, but we totally buy the bigger, more intense version of that fire when it's layered with CGI fire. However, sometimes the final visual designs are so dissimilar to reality, that you might question the value of shooting real images that get VFX enhanced. VFX people prefer to work from real images, even if they are eventually totally replaced. The result will be more organic. The movement, scale, dimensions, or reactions to stimuli of real animals or moving objects are a useful basis for the final CGI imagery. Start with as many real elements in the frame as possible and work backward from there. With that being said, it's easy to see how the specialized fields of special effects and visual effects are merging. To recreate environments and characters that can only come from one's imagination, visual effects make this more possible than ever. But for aesthetic and even cost considerations, the foundation upon which the most sophisticated and realistic visual images are created is built on real images that a special effects team helped create with other departments on a traditional production crew.

JOHN HARTIGAN: *CGI has taken a lot of effects work away, but it's also opened up another avenue for a different type of effects work. Special effects and visual effects work more hand in hand. It's a different way of doing it, but you still need the special effects to make the visual effects work. When I did* Walking with Dinosaurs, *the visual effects supervisor and I had to work out exactly where everything was going. I built pneumatic rigs buried in the ground to create dinosaur footprints prior to the shooting of the plate at the practical location. They surveyed it all with engineers, identifying exactly where everything needed to be in order to line up the shots properly. We preloaded devices in the ground behind the bushes, and had cables rigged to pneumatic rams to be able to move bushes so they could do a traveling shot. When they were done shooting, they CGI'd the creatures on top of the footage of the footprints and moving bushes we made. Together they made an amazingly realistic scene.*

Just to give you an idea of another way in which special effects are called for, this glimpse into the movie magic created by a special effects team will further reveal the range of their responsibilities and talents. This team created a natural environment, a raging storm in freezing Alaskan waters. A real commercial fishing boat was transported to a controllable location, a dry dock, to shoot the recreation of this event.

JOHN HARTIGAN: *On the TV show* Deadliest Catch, *we shot the commercials for that show in San Pedro. We shot it on top of a hydraulic boat lift that is used to move the boats when they do repair work. We surrounded the boat with giant rain towers that were mounted on top of condors (very tall hydraulic lifts). I had 50 gallon air mortars flowing water up over the decks of the boat. All that was shot in the harbor. We took 24 sea containers and built a huge U-shape around the boat, green-screened it all right there in the harbor. We had rain and wind blowing all over it. The boat was supposed to have ice all over it, so we made icicles using these big hot wax guns. It looks like there were icicles hanging all over the boat.*

Fights

The most fundamental and universal use of stunts in movies is *the fight*. Fistfights or sword fights. Old-fashioned fisticuffs or balletic kung fu. Fights have thrilled audiences since the earliest days of motion pictures. In Charlie Chaplin comedies or Tom Mix cowboy action adventures, the sheer entertainment value of watching characters engage in a dangerous and tension-filled conflict in which somebody's gonna get hurt...bad is as surefire a way of entertaining an audience as there is.

The most foundational requirement of any story is conflict. Without conflict, there is no drama. If you attempted to tell a story in which all the characters are in agreement, that will be numbingly dull. Characters should want something...badly. They should want or need something so much that they're willing to go to any length to get it. In many cases, they're willing to risk their safety or even their lives. That's high stakes. Without the highest stakes plausible for your characters, your story may run out of steam. In our own lives, the more we want or need something and it's very important to us, the harder we try to get it. This makes sense in our own lives, and it makes sense in the lives of the characters that inhabit your stories. Even though many movies or TV shows have a heightened sense of reality, those stories still turn on these principal elements of need, high stakes, obstacles, and an active effort to achieve objectives. The fight is the natural outcome of many a conflict. In our own lives, fights rarely turn to violence. In movies, where the interior world is one in which conflicts are often bigger and more challenging than the ones we normally face, violent resolutions to conflict are the norm. Fights in movies take many forms. A fistfight, a gun battle, or a kung fu contest are standard manifestations of violent conflict resolution. Even a car chase can be a violent battle for survival.

Believing that the combatants in a high-stakes fight could get severely hurt or even lose their lives is critical to the connection an audience makes with your story. These are vicarious thrills. In a sense, the storytelling principles are the same as in a drama or comedy. As storytellers, it's our job to make the audience share or experience the emotions of the characters, to feel their joy or pain. If the characters on screen are acting in a way that they risk injury or death, we need to believe that. We must share their fear or exhilaration or terror. By watching characters fight, we should be saying to ourselves, "No! Watch out!" "Phew, that was close!" Or we should be thinking, "Oh! That must've really hurt!" The thrill of danger is the thrill we all seek, but from the safety of a theater seat or our sofa. The fight can therefore be viewed as the ultimate expression of characters desperately attempting to resolve their interior and exterior conflicts. We can understand why the big fight is at the end of the movie. It tells us who among the characters we've been following is going to win. Who's going to achieve their objective and who will fail in that quest.

Stunt choreography

Part of what makes movies, "magic," is the endless planning and preparation filmmakers engage in to faithfully recreate swatches of reality. Rarely will any idea a filmmaker hopes to bring to the screen turn out successfully without planning and preparation. Movies are as collaborative a venture as any you can imagine. There are no one-man bands or solo acts in professional moviemaking. The trend in the field of stunts and special effects is moving toward specialization, which ultimately requires collaboration.

While it is certainly true that stunt coordinators or stunt performers can confidently and competently plan a fight of any kind, often those experts will look to team up with people who specialize in the kind of action the script calls for. The most obvious category is martial arts. Bringing in a martial arts expert, one who has experience in planning how to most effectively execute and shoot a fight, makes sense. Later on in the book, I'll talk about the special considerations martial arts combat requires. But fighting is fighting, no matter the style of combat. It is universal in its principles, and how it is shot remains consistent with those fundamentals, no matter the style of combat. An expert's intimate knowledge of a particular style of fighting is helpful in making sure the finer points of that style are featured or shown in the best light possible. There are, however, some fundamental laws that apply to all forms of combat, such as you don't really hit the other person in the scene and the ways of accommodating that apply to boxing, martial arts, or street fighting.

If you have a story that includes a boxing match, there are experts who not only know the mechanics of that very specific activity, but know how an exciting and realistic boxing match has to be shot. The stunt legend Jimmy Nickerson is as respected a fight choreographer as there is. He choreographed the fights in *Rocky*, *Rocky II*, and *Raging Bull*. Respected directors John Avildsen and Martin Scorsese relied on his knowledge of boxing technique and camera placement to bring a level of realism never before seen in the 400 or so boxing movies made to that point. Experts in specialized fields understand the dynamics and fundamentals upon which style is based. They know what a fighter will do in certain situations. They understand the ebb and flow of a fight, what is realistic or plausible and what is not. These are clear examples of the concept of experts collaborating with experts. Not everyone is equally familiar with or experienced in all forms of combat and how to effectively shoot it. This is a critical concept I will repeat from time to time. Having a talent for dreaming up exciting fights or combat of any kind is an important talent. However, there is a second component to that package of skills one needs in order to serve the story, and that's staging or executing.

Staging combat scenes must be done in the context of how it will play on the screen when all the pieces (shots) are cut together. Don't forget that recreating exciting events or actions is often about creating the *illusion* something has taken place, not about faithfully or graphically recreating that event or action. Directors and editors will tell you that you can dispense too much visual information. If you're relying on a real stunt, not enhanced or replaced by a CGI version, it has to look like the real thing, if you show the whole action from a clear and all-inclusive perspective such as we see in a wide shot.

> DAN LEBENTAL: *Stunts are about creating the illusion, not the reality. And in a way, the editor is certainly the partner in making sure that we see just enough to create the illusion.*

So if you look carefully at a stunt shot that employed the methods often used to create the illusion that something violent just occurred, not many actions could withstand that scrutiny. If they did, the stunt was possibly too risky to try. The art of creating the illusion is to show parts of an action and allow the audience to use their imagination to "see" the complete action. Show the fist arcing toward a jaw, but do not show contact. Show the split second after impact. It works.

> DAN LEBENTAL: *Length is everything. If you look at a movie like* Jaws, *it teaches you a lot. Actually, how few frames you really do see the shark is a very good example of how less is more and how reality can be broken so easily. You have to find the line and then keep yourself safe from the audience crying BS.*

Understanding that a punch can, in some instances, miss its target by up to a foot is important to appreciate when choreographing combat. Understanding where to place the actors, when to employ stunt doubles, what shots are important or not important to sell an action or series of actions, what direction the action should flow and at what tempo are among the many considerations a seasoned fight coordinator/choreographer can uniquely contribute to the successful execution of your story.

> DAN BRADLEY: *If you want to do a fight, a good fight, have the same sort of elements of a good dialogue scene; there's a beginning, there's a middle, and there's an end. There's a story being told.*

Throwing a punch seems to be a pretty straightforward act to execute in front of a camera. How many of you guys have faked a punch or as a kid engaged in a "play fight" with your best friend when acting out a scene in a movie or just messing around as a teen? We never thought twice about any danger such a simple act might present. Agreed, a fistfight doesn't present the dangers inherent in a high fall. But a closed fist can do damage. A punch thrown off target can break a jaw or nose. It can knock out teeth. It can cut or even break the hand that threw the punch. From a business perspective, you could lose a principal player in your movie for days or weeks while they heal sufficiently to appear in front of a camera again. That can cost you money. Insurance deductibles will be in the thousands of dollars. In fact, insurance companies will most likely take the position that you took an unreasonable risk by not hiring a stunt professional and may not even pay a dime if an accident occurred involving that stunt. That can shut you down and threaten your whole production. It was just a punch!

Hire the qualified pro. Here's what you will learn. You may be surprised that when punches are thrown, they intentionally miss by a mile, in reality maybe as much as a foot.

> DAN BRADLEY: *Boxers spend a lot of time training how to hit somebody. You know, stunt guys spend a lot of time training how to make it look like you hit somebody. When you're doing a fight, the guy throwing the punch is less important than the guy acting like he got hit by the punch.*

The experienced stunt person knows that by placing the camera directly behind the actor throwing the punch as straight as possible and using a long lens that compresses space, that gap of up to a foot shrinks to an imperceptible distance and the punch appears to have squarely landed. In order to sell the punch, the actor or stunt performer receiving the punch must time their reaction to being punched perfectly by snapping their head or doubling over. Add a great sound effect and you've captured your devastating punch, and the audience totally believes it.

Ok, now I have revealed the secret as to how to shoot a punch that is believable and safe to perform. What's stopping you? What should stop you is appreciating the breadth of a stunt pro's knowledge and experience. Just because an actor or inexperienced stunt person knows the concept behind throwing a punch, that small bit of knowledge certainly doesn't guarantee they can throw that punch with accuracy and consistency. There's still a target to "hit." The target may be a point in midair between a moving fist and a moving jaw. But a target exists nonetheless, even if it's not a solid object. You've heard the phrase "a little bit of knowledge can be dangerous"? Maybe stunt performers came up with that or maybe not, but they can certainly appreciate the wisdom expressed.

There are numerous factors in performing a fight in which punches and kicks are used. Timing, distance, energy, and camera placement are all critical elements of the realistic fight. For instance, different kinds of punches are best delivered specific distances from the target. Straight punches, hooks, and uppercuts all require specific choices in distance, speed, energy, and camera placement in order to best sell those strikes.

A professional has performed a punch like your script requires thousands of times. He understands where the camera can best capture the action. He has practiced the speed, energy, and distances countless times. He has encountered unexpected occurrences that he has had to adjust for … quickly. The experienced professional has experienced the anticipated and the unanticipated so many times that you can have a certain level of comfort that the punch will be performed safely, convincingly, and with consistency.

Part and parcel of effectively staging and shooting action is understanding how the use of the camera to best capture all the action in the most exciting way is essential. Where to place the camera, what lenses to use, what frame rates, shutter angles are all in the province of who choreographs the fight and who will shoot it. That collaboration between the stunt team and the camera team is essential. If your story is heavily loaded with stunts, action, and special effects, then you should know there are cinematographers who specialize in those kinds of stories. They have vast experience in shooting action and special effects. Not all directors of photography have that experience. So it's quite possible you should be looking to employ a DP (director of photography) with an appropriate resume. There's a specific cinematic language to shooting action. Your DP needs to speak that language to effectively and clearly communicate with your stunt performers, choreographers, and coordinators. The other quality I find highly valuable is having a DP who is fearless, who will do what it takes to get the shot or die trying, in a manner of speaking. That can-do attitude is so much a part of the ethos of filmmaking that it's hard to imagine someone who doesn't say when you ask them to jump, "how far and how high?" But I have worked with one or two DPs who have resisted doing shots that they felt wouldn't meet their standards or the standards they had set in the movie.

> ROY WAGNER: *There's always someone who can tell you why you shouldn't or can't do something, but finding someone who can tell you how you can and why you should do something is what you want. My mentor told me it's not my job to say no, it's my job to say yes. Certainly there are safety issues, there are risks that can put you in jeopardy, but that's different. Find a way to say yes.*

A cinematographer's job, like everyone else on a production, is to help a director realize their vision. Especially due to the specific role a DP plays on a production, that of the person assigned to capture the visual images in such a way as to tell the story in the most truthful and faithful way possible, the cinematographer is faced with constant challenges, both technical and aesthetic. Your DP must be a problem solver of the highest order.

> ROY WAGNER: *It's our responsibility to find a solution that will not be inferior. It's not the director's job to protect our integrity or our aesthetic. It's our job to protect his integrity and that of the show. In doing so, you have to find the solution that will preserve and protect others. As I said, there's never enough time or money, but there's always a solution.*

Since I've brought up the subject of the importance of the choices made regarding the camera, I want to point out a fact. All scenes require the careful and informed use of camera in order to be realized to their fullest. Camera placements, movement, lenses, etc., are all critical factors to consider when planning and shooting a shot or a scene. These factors are as important to a dialogue scene as they are to an action sequence. Same importance, different applications. How high a camera is positioned supports a specific point of view. What lenses are employed in a scene allows the audience to connect with a scene and its characters in a specific way. Lenses, composition, and blocking focus an audience's attention on what we, the storytellers, want them to see. Don't take these decisions for granted. Make sure you or someone of experience has thought through how the camera is to be used and what the frame will reveal.

ROY WAGNER: *If you find somebody who's willing to find solutions,*
obviously experience is everything, but you can have shot for 100
years and have all that experience in your suitcase, but there's another
way to look at that if somebody thinks outside the box. If I do this, I
may get the same result, but I'll do it in less time and cost less money,
with less risk.

If your script calls for a fight of any sort, there are numerous things to consider
and be aware of. Once again, I will start with safety. The risk of someone
getting hurt in a fight scene varies from low to certain, depending on the
requirements of the scene and the stunt personnel executing it. For the
moment, let's assume the description of the fight poses no unusual risks.
Who on your team is prepared to make the judgment? Most likely, no one.

The person you should rely on to assess the practicality of the stunt and
to plan the execution of any stunt, in this case fight, is a professional. Of
course, I mean a stunt professional, but I also mean a first assistant director
(1st AD), who should have experience on shows that required action and
special effects. Here's why that is so important. The 1st AD runs the set.
According to the rules of the Directors Guild of America (DGA), they are
ultimately responsible for the safety of the cast and crew as well. So any and
every thing that happens on a set must be reviewed and approved by the AD.
They have the authority to prevent anyone working on the production from
doing anything the AD feels poses an unacceptable level of risk, no matter
who disagrees. That includes the producer, director, stunt coordinator, special
effects supervisor … anyone. So your AD better be experienced in stunts
and special effects. Otherwise they are not in a position to make the best
decisions, which can have enormous impact on your shoot.

DAN BRADLEY: *If you're working with somebody who's not*
experienced doing action, they may see things that scare them. They
don't understand and they may pull the plug, not based on any actual
danger, but their perception of danger. If you'd never seen a car stunt
performed before in your life and you're seeing somebody set one
up, that can look terrifying. Contractually, the AD has the last say on
allowing a stunt to be done, but in reality, they may not be qualified to
make that call. So, there is kind of a dance that happens between the
stunt coordinator and the AD to reassure them that what we're doing
in the stunt is safe.

Based on the DGA minimum basic agreement, the director can choose
the 1st AD. The director and AD will be working very closely together from

preproduction through production. The director's vision depends on the managerial skills of his AD. So it's a critical choice. When going through the process of finding the best AD for your show, you will think through many of the same considerations you had when hiring others on your team. In what ways are they qualified to best support the specific needs of your production? Eventually you get down to compatibility as well, but the first order of business in this very important position is, is this person qualified? Have they been around stunts and special effects? Do they know how these things are done and when it's being done properly? Do they understand the length of time these things may take so they can accurately schedule them? The AD is at the organizational and authoritative top of this pyramid. They organize and marshal the people and resources to bring about a stunt or effect. They don't actually design, plan, or execute the stunt or effect, but they do need to know how it was planned and how it will be executed to assure efficiency and safety. The AD is brought onto the production relatively early in the process. Because their responsibility is to schedule the production, many other decisions can't be made until that happens. The schedule will impact the budget. The budget will impact the schedule. Until that is sorted out, other decisions will have to wait. So the AD is a critical member of the team. At the point at which stunts and special effects such as pyrotechnics or rain effects, dust, wind, etc., must be planned for, the AD will be at the forefront of that effort. Many meetings in preproduction will take place addressing the issues connected with stunts and special effects. It may be one meeting for a simple straightforward stunt or effect, or it may be a series of meetings, depending on the complexity of the event. On larger shows, it takes a community of technicians, craftspeople, artists, and performers to serve the requirements of the story. In cases such as those, where things need to be built or customized or outfitted to fulfill the demands of the scene, constant meetings are held. This is simply a matter of organization.

> LINDA MONTANTI: *On a tv movie,* Turbulence, *we have them every Friday morning, all the departments. It would be like a production meeting, "OK, what do you have to tell us this week? How's it going? How's the construction going? What's happening with the plane? What's happening here? Did you order the windows? When do the seats come?" All these things everybody has to state where they are. This can last for an hour, and then, all the departments go back to work. You gotta do this or things will get lost or dropped.*

Everything runs through the AD. It's their job to know everything that has to be accomplished on set. They know the list of shots and at what time they should be shooting them. They know what resources are necessary to shoot those shots, that is, equipment, design, and labor. The success of any day's shooting depends on how well they do their job. They must be masters of organizational skills, cool under fire, and respectful of their responsibilities to guide the production through its schedule in a timely manner, and also serve the creative goals of the production. After all, it should be everyone's aim to make the best movie possible.

> LINDA MONTANTI: *An AD has to be around in prep and on the set and work with the other crew, work with the DP, work with the stunt coordinator and with the grips and the special effects people and put them all together and figure out, starting in prep, how we're going to do this. OK. This is a wonderful thing. The script says, we're going to do this huge stunt. I need to know how are we going to do it? I gather everybody connected with the stunt or special effect … we just sit around the table and I say, "How are we going to do this stunt?" I just say this to the stunt guy and the special effects guy, "OK, make believe I don't know anything. I'm just a dummy. What are we going to do? What do we do after I say roll, what happens?" And then, let them go through it. And then, we can say what we need to have and what we don't.*
>
> BUDDY JOE HOOKER: *The first assistant director runs the set. They're involved in the scheduling. They know what they have to accomplish within the day's work. They have everything ready for the director. It's kinda like, the director's the artist and the 1st AD provides the pallet and the paint … and the rags to clean up.*

I've worked with a few 1st ADs who are efficient and responsible, seeing the timely completion of the day's work as paramount above all else. This is not necessarily a bad thing. A well-known director's rebuke to the AD who is a slave to schedule above all else is "are we making a movie or a schedule?" The truth is, both. It's a balance. If the production isn't organized properly and run efficiently, the creative aspirations of the production will be suffocated. There won't be sufficient time to stage and shoot the show as planned. Time equals quality, if the time to plan and execute your production is well managed. The good ADs understand this dichotomy very well and will be hired over and over again. In fact, the DGA contract requires that every production allow the director to select their 1st AD. The reason for that rule is that a director must feel confident that the AD not only is qualified and well suited for their production, but will in a sense be the practical expression of the director's creative thinking.

With all this being said about how critical the director–AD relationship is, the first assistant director's role is a little tricky. Once the AD has created the shooting schedule, it is their responsibility to do everything in their power to deliver, meaning shoot the schedule on time. In a sense, they are also the producer's representative on the set. The AD is looking out for the areas that concern the producer and the money people as well as the creative intentions of the director. It's a balance. It's their primary job to assure efficiency, but in the spirit of delivering the best movie possible.

> BUDDY JOE HOOKER: *The ADs make things run smooth or not smooth. When I'm working with a bad one, it makes my life real difficult. Real difficult.*

The longer the resume, the better. The more specialized or experienced the stunt person is in executing the kind of stunt your movie requires, the better. The more times your 1st AD has had to plan and support a stunt on a production, the more qualified they are to assess risk from a stunt. That is a crucial part of their job description.

> BUDDY JOE HOOKER: *I would say anything involving a car or any kind of high fall stunts, don't compromise on your first AD. Get somebody who understands all of the safety elements and knows who is needed for a stunt team. Somebody that will respect the amount of time needed to set everything up. If you have a simple fight scene, something kind of small, it's different. But the bigger you get, the more important that AD is ... the stunt coordinator doesn't do it alone. The things that frequently go wrong is if there are people in the wrong place and at the wrong time.*

If you hire someone you have a personal relationship with, such as a friend from film school, someone you've worked with at another job, or just a buddy, this can pose a conflict of interest. The professionally minded AD will never let their personal feelings for anyone on the film set affect their judgment or final decision as to whether a stunt or special effect is safe enough to proceed. They know there's no room for skirting safety protocols or going against your judgment for the sake of friendship when lives are at stake. The fact that the AD can be legally liable for on-set safety may enter into the calculation, but it seems beside the point. The AD can never be thinking, "can I get into trouble for this?" Their interior conversation always has to be "Is this safe? Am I totally convinced that all reasonable measures for safety have been taken, and based on what has been explained and shown to me, the stunt should be successfully executed as planned?"

> DAN BRADLEY: *If you're going to be doing a big action scene, it's best not to hire your best friend as your AD. Find an experienced AD who's done action. It's a surprising reason because it's the AD who has the final say on whether a stunt or special effect is safe or not. Contractually, it falls on his shoulders in a big way.*

The AD will request that the stunt coordinator and possibly his performers share any planning that has been created with models, storyboards, animatics, or any other form of preplanning or visualization. This meeting may occur in preproduction or, in many cases, since stunts and special effects are often devised or revised during production, may take place at the start of a work day, during a break or the night before the stunt is to be shot. If you have a modest budget and you really can't afford mistakes in conceptualizing, planning, or executing, find some way to allow as much preparation as possible for those who are executing the tricky stuff, stunts, and special effects. Your stunt team will bend over backward to make rehearsals as inexpensive as possible. They want the stunt to succeed and go on their reel. Maybe they will give you a rate break and pull in some favors from their resources as well. These people want you to succeed to get what you want. In most cases, they will move heaven and earth to make it happen. That's just the kind of people they are. They love what they do and want nothing more than to pull off a great stunt or spectacular explosion.

On larger-budget movies that require complicated or very precisely timed stunts or large-scale pyrotechnics, the coordinators or technicians will do extensive rehearsing and experimentation. Vehicle stunts in particular will be practiced and perfected well before the day to shoot arrives. The stunt coordinator or driver may rent a large empty parking lot or field where he can safely figure out the stunt. A pyro expert will also secure some remote location where he can rehearse his gag, so he can be certain that on the day he'll deliver the bang everyone expects. Now it takes a hefty budget to provide this kind of preparation. Extra cars, mechanics to repair and adjust them, extra stunt drivers, transportation department drivers, and more. But when a major stunt can only be done once, this kind of prep is a smart investment. But what about those of you who don't have that kind of budget? It's unlikely and certainly inadvisable to tackle any kind of stunt or effect of such a scale that in order to prep and execute it well, you capsize your budget. But many less demanding driving stunts can and should be rehearsed to some extent before the day of shooting to make certain everything goes as planned.

On the day, before the stunt shot is to be actually performed, the AD will walk through every step of what the coordinator describes will happen, step by step. On the day just before shooting, everyone goes through it again.

> LINDA MONTANTI: *On the day we shoot I get everybody together for the safety meeting or even the pre-safety meeting earlier in the day and just say, "OK, what happens after I say roll it?" And I want to know who is doing what, who's rolling what camera? OK, OK. I say roll it, sound rolls, says speed, now what happens? And I want to know from the camera department who's going to tell me what all 15 cameras are shooting, and then who's the last camera to roll? Usually, an Eyemo [an inexpensive film camera] is the last camera or a camera positioned in a spot too dangerous to allow an operator. And then the first AC on the A unit, on the A camera, is usually the guy who says, "OK, we're ready," because then I can give the signal that everyone is ready. Either the director says action or the stunt coordinator.*
>
> JOHN BADHAM: *I will always have the stunt coordinator say action. There's no confusion that way.*

This discussion is specific. It's not "the car drives over in this area, it hits that guy over there, and stops around over there." It is a highly detailed description, walking the path of the action, describing exactly where and when every part of the whole stunt will take place. You clearly identify boundaries and spots where different beats of the action are expected to take place. You identify where a car will land, how high an explosion will be, where a character will be falling down, etc. That includes the run-up, any actual stunts, and the aftermath.

> GAYLE HOOKER: *The AD, director, and stunt coordinator hopefully have diagrams for car stunts; that's really important because that's how they communicate with each other and the stunt performers. The stunt drivers may say to everyone, "We need to make sure the gap right here is big enough because we're driving here and it's really important that we do this exactly like this." Then everybody gets to see what the drivers need and it becomes not just a getting the shot right, but in fewer takes. It also becomes a much safer thing.*
>
> JEFF TUFANO: *Every time a new situation or gag is created by the stunt folks or the special effects people, there's a meeting. Everybody stops what they're doing, the assistant director calls the safety meeting and you better pay attention. 99% of the time, things go right. But sometimes things don't go right and when they don't go right, they can go very wrong. I've seen bad stuff happen.*

Here's the safety meeting in broad strokes.

> JEFF TUFANO: *The safety meeting usually starts out with the AD presenting the broad strokes; this is what's gonna happen, this is how big it's going to be, this is how long the duration will be, where's the safety zone. There's always a place to watch, everybody wants to watch. There's a line we don't step over. We are especially careful with the special effects, because what they're working with is always hot, so to speak. And then it would not be unusual for the assistant director to turn the meeting over, one by one, to the different departments that are involved in making the stunt or special effect happen. The coordinator is going to have something to say, the visual effects supervisor may have something to say, the special effects people will tell you if there are explosives, where they are, how loud they will be.*
> ROY WAGNER: *The most experienced people I've ever worked with don't tell you what's going to happen, they'll let the people who are actually doing the stunts explain what they're going to be doing. The person who is going to be rolling the car or the person who has their hand on the button to explode the building will be explaining what's going to happen.*
> JEFF TUFANO: *Everyone explains what their part in the stunt is and what they expect to happen based on their experience. Sometimes I like to hear what to expect based on their experience from someone with a little gray hair. But if a guy comes to me with an attitude that is safety first and he seems to have done his homework, then I give him the benefit of the doubt.*

Let's not forget the producer in this beehive of activity. The producer should attend as many of these meetings as possible. A producer has a responsibility to make sure everyone is doing their job safely and appropriately in all ways. A good producer asks many questions. Of course, the best time to ask important questions is not as you're about to shoot; it's long before that time. But if that's the time an important question occurs to you, by all means, ask it. Your questions can save someone from injury or worse, not to mention money.

> JEFF TUFANO: *My favorite kind of producer is the kind of guy who stands right next to the first AD at the safety meetings and looks everyone in the eye and means it and there are a lot of guys like that.*
> *Most of the people I've worked with do good work and safe work. We work a lot at night. We work crazy hours. We were in the proximity of explosions, smoke effects, water hazards, and high-speed*

vehicles. I worked on the first Fast and Furious *movie. Some of the things we were doing were breathtaking, to put it mildly. So you want strong people who have done it before. Once again, the big thing is, it's got to be done safely. Anybody that even in a whisper tells you safety isn't the first thing to think about, is not the person you want to be working with.*

The director and the director of photography must be included in safety or planning meetings as well. Anyone connected with the execution of a shot needs to know what to expect before shooting it. That's why rehearsals are a time-honored tradition. They save time by familiarizing everyone with what the shot will look like and make any adjustments or calculations necessary to successfully capture the shot in a camera.

ROY WAGNER: *Sometimes in the safety meetings you'll find somebody says something opposite of what's been discussed and you either correct and adjust what their interpretation is, or you embrace it. Until you push the button and capture the moment, the film is a constantly malleable medium.*

It's about communication. Everybody needs to know what everyone else is doing that directly impacts their job. If you're a camera operator and you've set your camera in the most advantageous position to capture a piece of action, you want to know from the stunt or special effects people that where you are placing the camera is safe: no explosives, shrapnel, or careening cars have a reasonable chance of harming you. There's lots of talking these things out: lots of questions and lots of demonstrating. The more experienced the team is, the faster these conversations go. I don't want you to think there's so much conversation that takes place that the rest of the cast and crew is sitting around doing nothing most of the day. But like most other aspects to the shooting process, there is more planning and talking than actual shooting, just more so when it comes to scenes where safety is a concern.

LINDA MONTANTI: *On* LA Confidential, *we did hundreds and hundreds of squibs in the hotel scene at the end of the movie. And we could only do it once. The special effects people had this place wired, took them days to wire all the walls and then repatch the walls and repaint the walls and all the charges in all the walls, hundreds of them. And we set four or five cameras. Some cameras could not be manned because they were too close to where they're going to go off, but that's for the effects guy to tell me and the stunt guy to tell me. I can guess and say*

*to myself, "that looks like it's going to be too close," but they are the
guys who really know.*

With stunts, rehearsals can be problematic but are absolutely necessary. The
director must see a rehearsal. They must be able to confirm their expectations
or be able to see one last time before they shoot that no problems or flaws
in the planning can be discerned. When there is destruction of any sort such
as a car, a piece of furniture, a wall, or anything that is expensive and/or time
consuming to reset after a take, full rehearsals may not be practical. It's very
important to demonstrate whatever is possible with the actual elements of
the scene, such as cars, utilizing them in showing the scene for the crew and
director. Cars can be slowly driven through the path of the action.

JOHN BADHAM: *Just before we shoot a scene with a stunt or any
dangerous element, I see the people involved show me what's going
to happen. They walk it through, first at half speed and then if we can,
at a speed closer to how it will look when we shoot. I must be sure I
understand what they're going to do and that it will be what I asked for.
I'm also thinking safety as I watch, not just how cool the stunt will be.*

Fight scenes are somewhat easier to demonstrate. The choreography can
and should be precisely shown to the crew. Everyone needs to see within
what parameters it will take place in order for camera positions, lighting, art
direction, and safety to be made ready. Painstaking steps must be taken to
ensure safety, but also a successful execution of the stunt or pyrotechnics. If
due to a lack of knowledge about any aspect of a stunt or effect, it isn't usable
in the movie, that could be a very costly mistake.

LINDA MONTANTI: *We blew up a building in downtown on the tv show
Boomtown and it's a huge explosion. We're on a split-day schedule
and we had one scene, a four- or five-hour scene. And a character
was inside of a store. Across the street was the place the explosion is
going to take place. I check in with the stunt guys. "How's it going?"
"We're fine, we're fine. We'll be ready to do this right after lunch." And
so, right after lunch, it's maybe 10 or 11 o'clock at night, and we got
it ready. We have five cameras on it, and some of the cameras were
manned and some of them weren't. I asked the special effects guy,
"Where is it going to go?" And he said, "It's going to go up to 20 feet
high, maybe 30, but it's going to go up to the top of that building."
The director doesn't look because everything is fine, everything is
checked. Then we go through the safety meeting, check everything.*

The director was going to say "action." And we rolled cameras and it was so much bigger than everybody was told it would be, everybody's camera missed it! Everybody missed the shot because they were all framed too low except for one of the guys, an assistant working for the director ... some kid who had a video camera. He got it and that's in the movie! The director was so pissed. It came very close to one of the cameras. It didn't hit them, but some debris came close to one of them. He was also upset because he thought somebody was going to get hurt. Nobody did.

JEFF TUFANO: *Even the best guys have off days. For the most part, explosions seem to go the way they are supposed to. There are certain things that special effects people do that have become pretty routine and predictable. Any time you have to redo an explosion, you can expect it to be twice as big. Also, sometimes explosions can go off ahead of time by accident. I saw a special effects guy go into a stunt car to set a gas bomb and it went off right in his face. They had to put him in the dirt and roll him around to put out the fire. All you can do is hire the best guys you can find. Based on what they do and how things have gone in the past, they can only say "this is what you can expect."*

Some stunts or explosions just cannot be done twice. Not everyone has the time and money to reset and do it again in a day or a week later. You combine that reality with the unpredictability of some stunts and special effects, and it makes one appreciate the folks with the long resumes who have performed their jobs over and over and over again and well. Stunts and special effects are not a crap shoot. They can be controlled and their results can be reasonably predicted, but not guaranteed. The more complex the stunt or the bigger the explosion, the less controllable these efforts are. There's always Murphy's law, which people on movie sets like to quote. "Anything that can go wrong, will go wrong." I don't take that to mean every time or even often. I think it means that someday what went right dozens of times will, someday, go wrong. The professionals, the assistant director and the stunt and special effects team you work with in these dangerous areas of production, know this and take this seriously. These professionals should be assuming that something can go terribly wrong every time a stunt is performed or an explosive charge is detonated. That's how you stay safe. And your first assistant director is the one person who must oversee it all. They must review and check and double-check that everyone is following safe protocols and that everyone knows their roles and what to expect. They are the ones with ultimate responsibility. Even with all the best people, with the best of intentions, accidents can happen. Something impossible to anticipate can happen. It's part of the deal.

JEFF TUFANO: *The director decided from the cutting room, after we had finished shooting, that his movie is lacking punch, so he decided to shoot one more big stunt. The stunt was going to be a car going off a ramp and landing in the Hudson River. The director was in California and directed the sequence by telephone. The stunt coordinator had set it up. Apparently at the 11th hour, the director decided the car going off the ramp into the river was not exciting enough. So he decided he wanted it to corkscrew as it went off the ramp. Based on that change in plans, the coordinator decided it was too dangerous for the guy who was going to do it, so then he decided at the last minute, he was going to do it. He had plenty of experience and we understood why he decided to do it himself. There were five or six cameras. It was January and freezing. It was magic hour with the last little tiny bit of light over New York from the New Jersey side. The car goes off the ramp, it corkscrews perfectly, and it hits the water. Everything looks cool. Now we're waiting for the divers, who were waiting in the water, to go down and help the driver out of the water. The driver had an oxygen tank in the car. He was harnessed in and had a knife, in case he had to cut himself free. He had everything you could possibly need to be safe. It was almost dusk before the shot and now it's nighttime and he's still not out of the car. Finally, they sent a diver down with the cable and he hooked it up to the car. They pulled it out of the water while we all watched. The guy was still strapped in. He had apparently broken his neck on impact. It could have been for one of the greatest movies of all time, but it's still not worth it.*

There may be times when even the most experienced, but frankly it's usually the least experienced film crews, don't practice ideal safety procedures. Crews are often a mixture of experienced and less experienced workers. If a stunt is being rushed or a particular step in the protocol is being avoided, the seasoned pro may have his radar up and sense potential trouble or danger and air his concerns to the proper parties despite the culture on sets that discourages anything that slows down the day's work. Delays can be very costly, so everyone is always conscious of being efficient and being a team player. That gives most people pause before speaking up in a way that might be considered disruptive. If a stunt looks dangerous to a crew member, it may be meaningful or not. As I've pointed out, the inexperienced AD may get nervous when presented with a plan for a stunt because they don't have enough experience to evaluate its safety. Many stunts look scary and impossible to the uninitiated. If you're a young crew member who hasn't seen someone roll a car at a terrifically high rate of speed, you may feel like you want to scream for everyone to stop the madness. More often than not, everyone would get a good laugh, but not always.

> ROY WAGNER: *Every show I've been on, there have been questions addressed about safety. Every show and every shot. Sometimes the people are right. Sometimes you're dealing with fear. If the fear continues and is unfounded, you've got the wrong partner. If the fear is well founded, then you have to be very cautious about the implementation of those effects and make sure you protect those underneath you and yourself.*

As importantly, if you see how anyone on the crew or cast might be in harm's way, your concerns must be addressed. This is an area of focus that is sometimes not given enough attention. There's always much attention given to what's about to happen in front of the camera. Less experienced crews may not foresee danger lurking off set or just off the intended path of the action. People miss marks, conditions change, and equipment fails or becomes unexpectedly unmanageable. You and others may not appreciate how much of a margin for safety is advisable or what other precautions would be smart to implement. I won't deny there's politics to consider. There is a hierarchy on sets. Speak to the head of your department; share your concern, quickly and without drama. Either that person will be more willing to speak up to higher authorities if they agree with your concern or they will be able to explain to you why your concerns are unfounded; you learn something.

> ROY WAGNER: *It's always your place to speak up or to say I'm not comfortable with this. Your safety issues will be addressed. If you're still not feeling comfortable, you can bow out of it and step away or you can trust your partners. But generally if you're on the right team, people will adjust whatever is required in order to make it safe.*
>
> JEFF TUFANO: *If you have a safety concern, you would mention it to your assistant director or the second assistant. You also might mention it to the key grip, who often is considered in charge of on-site safety on behalf of the crew. In a union crew situation you have a shop steward, who is another avenue through which you can go. But again if something is 60 seconds away from happening I'd scream it at the top of my lungs. There are channels and there are politics, but safety is always first. Interestingly enough I've been in many dangerous situations over the years, but I didn't feel I had the clout to stand up and say "I'm not doing that." But now with more experience and stature on the crew, I will do that, and I have done that. But when*

you're younger and you're new, it's tough. But you have a boss and you hope that sometimes your boss will stand up and say something. But the bottom line is, we're each responsible for ourselves and we're each responsible in some ways for the people around us, whether they like it or not. I've never felt any repercussions and I encourage people to speak up. I'm probably one of the first few people who would stand up and say no instead of just thinking it. You develop a sense for what feels right over time and with experience.

I remember a director saying "lower, lower, lower…" to a helicopter. We're underneath the helicopter and the dirt is blowing and it's only 25 feet above our heads and we're shooting straight up and he wants "lower, lower, lower…" Not long after that, the Twilight Zone disaster with the helicopter happened. And then the next thing you know, there's no more "lower, lower, lower…" with the helicopters. I knew when the helicopter was getting lower and lower I didn't like that. But back then, I didn't feel I had the power to say something. But nowadays, I jump out of the chair. I have a 25-year-old son in the business and I am trying to imbue in him some sense of "don't be a sheep." I understand not everyone wants to speak up, but sometimes on a film set, if somebody doesn't speak up, something bad can happen. I will always tend to err on the side of caution. There are what we call in New York "knuckleheads" out there. There are some in every business; it's not unique. The only thing is in our business, somebody can get hurt.

The *Twilight Zone* incident in 1982, which is mentioned a few times in this book by various filmmakers, was a horrible catastrophe on the set of that movie in which three actors were killed (including two small children) by a falling helicopter, which was basically blown out of the sky by an explosive charge that was set on the ground. The helicopter, on orders of the director, came too close and was disabled. Many safety regulations in force at the time were ignored. Arguably, an overeager director with a forceful personality and elevated status in the industry lost sight of reasonable safety precautions, and the worst-case scenario occurred. This incident became a bellwether for film set safety. There are cases, to be sure, that if someone had spoken up, raised a safety concern they harbored deep down or even just below the surface, someone's life would've been spared or a serious, life-changing injury avoided. I think that statement, while of course not provable, is inarguable.

How Do You Find and Hire Your Stunt Coordinator?

The job of stunt coordinator is one in which a great deal of experience and good judgment are especially important. The safety of many people is in their hands, cast and crew alike. You want someone who has the experience to come up with creative solutions, someone who's been there before. You also want them to exercise good judgment and prudence due to the many challenges stunts pose. You don't want thrill junkies and yahoos who take unnecessary risks. Stay away from the guys who seem to diminish safety in favor of bravado.

> DAN LEBENTAL: *I always found interesting with young filmmakers wanting to do big Hollywood stunts and have to show what they can direct, which is always funny to me because the big directors have big stunt coordinators and that's what they do. They don't even plan these stunts, they just bless them.*

The more experience, the better. It indicates a few things. It shows you that people are happy with their work and that they did it safely. Stunt people who don't practice safety seriously aren't around long enough to get a reputation of any sort, even a bad one. If you're going to have open heart surgery, do you want the guy who promises to do it quicker and cheaper because he's just starting out? Or do you want the doctor who has performed this very surgery hundreds of times with perfect results? This is not an exaggerated question I pose. The decision you make as to whom you're entrusting the safety of your cast and crew to can very well be as critical as choosing a highly qualified heart surgeon. You want someone with as much experience and success as possible, and there must be a bottom-line threshold you are not willing to cross in assessing competence. If you plan on a high fall and the only person available to do it or who will meet your price has done it only once or twice, STOP! Rewrite the scene, or keep looking for a more qualified stunt person who has performed this stunt time and time again.

A commonsense approach to finding a qualified stunt coordinator for your production is to research other productions you feel have elements in common with your production. Similar action such as car chases, hand-to-hand combat, martial arts displays ... whatever. Simply look at the credits of that movie on IMDb and identify the stunt coordinator. You can call the Screen Actors Guild (which also has long lists of members who are categorized as stunt performers) to get contact information such as their agent or professional association. You can call the agency and express your interest in meeting their client for your production. They are happy to field calls from people like you who have money to spend on their clients. The agent will ask you a few questions about your production: its dates, its budget, location, and other pertinent details that are both practical and qualifying. If your dates of production conflict with a job their client already has booked, then the conversation will be brief: that is, however, unless the agent takes the opportunity to sell you another client. If you are unfamiliar to the agent either personally or by reputation, they may ask you some questions that will satisfy their fiduciary responsibilities to their client. The agent must be satisfied that you are a legitimate production, the real deal who has money to spend. They can tell this if there has been anything published in trade papers about your production such as announcements of other hires. If you have signed any actors to contracts or they can confirm that other artists, craftspeople, and technicians have been hired, the agent will be satisfied that they are dealing with a genuine potential employer. I mention this because many producers and directors often represent they have more "assets" or valued personnel secured than they really do. They resort to such "exaggerations" in order to leverage those assets into landing a real and potentially valuable creative element to their production. This is significant, because when you actually sign your first person who has commercial value or the status in the industry to attract financing, it can often beget others. When people in the creative community see a production has hired one of their own, attitudes change. Suddenly they show interest. Now it's real and more attractive. So to create some capital-raising momentum, producers will work very hard to land that first valuable name, whether it's an actor or possibly a well-known cinematographer. If a producer represents that they have signed well-known talent to their production, that fact may favorably influence other people they approach to come on board: a domino effect.

If you're already part of that creative community, another easy way to identify candidates for the coordinator job is to start asking around. Ask friends in the business, colleagues ... anyone that has possibly worked with someone who fits the description you're looking for. Later in the book, I will describe for you other businesses that interact and intersect with the world of stunts and special effects. Two businesses in particular that can provide referrals for stunt and special effects coordinators are entertainment insurance brokers and completion bond representatives. Their jobs require that they intimately know the qualifications and track records of stunt performers and special effects technicians, because their companies insure productions against risks that may emanate from stunts and special effect gags. Depending on how long after this book is published you research which those companies are, there may be some new players in that market and some of the established companies may have left the market. I can only say that Fireman's Fund has been a major insurer of entertainment productions since the silent film days of Hollywood. Try them first.

It makes sense that you identify other movies that call for similar kinds of action as yours. It also stands to reason that you may assume productions that have much larger budgets than yours might not yield useful candidates for your modestly or cheaply budgeted production. That's not necessarily true. Don't presume that stunt coordinators on studio-sized productions won't help you. Most successful people in the entertainment industry started at the bottom. Few were handed jobs they weren't qualified for, although it happens; they worked their way up. If you're a producer or director who's just starting out or has a limited resume, the folks who have been there and have now "made it" understand your situation and are often very willing to help you.

> MARTIN CAMPBELL: *My advice is that it's all about personal relationships. You should get the phone number of the top stunt arranger you can think of, meet, ask his advice, and inevitably they know people who are up-and-coming who are eager to do something. I found Gary Powell that way. When Simon Crane went off to do a Bourne second unit, he had to drop out of a film of mine. I asked who he suggested and he said Gary Powell. Gary hadn't stunt arranged anything, but he said he would be terrific. He's due now to do something on his own. So he did the second Zorro for me and he did a terrific job. That's the way I would go about it. Find the top stunt arranger you can think of. Ring Dan Bradley and ask him out for a cup of coffee and say, "okay Dan, I've got a small film and I know you can't do it, can you suggest somebody who is hungry, talented, up-and-coming that perhaps would do it?" Don't be afraid to go to the top. Ring them up, ask their advice.*

Then again, they might surprise you and jump on board. There are stunt performers' organizations whose membership is comprised of the very people you want to work with. These are professional organizations that help promote business, safety, and the exchange of ideas concerning their industry.

One of the most prominent is Stunts Unlimited (stuntsunlimited.com), which is headquartered in Sherman Oaks, a suburb of Los Angeles. Stuntmen's Association of Motion Pictures (stuntmen.com) is another well-regarded organization that can be a valuable resource for locating stunt coordinators. They are located in North Hollywood, California.

> GAYLE HOOKER: *You should actually reach out to your best choices… do not be afraid of picking up the phone, finding out through stuntmen's associations like Stunts Unlimited or other organizations. They all have folks in the office who can help you locate a member. "I am doing a movie. I have a low budget. I saw so and so's name in this production. Can I just send him an e-mail or can you please give him my phone number?"*

On one side of the spectrum, they may just say yes to your job offer, if only to get you started on the right foot.

> BUDDY JOE HOOKER: *Don't be afraid to ask for favors. That happens a lot in this business. I still do it, although I don't do it as much. It depends on the person and the project.*

But if your budget and resources just don't make sense for them to accept the position, they may have some very useful suggestions. They may have a stunt person who has stuck by their side for years, learning and gaining experience as their apprentice or trusted go-to guy. The master may feel it's time for their disciple to go out on their own, on your production. Coordinators come into contact and work with multitudes of stunt performers. They can often recommend stunt performers they have full confidence in and are ready for the promotion. Big-time coordinators also may refer you to other coordinators they know by reputation, giving you leads to follow up on without their informed endorsement. Hopefully, they will be clear that they are not personally recommending them, but know they have good reputations.

> GAYLE HOOKER: *All of the big people have sons, daughters, associates, or protégés, who they would love to give or to start building up their own stunt coordinating resumes.*
>
> BUDDY JOE HOOKER: *We're not going to put them up on a job where they're way over their head. But people will do that too and that's one of the pitfalls. Some less reliable guys are going to give you somebody that they're trying to help out that really doesn't have the qualifications.*

The motion picture and television business is well stocked with sketchy characters: people who represent themselves to be more accomplished than they really are. By exaggerating their resumes or abilities, some people think they'll get ahead in the business. Sometimes, that makes for a very heartwarming story of success. Other times, it proves to be a cautionary tale about how someone gets in over their heads and does some damage to themselves and others who bought their story. The business is also rife with people on the fringes: well-meaning people with verifiable experience who have managed to get by, but have not progressed in their careers. This may be due to a lack of quality work, talent, managerial skills, or other problems that have held them back. You want to know what you're buying when you select a stunt coordinator or special effects technician. These are positions of enormous responsibility, where mistakes can be disastrous.

Get references. In our businesses, references count for a lot. It is common business practice to ask for references and CVs. Call the references; confirm what the CV states. Don't be afraid to ask a previous employer if what a stunt person did on their show accurately reflects what the stunt person claims on their CV. Did the stunt person do exactly what his resume says he did, or is there some puffery or exaggeration? Was he really the person who fell five stories or was he on the support team?

> DAN BRADLEY: *You can talk to other directors or assistant directors and get recommendations, because you definitely want to work with people who come recommended or who have resumes that perhaps have work that you recognize, work that you admire, that's similar to what you're looking for. But I would still try and follow that up with calling people they've worked with, find out how responsible this person actually is for this work.*

Don't be surprised if in your vetting of any of your team, someone exaggerates or lies outright about their experience, accomplishments, or skills. It's a code in the acting business, for example, to never say you can't do something. "Can you play the piano?" Despite no experience on any musical instrument, the dedicated actor will say "of course" and then prepare to prove it when called upon. "Can you ride a horse?" The hungry actor who can't pay his rent replies, "like John Wayne." This canon of behavior can trickle down to crew as well. So always ask for and conscientiously follow up on a reasonable amount of references any stunt or special effects professional you are considering working with provides. It's expected, never a bother. All professionals rely on that network of information to ensure safety, competence, and reliability. References are usually happy to provide positive information to people they have worked and had a good experience with. They wish them only the best when it comes to getting their next job. Everyone relates to that. Most references are honest as well when their experience was less than ideal with the prospective employee. You want people to be honest with you, so you better be honest with them. If you were to find out that you hired someone a reference knew was not qualified or did a poor job for them and someone got hurt or performed poorly, that would be indefensible, certainly unethical.

When you identify your candidates for the coordinator position, ask for resumes. Those may come in a few forms besides the standard CV. The coordinator will most likely have a show reel with examples of their work. You probably can view the productions they worked on online or other media and view what they claim to have been involved in.

> BUDDY JOE HOOKER: *So that's where you have to read the resume. What have they done? Have you done this? Can you show me something? What's very important is to start narrowing down lists and start to make phone calls to arrange interviews. So they can come prepared for the meeting, you must let them know the budget, what the stunt is and then, you can interview them. Have them read your script. The one to one is very important. It puts you both on the same page. I think it's imperative that every producer and director interviews a coordinator for the position.*

The interview itself should be a candid and clear exchange of ideas. Many producers and directors express exactly what they want, how they visualize the story, the look, and the stunts. They don't hold back. Others take the approach of not revealing too much. They keep their thoughts closer to the vest. They want to hear what the interviewee thinks without being prompted. Both of these strategies have their advantages when interviewing anyone who will be making a creative contribution to your production.

> ROY WAGNER: *You should listen to what the person says and determine instinctually if that's what you're looking for in a person. Truly, you're looking for a person who is like-minded and you feel has enough experience to create the illusions you're looking for.*

Maybe your production is more than you can handle, but don't assume. The coordinator you're interviewing may tell you it may be possible to pull off exactly what you want, with your resources, in a way you never imagined. He may also tell you the stunt is beyond your reach as described, but here's another way you might consider that will also serve the story and be entertaining. He may reimagine the stunt in a creative way that appeals to you, lifting your creative spirits back up.

He may be just the man for the job. You don't just want a guy who can simply execute the stunts as written. You want more than that. You want a creative partner, just as you do in other positions on your production. Also, it's not at all unimportant to like the person you'll be working with. Chemistry is helpful, maybe not absolutely necessary, but as with any creative collaboration, it enhances the creative process.

> BUDDY JOE HOOKER: *Creativity is key in the interview. I think that's really important.*
>
> JOHN BADHAM: *A friend of mine, Connie Palmisano, is a great stunt coordinator who works with Jackie Chan and coordinates a lot of Hong Kong movies. And he's constantly asking about the story, "What could be worse than that?" A helicopter comes along and is likely to chop our hero in half with the helicopter blades, but he grabs onto the skids and holds on. What could be worse than that? And Connie dreams up a gag that is an escalation of the action. That kind of playfulness is how you get your stunts to the point where you're doing things that people haven't seen a hundred times before. There's a lot of standard stunts, but your audience has the tendency to see them and go, "Oh, this is fistfight number 24. Boring."*

By the time we're six years old, we've accumulated and catalogued much of the vernacular of visual storytelling. We innately understand story structure, having seen it played out on screens of all sorts almost daily, through various media. We quickly acquire an understanding of how stories are set up and resolved after a series of confrontations. We know that a violent confrontation is the expected, the de rigueur way an action movie resolves at the end. It's the final fight or assault on the enemy that concludes the movie. Without being aware of it, we are inculcated with the basic shapes of most stories, and therefore we have certain expectations. When those expectations are either played with or defied, it grabs our interest. We're likely to think that the movie or show seemed original or fresh. There's an axiom many writers follow, *a story should be surprising, yet inevitable.* This means how the movie turns out should make sense. The ending should be built on events that lead to an inevitable conclusion, but those events should have an element of surprise. So a creative stunt coordinator will avoid the norms. It's easy for someone designing a stunt or making story decisions of any sort to reach into their mental archive of stories and situations that resemble one in your movie and choose from a list of likely events that audiences are familiar with and make sense for the story. John Badham obviously greatly values stunt coordinators like Connie Palmisano, and the directors, including me, who have worked with Dan Bradley (and I can only assume Paul Greengrass, among others) all treasure these people, because of the fantastic extra value these pros bring to our movies. They work hard to bring the element of surprise and originality to the stories they're helping to tell through their exciting craft.

So when interviewing coordinators, part of the interview should be their presentation of their ideas on how they would approach your stunt work. You must try to gauge their creative potential. They may bring diagrams or other visual aids such as clips to view. As director, you too should be prepared to help the interviewee understand completely what you have in mind. Words often fail us in making movies. "Show me, don't tell me" is a key pillar of the visual storytelling canon. Show clips, suggest movies to see in order to illustrate a particular scene or stunt. Storyboards or an animatic are excellent ways of expressing a vision.

> GAYLE HOOKER: *Buddy Joe did a TV pilot that got picked up:* King & Maxwell. *It's Rebecca Romijn and Jon Tenney, and the director of it came to Buddy Joe and said he had a vision of the beginning of this pilot. They spend a lot of money on pilots because they want it to go to the full series.*
>
> BUDDY JOE HOOKER: *The director said, "I want you to watch* Children of Men." *I knew the sequence that he wanted to redo. I got it right away. So it was really helpful.*
>
> GAYLE HOOKER: *It was important because the way he was describing it didn't do it justice…That sequence is very hard to describe. I think stunt coordinators are very tactile people. They are physical people. It doesn't always mean what you're saying is what's being heard. Let me see it.*

There are other benefits to the interview, even if it doesn't result in a professional marriage.

> GAYLE HOOKER: *A director wants to be able to say, "I can afford to crash two cars. How could I make this happen?" "How do we make this look amazing?"*
>
> BUDDY JOE HOOKER: *How can we make this little thing more exciting, within our structure and budget? A director or producer is going to get some real good creative input that they can use later, even if the stunt guy says no. And you're gaining knowledge too. Every time you*

sit down and talk with a stunt coordinator, you're getting information, useful knowledge that you can use down the line.

These meetings aren't always and don't have to be conclusive as to how to accomplish a specific stunt or an approach to the movie. If a coordinator has the right resume or, for some compelling reason, appears to be the right person for the job, figuring out how to pull off a stunt may come much later in the production process. Deciding how to execute or create the means by which a stunt can be executed may take research and trial and error. Feel like you have a creative partner watching your back and walking you forward.

The complexities of film production and the stunts in particular call for voices of experience on the team. I've stated the obvious reasons, safety, reliability, creativity, and precision. Another reason that hiring experienced professionals is a wise investment is because these old hands can save you money in many areas. Experienced pros know what equipment you'll need and what you can do without. They can organize your resources of manpower and material. They know, for instance, that by hiring a stunt double for a situation that doesn't seem that dangerous, the production can save an hour or two shooting a scene because they can help rehearse and teach the A-team talent some moves they have to make look realistic, while the shot is being set up.

DAN BRADLEY: *There are a lot of things…that may seem counterintuitive, like if you're going to do a fight, very often you'll save money in the end if you bring the stunt guys in a day in advance to have them rehearse. Sometimes if you're doing really complicated fights like in the Bourne movies, the rehearsal process can go on for weeks. But that's a smart investment.*

JOHN BADHAM: *On the* Nikita *TV show that I direct, the stunt guys are there and they know what shots are coming up. There's actually two of them on that show and one guy is rehearsing the actors before the shot because they'd like the actors to do as much as they can, but they're always prepared to double them, which is the other question and a big question, "When do you use doubles and when do you not use doubles?" So they're constantly rehearsing the actor. Even if the actors may only be in part of the sequence of shots, at least they can keep acting in the scene right up to the dangerous bit and look like they're still in it and I don't have to be focused on the back of a stunt double's head. So it's good to break in your actors and get them into the spirit of things. Actors always, always want to do their own stunts, short of diving off buildings.*

Extra stunt performers on set can also make things move faster in terms of preparing a shot. Three people can make something happen much faster than one in some cases. The $1000 or $2000 you might spend on extra help for the day pales in comparison to the amount of money you may be spending per hour for the whole production. So it may be worth spending $2000 to save an hour of shooting time, which can cost anywhere from $10,000 to $100,000, or much more. This is a calculation you'll do that suits your specific budgetary situation. Benjamin Franklin was so prescient when he said "an ounce of prevention may be worth a pound of cure." I actually think he was misquoted. I'm told he actually said, "An ounce of prep is worth a pound of prevention of delays." You might want to look that up, although whether he said it or not, other people say it all the time. Spend wisely. Spend a few more dollars to assure things go smoothly because the downside can be ruinous. A few more stunt guys can be a shrewd investment. I'm not suggesting that they be hired just in case an extra body is needed to help rig or rehearse. Your coordinator will lay out each day of shooting and what resources will be needed. He will assess his manpower needs and suggest how many people he will need to assure safety and efficiency. He knows a mistake on his part can cost the production dearly.

Stunt Doubles

Another important function a professional stunt coordinator or fight coordinator fulfills is to decide when to use your on-camera talent, also known as your principal cast or "A team," and when to replace one or all of your "A team" with stunt doubles when shooting a potentially dangerous shot. Stunt doubles are stunt professionals who are employed to replace your actors when the shot calls for any risky, on-camera action or for action that may have to be performed in multiple takes and angles.

GAYLE HOOKER: *The stunt coordinator works with the producer to determine exactly whether the double is going to be needed or not. But the double is always on set if there's any question of safety or ability. Because actors frequently turn around and say, "I can do that." Actors say that all the time.*

BUDDY JOE HOOKER: *They all do.*

JOHN BADHAM: *On the film* Bird on a Wire *with Goldie Hawn and Mel Gibson, Goldie is driving a car through downtown Vancouver being chased by police and the car has to do a 360 degree spin in the middle of the street. She comes up to me right before shot and says, "I spent all weekend out at the fairgrounds and I can take my Porsche and I can spin it all over the place." She'd driven her Porsche up to Vancouver, "And I'm really good at it." And I said, "Well, I'm sure you are, but this is in the middle of a street and on this side is the railroad station and on this side is a skyscraper and here are these concrete abutments and if you hit any one of those, it's all over for you. Certainly we're going to be out of business for a day or so. So no, you can't drive it." And this is where you look for cleverness among your crew. My transportation coordinator came up and said, "I just found a right-hand-drive version of this convertible and…," like they drive in England with the steering wheel on the other side. So we put a fake steering wheel on the left of the car. We put Goldie in where the fake steering wheel is and our stunt guy will hide and drive the car and spin it around. Even that made me nervous. It was a close-up on her and just to make it even more fun, she supposedly has Mel Gibson with his head down around her feet and his legs up around her neck because he's dived in the car head first and she's trying to control the car while it's doing this wacky thing. I mean it worked fabulously. Absolutely, totally believable, better than we could've done with green screen where the motion wouldn't have been quiet so real.*

Another important factor to consider when determining the need to use a stunt double besides the danger quotient of a shot is the ability to perform the stunt take after take. Remember that this is one of the major attributes a professional stunt performer brings to your production: the ability to perform a fall or car crash take after take in precisely the same way. Those moments of action are "money" in more ways than cost. As a filmmaker who has responsibility for the cost and *quality* of a production, you can't rely on luck that a stunt will be performed over and over again with visual consistency for purposes of cutting together a coherent scene or sequence. You must be able to rely on uniformity of action. Even if safety is not a factor in using a double, you can't rely on an actor being able to repeat the action more than once or twice. They may have only one good take in them, at most.

GAYLE HOOKER: *Actors not only say they can do the stunt, they say how high? How many times? And they can't. The question is, can they do it eleven times without getting injured for every different camera angle? Can they do it eleven times and show up the next day for work with all the bumps and the bruises and still be able to maintain their acting? There's sort of a fall-off curve with an actor. They might be able to do it one or two times. So the idea is you want to have that double there because there is almost always a chance that more than one take will be needed. So if the action is going to need anything more than one take, and they usually do, you are really increasing the chances that stunt could compromise that actor, meaning injure… lost to the production for a few minutes, a few hours, a few days, or worse.*

DAN BRADLEY: *You need to put your actor in a parking lot somewhere and see if they take direction, if they have any sense of what's going on because there are people who the rest of the world evaporates when they hear action and they just lose their minds and can completely forget they're driving something real. They can do real damage. It becomes more critical when they're dealing with equipment that carries a lot of power and their ability to hurt other people is greatly increased. If you think they're crazy in the room, wait until you see them in a car.*

Actors want nothing less than to be able to create a truthful, fully believable character in wholly believable circumstances. They worry about that "curtain" falling away, revealing the artifice of it all. No one wants to break the suspension of disbelief. A badly executed stunt sequence can reveal in a very awkward way the artificiality, the process behind the work. The delicate sense of reality is blown. They want to do the stunt (within reason ... usually) as to not risk revealing the "seams" of the sequence. While this is, of course, commendable, good judgment must prevail. Weighing the pros and cons of allowing an actor who may even be able to perform a stunt to actually do it on camera can be a crucial decision, one that averts the actor and the production from disaster. Your stunt coordinator must be involved in those decisions. You are flirting with disaster if you do not seek and heed their counsel. Issues of insurability may also be raised if you choose not to consult with and follow a professional stunt coordinator's advice.

> BUDDY JOE HOOKER: *Your actors will fight to want to do something. So as a producer, you know, as a young producer, as a young director, as a young DP, but especially as a young producer, the important thing is that actors will want to fight you and especially if they're your leads and they have some kind of a name and they will want to do something. So, it's a matter of navigating what their ability is. Some of them, even after years, will turn around and say, "They'll know it's not me. They'll know it's not me!"*

In these situations where you have an enthusiastic actor who insists on doing their own stunts, you have other problems beyond the practical issues of competence and safety. The production has a personal as well as business relationship with its cast, especially its principal cast. If you're the director or producer, you will most likely be relying on your lead actors to cooperate with the production in ways that transcend their duties on set. When the movie is released, you may want the lead actors to promote the movie, say nice things about their experience while shooting. "The director is a genius and the producers were amazing. It's the best experience I've ever had in all my years of acting in movies!" You may have to ask for special favors while shooting such as the occasional forgiveness on meal penalties or indulgence on a slightly shortened turnaround.

> RON SHELTON: *Kurt Russell is a very good driver and he could be very convincing too. It's really him driving so we put the camera over his shoulder, that's real crazy shit flying by. And then when you want the car to clip something, it's a stunt driver. That's a little bit more of the*

athletic model because how many actors can stunt drive? I had another actor on my show Hollywood Homicide *who insisted on driving and he wouldn't listen to reason. He drove anyway and ran into another car. We had to buy a new car. It was a short day and the guy went to the hospital. Next day it's on TMZ and everything.*

Everyone should be "playing ball." So when your star wants to crash his hero car into a brick wall and walk away in the shot, you will pause to consider it. This kind of politics is ever present. Will you lose the actor's confidence or support even though their request is ill considered? You may have to risk it. And there's always your trusty stunt coordinator whom you can point to and plead. "It's not me that's worried, it's him."

> BUDDY JOE HOOKER: *Sometimes it might seem like a shot or scene does not require a stunt coordinator to understand how to make the action appear seamless, but they save you the time, they save your actors and … producers can use them to mitigate any of the egos on set with the actors. "I want you to do it too. But it's outta my hands, the coordinator won't go for it," says the earnest producer.*

As a producer or director who is dealing with an actor who insists on doing a risky action, there is besides the stunt coordinator and AD another party to point to as having some "skin in the game"—the insurance company. You may be absolutely accurate in telling an actor they are prohibited from performing certain stunts by the terms of your policy. Such language exists in most policies. But even if that's a gray area, it's a useful tactic when your gut tells you that the risk to your actor and therefore to your production is unacceptable.

> MARTIN CAMPBELL: *You can always resort to the insurance company and explain that they won't allow it. If you get the side of your head bashed in or your teeth knocked out, you're putting people out of work for months. And there's no downside to using stunt doubles except the macho "I did my own stunts" kind of thing.*

Many times the risk is not apparent. A director or producer must still weigh the minimal risk against the consequences of an unexpected injury. Sometimes, it's just best to say no.

> JOHN BADHAM: *Richard Dreyfuss in* Stakeout *has to pretend that he just jumped over a 5 foot fence into somebody's backyard. And*

so I have his stunt guy do the jump over the fence because Richard
says, "No, no, I can't do that." And you go, "Fine, that's alright. Not a
problem, but I need to have you just landing on the ground. So here,
jump off this little apple box which is only a foot tall, onto the soft grass
like you came over the fence and it'll be fine." Great! "Okay, here we
go and action!" He jumps off the apple box, less than a foot, and he
twists his ankle and can't walk for two days! One foot high! "Well, I
got weak ankles," he informs me. We're not totally out of business, but
we were kind of screwed for a day or two.

Risks lie in wait in every stunt shot. You can have the level-headed actor
decline to do a stunt other actors might be more willing or capable of doing.
He knows his limitations and understands the consequences if he is injured
doing something over his abilities.

But … here's the other side of the argument as to whether to use your actors
in stunts or fights. As actors and directors are aware, there's no replacement
for the real thing. *If* safety were not an issue and the actor could be trained
or had the skills to do their own stunts, that would be the unequivocally ideal
situation. No doubt about it. But there are lots of risks associated with that
decision, so we make other plans quite often. But if the actor were to do their
own stunts …

DAN BRADLEY: *I much prefer doing fights with the actors because*
when I get to see them, the look on their faces, I get to see their
characters. I much rather have a fight that's less technically spectacular
because it relies on the actor's ability to pull it off, than to watch even
the best stunt guys in the world do their stuff from camera positions
far away or on their backs. I don't think that's interesting. I want it to be
as real as possible.

Not all actors have an objective view of their athletic abilities. Their desire to
do their own stunts may be for all the right reasons, that is, the desire to be
as truthful as possible in portraying a character. As has been stated, they may
also be looking to validate their macho cred. But they may also be looking to
validate their self-image, a valuable asset to an actor. The more experienced
actors have often come to terms with that issue and understand what their
strengths and weaknesses are and what's best for the movie.

MARTIN CAMPBELL: *If you shoot it correctly, it's very easy to swap*
your talent in where they need to be swapped in. And by the way,

the clever actors know this too. They'll know they look better with the stunt guy and it's just safer. I once had actors that I want to do all my own stunts and he was actually terrible at it. He was hopeless. He ran badly, his stunt work was just awful. What I would do was I would call lunch. He'd go off. I get the double and I'd say we're working through lunch and off we go and redo it. The actor fought me for about 10 days until he was getting so beat up, he finally opted out himself. "I'm not doing my own stunts."

DALE GIBSON: *You get an actor who gets in and out of the car a bunch of times and suddenly he thinks he's a driver just because they're on a set acting and pretty soon they convince themselves that they can do it. Let the professionals do the drifts.*

There are also times when it makes sense to hire a stunt actor. There are stuntmen who are pretty decent actors. There are often scenes where you need an actor to say a few lines and then get shot and fall off a roof. Lots of cops stories and Westerns call for scenes where some bad guys push around the hero or harass a damsel. Those scenes end in violence. Why not have a stuntman be the one to hurl an insult and then follow through with a punch, kick, or fall? You don't have to cut away to preserve the illusion. There is no illusion. What you see is for real. Stunt coordinators often recommend to directors that they audition stuntmen who can play those smaller roles that require some expertise, because it reinforces the illusion of reality. Every time you have to cut away just before the moment of contact, you risk revealing the illusion. Cutting away to a shot of a stunt double or reaction shot can be employed very effectively so that audiences never think about the artifice of it. But if you don't have to use those techniques, why go there?

DALE GIBSON: *Dan Bradley did a film called* Red Rock West. *He had the director, John Dahl, cast me as the ranch hand. The reason they cast me was so they wouldn't have to cut around me when I get hit by a car driven by Nicolas Cage. They actually put cameras in the car so they could see my face as I was going over the car when I got hit, without having to cut away. They could do this because they used an actor who could also do the stunt. I'll say to a director when they're casting, let me send you these cowboy stunt guys.*

Another wrinkle in the actor–stunt dynamic is when you have a perfectly safe way for the actor to be in the shot, to do their own stunt, and they are afraid to do it. You really can't force an actor to do something they perceive is dangerous. If nothing else, their performance will suffer if all they're thinking about is their imminent demise.

> DAN BRADLEY: *If you don't see the actor's face, don't use the actor. But I will often try and find ways to put the actor into apparent peril. Nothing looks better or tells the story better. Sometimes that's working underwater, sometimes it's working in the air and you make it look dangerous, but it's not at all. I know the actor's capability. That's part of what I do, assess their abilities and mind-set. Are they willing to do any crazy thing or is everything just too scary for him? I've worked with actors, and you'll be shocked, but they're playing superhero characters and the actor is definitely afraid of heights. On one movie, the lead actor became incapable of movement: frozen. I demonstrated the action. I showed him the two cables on him that will hold three cars each! But he was incapable of functioning on the edge at the top of a high building. The very first time I met Christopher Walken. He just had to lean over the top of this building in a gargoyle kind of crouch. He was tied off. He had three anchors. He was completely safe, but I found myself talking to him and holding the cable tight, leaning against him, and I just kind of shoved him over the building to put him in position. That can sometimes work and not work for you. To his credit, he could still act. He could still do his job. He was anxious but he wasn't paralyzed. I've worked with actors who get paralyzed. That's when you have to go another route.*

But when you decide the risk is too great and you will employ stunt doubles, the stunt or fight coordinator will, at critical cut points, plan to replace the actor with their stunt double up until the point in the scene where a risk is posed. Cut. The director, in collaboration with the coordinator, will then shoot the continuation of that action (a punch, for example) using carefully chosen camera placement in order to mask the identity of the stunt double. This should appear to be seamless. At the point in the shot in which the identity of the stunt double can't be concealed any longer, the shot will be concluded. Cut. Then in separate shots, the continuation of the whole action will be covered, without the risky parts and using the A-team talent: a sleight of hand.

In a series of shots that comprise a fight, a stunt double may appear in only one shot out of four or five. By slipping in that one critical shot in which the talent has been replaced, but appears more openly in the other shots, the audience is rarely aware that the actor has been swapped in the scene. The closer the stunt double physically resembles or can be made to resemble the cast member they are standing in for, the more invisible that switch will be. In fact, some actions stars have stunt doubles they consistently work with on every job possible. Those doubles are the same size and complexion as their star counterparts. They may even be able to approximate their star's physicality, their walk, or the way they throw a punch.

Stunt doubles are also called upon to teach or demonstrate an action to the A-team actor they are doubling for. When a certain specialized skill such as swordplay is required at a critical juncture of the scene, the double may be inserted to perform that part of the action that requires his skill and consistency. But the continuation of that action may still require an authenticity that requires the talent to show some of that same skill. Their stunt double may be the perfect expert on set to demonstrate how they enacted the movement with the sword. "Watch this. This is how I did it."

> GAYLE HOOKER: *I've doubled actresses so many times. But I often don't get on film. I'll show them how to do something I think they can do on camera. I'll help them out with the rehearsals and everything but I'm there ready to jump in and do the shot, just in case there's too much risk or they just can't perform the action well or over a few takes. And God forbid if something did happen and Teri Hatcher didn't have me there on set and she stubbed her toe or she broke her little finger. That's when the attorneys get involved.*

Often stunt coordinators or fight choreographers are working out routines on set. They may be fine-tuning or trying to resolve a logistical or creative challenge before the scene is scheduled to shoot. Stunt doubles are a handy and efficient use of manpower to assist the coordinator in their process by standing in for the talent as the coordinator figures out some choreography. Because some directors are not skilled or even have a strong opinion about what a fight has to look like, the wise director will say, "It's a fight to prove this guy is man enough for a job, show me what you have in mind." The good coordinators will design a fight that serves that story element. Once the routine or routines have been worked out, the coordinator and or the doubles will show the talent what they figured out. They will teach them every move so they can step in and do the fight or stunt themselves, assuming it's safe. The double is there to not only stand in, but to instruct.

> BUDDY JOE HOOKER: *As coordinator you'll set up and rehearse three or four fight routines to show the director when he gets a chance. This could be in a car, in a bar location … it could be anything. When you starting working with your director, you got what his feeling*

was about what a character might do in a challenging situation. The director will tell you, "Hey, this is what this character is like. He loses his temper (snap) like that." He leaves you to figure it out while he does something else. You'll go through a lot of rehearsals and different routines with your doubles. So when the director comes to the set, especially in TV when you're under a strict schedule and you have to do things quickly, you want to have three or four routines worked out when the director comes on. So you show him, "OK, we can do this, this, this." "Nah, I don't like that." "OK, how about this or how about that?" So that way, you can utilize your stunt doubles to rehearse and organize, while the main actors and director are off shooting other stuff. So then, when it's time to shoot the scene, you'll plug in the actors and the stunt people where you need them.

The efficiency in this approach is a great example of how planning and utilizing your resources to maximum benefit is always on the mind of filmmakers. Stunt people will always be tinkering, figuring, and noodling creative solutions to challenging stories. It's the same mind-set of the family cook who finds ways to use every part of the vegetable or animal they have to work with. Make the most out of what you have. You'll get a bigger bang for your buck.

Compensation and Adjustments

When you employ a professional stunt performer, their minimum compensation is dictated by the Screen Actors Guild (SAG) contract that a production company must become a signatory to. If you think you can't afford the rates, fringe benefits, and other requirements associated with signing a standard SAG agreement, you may be pleasantly surprised. SAG can accommodate your production to allow you to employ SAG actors and stunt performers. There are three low-budget feature agreements to choose from that are tailored to meet the realistic needs of low-budget productions. There is also a Short Film Agreement that has no upfront compensation requirements (all salaries are deferred). It requires the budget to be less than $50,000 and the running time to be less than thirty-five minutes.

The Screen Actors Guild represents virtually all professional actors. You certainly want to access them to be able to cast the best actors available. But it is critical to be under a SAG agreement, because every stunt performer you want to work with is a SAG member. They cannot work on nonunion productions. I can't recommend hiring any stunt coordinator or performer who is not a SAG member as that indicates a dramatic lack of experience. If you use an inexperienced, nonunion actor, the worst that can result is bad performance. If a stunt person lacks enough experience to qualify for SAG membership, the stakes are much … *much* greater. Below are the main features of each modified SAG contract. They can be found online through the following link: http://www.sagaftra.org/production-center/documents.

Ultra Low Budget Agreement

- Total budget of less than $200,000

- Day rate of $100

- No step-up fees

- No consecutive employment (except on overnight location)

- No premiums

- Allows the use of both professional and nonprofessional performers

- Background performers not covered

Modified Low Budget Agreement

- Total budget of less than $625,000

- Day rate of $268

- Weekly rate of $933

- No consecutive employment (except on overnight location)

- Six-day work week with no premium

- Reduced overtime rate

Low Budget Agreement

- Total budget of less than $2,500,000

- Day rate of $504

- Weekly rate of $1752

- No consecutive employment (except on overnight location)

- Six-day work week with no premium

- Reduced overtime rate

- Reduced number of background performers covered

Depending on the contract, you may only have to pay as little as the pension and welfare owed for the standard minimum wage for the job. The rest of the compensation is deferred, meaning not owed to the payee until certain streams of income accrue to the production when and if it's distributed and produces revenue. Therefore, stunt performers are either on weekly or daily rates just as your regular cast is. Depending on whom you hire under the SAG agreement, performer may have a rate that is more than the SAG minimum wage guaranteed. No one is required to take the minimum wage—that's a starting point. You will find, however, that many stunt performers will agree to the prevailing SAG minimum wage. The Screen Actors Guild posts all their Minimum Basic Agreement online. You can research rates of compensation and working conditions related to SAG members for any type or size of budget.

But … SAG rates may not comprise all of a stunt performer's compensation. There's this thing called an "adjustment." If a stunt is determined by the stunt performer to have an added degree of difficulty or risk, a "bump" or flat rate increase to perform that stunt will be required each time that stunt is performed. Using the high fall as an example, if the stunt person's task is to fall off the ledge of a five-story building to the ground, an adjustment is appropriate. The amount may be negotiable, but, usually, the price is the price. The adjustment can be anywhere from a hundred to many thousands of dollars, each time the performer is required to do the stunt.

> DAN BRADLEY: *The stunt guy gets paid a Screen Actors Guild daily or weekly rate. That's set by the union. The stunt adjustment is what he is going to get paid above and beyond that minimum rate for performing a stunt that has risk. That stunt adjustment is based on how dangerous the gag is or perhaps how much experience or expertise this guy has. If he is the only guy in the world who can do this thing, you're going to pay him more than for somebody else.*

Once again, the need for thorough preparation and planning is crucial. Making sure there are backup systems in place, such as multiple cameras that cover the critical angles of the stunt, is essential. It may be a prohibitively expensive or time-consuming proposition to repeat a major stunt.

> DAN BRADLEY: *Very often, when we're looking over a stunt scene in preproduction, the best 1st ADs will tell you… "listen, let's have extra stunt guys here." I didn't bring it up, although I might've. That 1st AD who has stunt experience will know things will go so much faster with professional drivers who are experienced and have a lot more confidence and understanding of the situation. So, sometimes we even have stunt guys doing things that aren't typically stunts but the experienced 1st AD will understand the time savings and want it to help everyone complete the day's schedule.*

If you're a producer or responsible for making the deals with stunt performers, understanding all costs associated with a stunt is not something you want to wait to negotiate or be made aware of at a time when you have no choice but to agree (such as on the day). Make sure you understand and agree to all costs connected with stunt work well before those services are to be rendered. The stunt coordinator should present to the production, in advance, an itemized list of all costs associated with all the stunt team's work necessary to fulfill the requirements of the script and director. This will include labor and equipment costs.

Safety

This is the most important topic. It's the topic that cannot be shortchanged or shorthanded. It's one of the few line items on your budget that is not mutable. It is not negotiable. You will be given advice or instructions by your professional stunt coordinator or performer as to what safety measures must be taken to ensure the stunt is safely executed and that the production is reasonably prepared for any mishap. This can mean anything from furnishing enough padding on the set to the presence of an ambulance and paramedic team on set. Many stunts are the result of many "moving parts," many participants who each have a job to do precisely. People make mistakes. The potential for miscalculations or poor judgment exists. Equipment has been known to fail or operate improperly. As a filmmaker in any position of authority, it is your serious responsibility to be prepared for any eventuality that can plausibly happen. When shooting a scene with a stunt, not only keep all safety equipment ready to be employed and first aid measures ready to be taken, but also don't forget to communicate to everyone on set that day what will be happening. Your cast and crew must be aware of the dangers and sensitivity of the work being done. The daily call sheet will indicate the scheduled stunt or special effects work and what hazards may be present while executing the shots. The nearest hospital will be identified so that everyone knows where to take an injured person if that responsibility falls on them, for any reason.

This is particularly a critical thing to know if you are doing stunts in remote areas where hospitals are not easily reached or quickly accessed. On set paramedics are helpful if not essential when extra dangerous stunts are being performed. But transportation to appropriate medical facilities must always be pre-planned and arranged in case of serious injury to anyone on set. Ambulances or even medevacs must be on set to ensure quick evacuation to delivery to a hospital.

JEFF TUFANO: *We were doing a rehearsal on a film for Warner Bros. where a motorcycle is supposed to get pushed into the opposing lane of traffic. In the film the character is hit by a truck. We started off with a half speed rehearsal with the camera set up and I was watching through a 1200 m lens down the middle of the highway. On the first rehearsal, much to my amazement, the stunt driver went smack into the front of the truck and went airborne right out of my shot. I wasn't close enough to be really sure what happened. They found him in the weeds pretty badly hurt and his legs were broken, it looked like his kneecap was missing. He was in serious need of help. He's bleeding and is semiconscious. The point to this story is, we had a set medic, but we didn't have an ambulance! We're on the highway outside of Moab, Utah. So we're waiting and waiting for medical help for this guy, because the medic can only do so much. Eventually, someone did come in a helicopter all the way from Colorado. They had to airlift the guy to a trauma center in the next state. He could've easily died. Cut to a year later and I run into him on a set. He was so lucky to have survived. But that's what you call very poor preparation. I've never been on a proper job where there wasn't the ability to get someone to a hospital immediately. It's important to have an ambulance and paramedics standing by.*

As a postscript to this tale, Jeff Tufano's recollection speaks to the tough guy culture that declares "the show must go on". Money's at stake, egos need stoking and that next job is always on everyone's mind. It's not hard to see how the culture can produce a recipe for disaster; where common sense is left behind.

JEFF TUFANO: *The irony is we thought that day was over. As a matter of fact, a few of us were thinking his job is over. The second they airlifted the guy out, the stunt coordinator put on the guy's costume, got on his bike and proceeded as if nothing had ever happened. To those guys it's almost a badge of courage. Now he's got a great story to tell.*

That is the perfect example of the culture and tradition of the stunt man.

The safety meeting

The safety meeting that the first assistant director will conduct at the start of every workday is another key form of communication your production must never avoid or miss. Your full cast and crew need to know if there will be fire, explosions, crashes, falls, weapons, fights: any event that can cause injury. The 1st AD will conduct and document the safety meeting, which all crew members should attend, including the director. At the very least, each and every crew member participating in the execution of stunts should attend this meeting in which the stunt to be performed is described and examined.

The following is an excerpt from the Industry Wide Labor-Management Safety Committee Bulletin.

An on-site safety meeting, including all participants and others involved, must precede the performance of all stunts. This meeting should include a "walk-through" or "dry-run" with the stunt coordinator and/or effects people. An understanding of the intended action, possible deviations, and authority to abort should be made clear. Before rolling cameras, should any substantive change become necessary, the First Assistant Director will again call all persons involved in the stunt to another meeting to confirm everyone's understanding and agreement to said change(s).

The 1st AD, who, in California, is legally responsible and liable for set safety, will describe in detail the potentially dangerous work to be done that day, identifying areas of concern regarding safety, describe procedures in case of emergency, and make specific requests from the crew that will enhance safety. The SAG safety guide, also based on the recommendations of the Industry Wide Labor-Management Safety Committee, states the following:

All stunts and special effects should be reviewed by all participants prior to execution to help ensure that they are performed in the safest manner possible. Before filming a stunt or special effect, the involved parties should all perform an on-site dry run or walk-through. A safety meeting should be held and documented.

A few examples of the sort of those requests are the following: keep the set extra quiet; keep all exits unobstructed; make sure there is an unobstructed, equipment-free, four-foot perimeter around the walls of the sound stage (if indoors); identify all exits that have been preselected by the production as the safest paths to escape a fire or other mishap that may demand an immediate exit from the set. Often, the fire marshal, the stunt coordinator, and the special effects coordinator will participate in those safety precaution decisions. Their input is informed by experiences most directors or producers haven't had or have rarely experienced. They have seen more go wrong than most of us have seen go right. Communicate with your team. Do not make these decisions unilaterally or casually. The stakes are too high, the consequences too grave. If the production does not take appropriate precautions or steps to prepare for potential safety hazards or a medical emergency, it is no exaggeration to say these decisions can be life changing.

I strongly suggest that you and anyone in a position of authority on your production download and read the Screen Actors Guild Safety Bulletins (http://www.sagaftra.org/files/sag/Safety_Bulletins_AMPTP_Part_1_9_3.

pdf) and the Industry Wide Labor-Management Safety Committee Bulletin documents (http://www.dga.org/Resources/Additional/Safety-Issues.aspx). These are detailed handbooks identifying all issues of safety to actors and crew members. They describe procedures and areas of concern in all situations that may pose a health or safety risk. They also explain protocols and avenues actors and crew may pursue when they have safety concerns. They are drafted by the National Stunt and Safety Department of SAG. They are also endorsed by the Industry Wide Labor-Management Safety Committee. This is mandatory reading for anyone in a position of authority on a production.

Also mandatory is reading and becoming familiar with the Occupational Safety and Health Administration (OSHA) guidelines for set safety. Below is a checklist that is included in this important safety guide for the 1st AD. It gives a clear list of compulsory areas of knowledge and things to do to ensure set safety. It comes from the *California Workers Compensation and Safety Guide January 2013* (https://www.capspayroll.com/live/upload/CAPS_California_Safety_Guide-Jan2013.pdf_2cd99.pdf).

First Assistant Director Checklist

❑	Health and Safety Manual received
❑	Health and Safety Manual reviewed and understood
❑	Legal responsibility reviewed
❑	Chain of responsibility reviewed
❑	Pre-pro meeting with Director and Line Producer
❑	Shoot day location hazards
❑	Health and Safety Bulletin Board
❑	Basic Safety Bulletin Board
❑	Location of safety facilities
❑	Crew safety awareness
❑	Shoot day meeting with Director and Line Producer
❑	AM safety meeting
❑	Rehearsals/run-throughs
❑	Location inspections/safety check list
❑	Bystander safety
❑	Potentially hazardous situations
❑	Condition of special equipment
❑	Health and Safety paperwork/reports

The following is another checklist that the line producer or anyone in a position of higher authority for the production as a whole (not just department heads) should utilize conscientiously:

Line Producer Checklist

1	General
❏	Safety Manual received
❏	Safety Manual reviewed and understood
❏	Legal responsibility reviewed
2	**Pre-Production**
❏	Storyboards
❏	Tech Scout
❏	Meetings with key people
❏	Potentially hazardous situations
❏	Health and safety bulletins
❏	Outside facility personnel / equipment
❏	Crew Experience
❏	Rehearsals and run-throughs
❏	Location Inspections
❏	Health & Safety Bulletin Board
❏	Proper casting procedures
❏	Safety meeting with Director and 1st AD
3	**Shoot**
❏	Shoot day meeting with Director and 1st AD
❏	AM safety meeting with all personnel
❏	Health & Safety bulletins
❏	Rehearsals / run-throughs
❏	Bystander safety
4	**Wrap**
❏	Wrap Crew qualified
❏	Final Site Inspected
❏	Paperwork completed
❏	Safety Suggestion sheet
❏	Record of Safety Meetings
❏	Hazard reports
❏	Accident /Illness Reports
❏	Reports to outside suppliers
❏	All other pertinent health and safety paperwork

This guide contains other checklists as well that are critically important to familiarize yourself with. Making movies or operating at any level in the production process requires a number of administrative and practical areas of knowledge and even expertise. If you don't possess sufficient knowledge in these areas, find someone who does, and either bring them on board as a part of your production or seriously consult with them. Your responsibilities go beyond craft or artistic effort. I hope these checklists are a loud and clear testament to the thoroughness of preparation necessary to make a movie, creatively and organizationally. These guidelines are just that, suggestions on how to avoid accidents and liability. They don't appear in civil or criminal law codes. However, in some very similar form, these safety checklists are company policy at all studios, networks, and other large production entities. These checklists, safety meetings, and other protocols are taken very seriously and are rigorously enforced. All major corporations have vast legal teams that assess risk and advise, if not dictate, on matters of liability. It's critically important for the production to exercise common sense and take all reasonable steps to ensure set safety. If something bad happens and it can be shown that the production did not exercise all reasonable means to ensure safety or initiate all reasonable precautions, the production company and its principals will most likely be held accountable in civil or possibly criminal proceedings.

Insurance

The first thing you have to know about insurance, regardless of you doing stunts or special effects or not, is that you have to have it to make a movie. If you're making a movie "guerrilla style" or "under the radar" and decide not to buy insurance, you've determined the narrow boundaries of your production. Maybe due to lack of funds, that's how it has to be. There is a vast array of resources you cannot access if you don't have insurance as you will learn in this section.

Most of us have insurance in our private lives. We insure against catastrophic illness and damage and loss to our homes and to our expensive cars. Movies are a high-stakes investment as well that demand financial protection against loss. An important aspect of the safety net every production requires is the part your insurance broker and underwriter will play in making sure a production is appropriately covered against the sort of loss your specific production could reasonably expect to suffer. Your broker will help you choose a package of different policies that your specific production requires and should have. They also advise productions on necessary protocols and precautions they feel will help avoid mishaps and resulting claims due to the myriad of things that can and do go wrong on a movie production. If appropriate measures recommended or required by the insurer cannot be demonstrated to have been taken, the insurance company will not insure that part of the production in which a stunt or special effect is planned or they may decline to insure the entire production.

There are independent production companies whose business models are to spend not one more cent than is absolutely necessary … or a little less. They often shoot overseas where governmental agency oversight is nonexistent, labor is cheap, and, sadly, shortcuts are often taken that put cast and crew lives in harm's way. Stunts may be performed without the rigorous safeguards and redundancies that are present on most North American sets.

PAUL HOLEHOUSE: *If you don't want to use permits. You want to go to Bulgaria.*

There are numerous forms of insurance every production must have in order to be in business. Practically speaking, it's not possible to make a movie unless the production is appropriately insured. The choices can be dizzying. Each category of policy offers many options. Rely on your experienced broker to guide you through this complex maze of choices in coverage.

Loss and damage insurance will protect against the loss or damage of equipment or property under the production's control such as a location. Most equipment used in production is rented. It rarely makes sense to purchase expensive equipment unless it's in constant use. Rental houses all require "certificates of insurance" naming their company and the equipment you're renting from them as "added insured" on the policy. Being an added insured party means that they have the same protections for their property as if they had initiated the policy themselves. Their coverage expires once their equipment is safely returned. These certificates can be obtained very quickly from your broker by fax or Internet, often the same day as your request. Almost every vendor will require you to supply insurance for their property. In a few cases, you might find vendors or independent contractors who carry their own insurance or at least workman's comp, which covers the insured party against injury on the job. You can save some money if the vendor or contractor will use their insurance while working on your production, or they may share the risk with you.

But this doesn't happen very often and never with stunt performers or special effects companies. Vendors do carry their own insurance but not to be applied specifically to your production. They carry something like an overall umbrella for liability like any business. It's worth asking if you need to purchase insurance for them or if their policy covers them and their work on your show. You could save a few dollars, which is always a good thing.

You will need liability insurance to protect the production and the principals of the company against claims arising from accidents, injuries, and negligence connected with the numerous things that can go wrong and can be litigated.

There's accident and disability and workman's comp for accidents and mishaps in which someone is injured on the job. Regarding workman's comp, which is essential, a common way of acquiring that coverage is by using a payroll service such as Automatic Data Processing (ADP), Payroll Services, or Cast & Crew. These companies provide numerous services ranging from handling all your payroll accounting and payments to providing workman's comp insurance for everyone on the payroll for your production. This makes sense for smaller companies, which may not be able to come up with large sums for a deposit. Technically, your cast and crew will be employed by the payroll service instead of by your company. That's why the payroll service's comp insurance will cover your employees.

PAUL HOLEHOUSE: *Workers' Comp is especially important when doing stunts. A fair amount of injuries occur in connection with stunts. You want to go with a payroll service which also includes the Workers' Comp in their services. If you or someone else on your crew gets injured in the course of carrying equipment or gets hurt in any aspect of the production, the production company is covered against loss. Workers' Comp also covers an employee as long as he's on his way to work. There's all levels and depending on the individual, the actors have a certain level of coverage, and the extras another, and the crew people, another. They all need some kind of coverage, so you don't have the catastrophic loss of some kind that shuts you down because of it.*

Errors and omissions policies protect the production against any claims arising out of copyright, underlying literary or musical rights, releases, use of likenesses, etc.

Cast insurance insures the production against any lost time and money due to sickness, injury, or loss of a cast member for specified reasons. It also pays the medical expenses for any cast member injured in connection with the production. Any claims arising out of the execution of stunts and special effects will most likely apply to cast insurance, loss and damage, and liability. This basic package or "portfolio" is mandatory.

If one of your stunt or special effects team members is potentially responsible to any degree for injury or property loss due to their negligence, you'll need insurance and lots of it. Because there is often unusually high risk associated with stunts and special effects, insurance underwriters will often charge additional premiums or surcharges. The basic package generally applies to "walk and talk movies," where no unusual level of risk can be identified. The many higher-risk, but common circumstances that are part of a production such as use of pyrotechnics, stunts, animals, large amounts of people, shooting in or near bodies of water, aircraft, etc., may require extra coverage. Common sense tells you what constitutes a higher level of risk. Insurance policies get constructed in layers of protection beginning with the basic package. Many productions can get along just fine with that basic portfolio. But once you enter the realm of stunts and special effects, that situation can change. However, if the stunts and special effects in your production such as any pyrotechnics are commonplace and in a very controlled situation, there may be no increase in the cost of the policy. Risk is assessed through a meticulous and orderly assessment process. Many factors are part of the risk equation.

If you think or are certain you have such extra risk elements in your script, your choice of an insurance broker is that much more important. You should always seek out brokers who specialize in entertainment insurance. It is critically important that they understand your business. This is not even debatable. If you live in Los Angeles or New York, there are numerous ones to choose from. However you don't have to live in those cities to access their services. They are very used to servicing clients from around the world, even Tallahassee, Tucson, or Portland.

The brokers who specialize in entertainment insurance are valuable in a few ways. They are familiar with your business and how it operates. They are often more expert in how stunts and special effects are done and the options and variables associated with them, than many producers and directors are. They often know who the members of those stunt and effects communities or talent pools are in your market and are familiar with their reputations and abilities. This level of expertise is available at the broker level.

> PAUL HOLEHOUSE: *If the broker is experienced and they're entertainment type people, and there's a small handful of them out there, and there's more and more who want to get into the entertainment side; you want to make sure that they're giving you the best advice on coverage, so you're covered for everything that you're doing.*

The broker is your personal representative and connection to your insurance policy. You apply through them, and they either complete the process of furnishing your production with the necessary insurance or lead you through a process that will connect you with the insurance underwriting company that actually finances or "underwrites" the risk to complete the policy application procedure.

> PAUL HOLEHOUSE: *Generally, the amount of coverage goes by units of thousands or millions of dollars, adding layers of coverage based on all the elements being proposed to shoot, and that's how we separate the risk. The insurance companies, the underwriters, may not take all the risk themselves. They move it around in a pool. Our company may take the first $5 million in risk and somebody else will take the next $5 million and maybe even another company taking all the risk above that amount.*

You should approach a few brokers and have them design a custom-made package and shop for the best deals from their various underwriters.

> PAUL HOLEHOUSE: *We always work through a broker system here where you have to be an assigned broker to deal with us and other underwriters. This gives you some idea that there's a broker out there trying to get you the best price whether it's Fireman's Fund or Chubb*

or someone else. You're comparing cost and risk and then coming up with a price. There's some groups that you can access online and fill in the form.

While the best price is important, the relationship you have with your broker is just as essential. This decision is not unlike the other personnel choices you make. Not every decision should come down to who will do the job for less. You don't hire crew people only because they will work for less pay than anyone else. Similarly, you don't choose an insurance broker based solely on who will provide coverage for less. You want a broker who will make sure you have the appropriate or sufficient coverage for the best price. You don't want to buy a "deluxe model" when all you needed was the "standard model." More importantly, you don't want to buy the cheap package when you needed the greater coverage because of the specific requirements of your production. If a significant mishap occurs and you have to make a claim, you want avoid financial disaster by having adequate protection.

Your broker and the team that stands behind them may save you money in ways not readily apparent. Their insight into your production and creativity in solving challenges can have tangible results. The benefit of their experience, wisdom, or creativity can protect or enhance the director's creative vision. They may be able to help figure out ways to make a high fall or explosion acceptably safe and, from an insurance standpoint, affordable. Their solutions to your production challenges can stop a worried producer from canceling or reducing the scale of a great stunt or explosion. So the relationship you have with your insurance team is important. The insurance representatives are not there to prevent you from doing any aspect of your production, although deep in their hearts they wish you'd just take the easiest path to filming a stunt.

PAUL HOLEHOUSE: *Of course, we probably suggest that you use stock footage and save somebody from any risk.*

It is up to them as to whether they are willing to take on the risk posed by your production or any aspect of it. They can decline to cover a particular stunt, but are perfectly happy to insure you if you agree to use a different approach to the "gag" that poses less risk.

So give a lot of points to the broker you feel will be the most enthusiastically on board, the one who gives ample attention to your production. If you have important stunts and special effects, stay away from the ones who merely suggest you fill out the forms for a premium quote. Go with the one who will be a de facto member of your team, the one who will be actively engaged in tailoring your insurance package and be a problem solver. You'll find them.

To start the process of getting your production and the stunts and special effects in it insured begins simply enough. There are forms and questionnaires to fill out. The insurers want to know who's on the team and what their resumes are. Experience and track records are important factors in this approval process. Are the special effects experts licensed? Which licenses do they have? You will explain the plan for your stunts or special effects in detail. Where will it be staged: on a soundstage or in an old abandoned warehouse? Where you plan to shoot the stunt or special effect is an extremely significant factor in assessing risk. Will the event be shot on a professional-grade soundstage where safety has been built into its design? Or will it be shot in an abandoned warehouse that poses a higher risk of structural weakness or flammability? Your insurance representative will be scrutinizing a practical location for any possible weakness. Is the structure strong enough to support equipment or crew who will be working in that area? If not, the production may have to have that area fortified. That could take structural engineers and contractors to do the job. Are all safety railings secured? If a few are loose, that'll have to be attended to.

> PAUL HOLEHOUSE: *Productions always like looking at abandoned or bad buildings as part of the look, but they also then have to shore them up or reconstruct it to make sure that it doesn't come right down on them as they're filming. If you've seen* Rent, *everybody is dancing on a fire escape. We had to go in with the structural engineer and inspect them. They had to reinforce them all because they were going to put two or three kids hanging on and dancing, We ended up with a lot of people with safety belts even though you couldn't see them while they were dancing on the fire escapes. We couldn't afford to have one of them come falling off the building because it wasn't put there as a permanent structure to inhabit. It was more like a façade to just take a picture of and not really use normally. Things that are built just to take pictures of don't have the same standards as permanent buildings.*

If the event is an exterior one, will your explosion or fire be staged on a city street where crowd control is challenging? Who will be in the shot, and how far away from the action or pyrotechnics will they be positioned? How many police officers controlling traffic and firemen ready to deal with any emergency do you plan to have? How many productions assistants (PAs) will you have stationed in the area to control foot traffic from civilians? Is there a need for an ambulance standing by or just a paramedic, in case someone breaks an arm or worse?

PAUL HOLEHOUSE: *We look at the plan to shoot anything that has added risk. Someone's going to do a campfire and it's going to be out in the middle of Malibu. We got wind and fire in the scene. If the fire department won't give them a permit, that would pretty much tell you that we don't want to be involved if they can't even get it approved from the fire department.*

Maybe your big "t-bone" car crash will be staged in the middle of the desert, where no one is likely to even know you're there. If that's the case, you will need less in the way of safety officers, but you may still need police support or fire department presence. If you're in a remote area, how quickly can you get an injured person to a hospital? Do you have transportation arranged prior to the stunt or special effect? The insurance rep wants to know and be able to approve all your plans. An abundance of safety and an absence of risk is their goal for your production.

If areas of vulnerability are not resolved, the insurer may decline coverage for that part of the shoot. Therefore, the options are really limited. If the insurer is wary about the safety of a proposed location, change the location to one that is more suitable to the needs of the production or upgrade the location you want to meet safety standards. It doesn't make a lot of sense to argue these issues with your insurance rep. What you'd be saying is, I don't agree with you about the level of risk (even though I have no qualifications to make that judgment) or I am willing to take that risk (which is foolhardy and negligent as people's health or lives are at stake). And they won't engage you in that argument. They will simply say, "If you don't agree, that's your choice. Our company cannot insure your production at any price; I'll be heading back to my office now. Have a nice day."

The application may be submitted and followed through by a producer, the unit production manager, the director, the stunt coordinator, and/or the special effects supervisor or any combination of these people who are necessary to completely and accurately inform the insurer of your intentions. It's common to find that these applications can be downloaded and submitted online.

Very often, the applications forms will suffice in the acquisition of an insurance package, because they indicate that requirements such as permits, licenses, and other legal requirements for doing a stunt or special effects have been met. Those permits and licenses are issued by governmental agencies such as fire departments, police departments, or city and county motion picture permit offices. Special effects technicians are often required to carry permits issued by the federal Bureau of Alcohol Tobacco, Firearms and Explosives, allowing them to possess and transport explosives. One or more of those agencies have examined the production's plans for stunts or special effects and have either requested modifications, not allowed them, or approved them. An approval by those agencies in the form of a permit or license can expedite your insurance application. Your insurer will most likely accept those approvals as confirmation that your production is following safe protocols.

If stunts or special effects are of a major scale with added complexity and risk, the risk specialist at the agency or at the underwriters who assess on-set safety will be called in to advise the production of their options. "If you do it this way, it'll cost x. If you do it this other way, which I believe is less risky, it'll cost you y." Some brokers are qualified to assess risk. If they are not and there's no one else in their agency that is, a consultant employed by the underwriter may be called upon. These risk consultants are employed by large insurance underwriters with vast experience in entertainment productions and events such as Fireman's Fund and Chubb. They will examine the production's plans for stunts and special effects in great detail looking for anything that may not be properly prepared or planned. After they have thoroughly scrutinized all the details of your proposed stunts and special effects, they will make their recommendations to the brokers, who will cost out a bid that will detail the various price layers of the premium. So if a particular stunt or special effect throws your budget for a loop, you can discuss how you might save money by taking a different approach to that part of the story. There may be various solutions your broker or risk consultant will suggest that will bring the price down and still deliver the entertainment value you hope for. They just might say "you know, I've seen this done another way" and suggest an alternate approach.

They will often consult with the stunt coordinator or special effects supervisor, or both, and discuss the event. Someone from your team will share all the preparations and planning they have connected with stunts or special effects.

> PAUL HOLEHOUSE: *If you have an art department, you probably have a storyboard. If you don't, you're going to have somebody sketching these stick figures.*

Sometimes sketches and diagrams will suffice, while other times computer-generated previz presentations are created and shared with the insurance people. Everyone will explore the options together and arrive at a solution that makes the most sense. These kinds of encounters are how brokers and risk consultants gain their valuable knowledge. They've explored stunts and special effects from the inside out with seasoned professionals. While they certainly are not qualified to be stunt coordinators or special effects techs, they are experts in those fields having a thorough understanding of how the jobs are best done.

> GERMAN GUTTIEREZ: *Productions have actually used my suggestions a more than a few times. It saved the stunt.*

It's difficult to give a rule of thumb by which you can calculate the cost of a policy, in part due to the many variables that come into play. On large-budget, action-heavy productions, the insurance premium can cost in the 4 percent of the budget range.

Sorry to sound repetitive, but production insurance is a nonnegotiable budget item. You gotta have it. No investor, lender, or financial participant in your production would knowingly capitalize your production if it were not covered with a reasonable level of insurance. So many things can and do go wrong on a movie set: to not protect you from worst-case scenarios or even less substantial losses is irresponsible, reckless even. I must point out that you will still suffer some financial loss because there are always deductibles on every claim the production must pay. It can be $2000, $5000, or more, depending on the kind of claim it is and the coverage you chose. If you're smart, you'll set aside some funds from your budget for that rainy day.

Imagine your camera team is setting the $150,000 camera on the tripod. The new assistant, right out of film school, forgets to lock down the camera to the tripod (this has happened on one of my productions), the camera is bumped, and it tumbles to the ground, damaging it badly. The damage will be the production company's responsibility, and the time lost in the shooting day will also be very costly. But this kind of mishap can be insured against becoming a financial calamity. One incident such as the loss of a camera can "break the bank." The cost of the camera and time lost shooting can jeopardize the completion of the production. Who would risk having the entire production collapse due to one instance of incompetence or chance? If a stunt performer is injured and taken to an emergency room for x-rays and treatment, even if the injury is minor, the bill can be $10,000 to $20,000. If it's more serious, we all know the cost of medical services; they are huge and potentially debilitating to a budget. You need insurance.

Completion Bonds

The lesson is clear. With the vast amount of money that is at stake on most productions, certain risks are unacceptable. And when I say vast, that can be a relative term. The first feature-length movie I produced had a cash budget of $22,000, a vast sum to me. The cast and crew worked for a small stipend and owned "shares" in the production. They endured baloney sandwiches for lunch. The only way their hard work would ever be compensated is if the movie actually returned a profit to the producers. That was a big leap of faith that thankfully was validated as the movie made a handsome profit. No one connected with the movie who had made "deferred pay" deals in the past had ever seen a penny. So there's a lot riding on a production being well run. Risks must be assessed and addressed in the best possible ways to protect and honor the investment of time and money made by the participants in your movie who helped make it happen.

When you're working on a "shoestring" or with "smoke and mirrors" to make the biggest and best movie you can for the money you have, every wasted penny hurts. If a piece of equipment is lost or damaged, that will have consequences in some other line item of your budget. Hopefully, you have a loss and damage category in your budget to pay for smaller losses and the cost of deductibles if you make any insurance claims. If you don't have that money set aside or if you use that money up, something else in your budget will have to pay for that loss (unless you have access to more funds). You'll have to "rob Peter to pay Paul." But on a $22,000 budget, a $5000 or even a $1000 loss is potentially catastrophic. It took me almost two years to raise the $22,000, and half of that came from my family and my savings! A $5000 loss would've sunk the production. This has happened many, many times, particularly in the low-budget, indie world of filmmaking. Everybody would've had to go home as the funds to finish shooting the movie would not be there. My grandmother would've been very disappointed in me. She probably would've been thinking and might've even said, "how stupid is my grandson that he didn't protect my investment better?"

So we did have a modest insurance portfolio to address some risk, but what we did not have was a completion bond, more formally known as a guarantee of completion. In our everyday lives, most of us don't accept the risk of losing our car in an accident or incurring huge medical bills when we get sick or injured. It can ruin our lives with debt we can never repay. Stuff happens. Lots of stuff happens on complex movie and television productions. On small-scale movies, large-scale liabilities can occur. Even small losses can cause a production to run out of money, jeopardizing the completion of the production. So that's where the completion bond comes in to provide added protection to the stakeholders in your production. If your production has one stunt or many, if it has a small fire or a large explosion, the bond company will determine the degree of risk those actions may pose. In practical terms, their risk is likely to be minimal because they will insist on adequate insurance coverage that will mitigate their risk. If something were to go wrong that was insurable such as an equipment malfunction or injury due to a stunt or special effect, the insurance would cover most of that loss. If, however, there was a loss of time or money that threatened the completion of the movie due to noninsurable factors such as incompetence, the bond company could be exposed. But don't forget, part of the application process and negotiation of the terms of the completion guarantee is an approval by the bond company of all key personnel, which would certainly include stunt coordinators and special effects companies. Risk due to human error exists, but it can be greatly diminished when seasoned pros are planning, supervising, and executing dangerous activities on a production.

Lenders and investors must be assured that the product (movie) they believed they were investing in is in fact what will be produced with the capital they provided. Any shortfalls that could threaten that assurance must be covered by the completion bond. It's clearly in their interest, and they have the authority to reduce financial risk by any means necessary. Part of the agreement between the production company and them is that they have the authority to take control of the movie if they determine the production is in jeopardy of not being completed as agreed to in the terms of the bond. They are empowered to anything they deem necessary within the boundaries of the bond agreement to protect their investment if called on to spend money to ensure the movie is completed.

Here's an example of how a completion bond would work in a non-movie circumstance. If you invest in a friend's start-up business, which essentially every movie is, to make and sell brownies with macadamia nuts, and your friend makes those brownies with broken peanuts because he has mismanaged the business and couldn't afford macadamia nuts, you'd be upset. That's not the same product. It's a cheap version of the upscale version your friend promised to make with your hard-earned money. This has market implications. The inferior broken peanut brownie may not sell in the same retail outlets or at the same price of the upscale version. This change in production plans was not intentional, but after your friend found himself with less capital, he made the best product he could with what resources he had. This turn of events would not be fair to you. Your friend made certain representations about the quality of his product that had implications on the relative safety of your investment. *If* you as an investor had insisted on a completion bond (and if they existed in the brownie business) to ensure that the brownies would be made and delivered as promised, the bond company would have had to step in and provide the necessary funds to purchase the macadamia nuts, so he could deliver the product he promised. They might've even seen the problem coming through their monitoring of the production and been able to avert the loss of macadamia nuts, saving them and everyone concerned the grief. Whether or not the brownies made a profit is not at issue; it's that the product is the same product that was planned and that all assumptions surrounding the business that were made are the same.

If your movie is independently financed or to some degree relies on bank loans, you may be required to provide a completion bond. This is an insurance policy that guarantees the at-risk investors or lenders in your production that the script agreed upon before shooting began will be shot and the production completed to professional standards. If the movie experienced a terrible loss and couldn't finish and deliver a finished product, the investment or loan would be seriously at risk. The bond companies, much like the insurance companies, are staffed with people vastly experienced in the production of movies. They often have production management, line producing, or producing credentials on their resumes. They have worked independently or for studios. They are well qualified to look at your production plan and evaluate the risk of not finishing the movie as it was envisioned prior to the movie being green-lit or at least shot. After reading the script, they will examine all the logistics and proposed safeguards. They will examine the budget to determine whether or not it is sufficient to cover the costs of the script once in production. They will examine the shooting schedule to make sure it is logically sound and realistic. They will want to know who is on board in the key crew and production roles to assess their experience and suitability. This includes the producers and director. Their experience or lack thereof is a risk factor. Assuming these factors seem to be well thought out or, more to the point, doable, a meeting with everyone from the production who have vital roles will follow. If the meeting goes well, a "letter of intent" will be issued by the bond company indicating their willingness to guarantee the production if all their standard requirements such as knowing the financing is truly in place, the right personnel are on board, appropriate levels of insurance have been arranged for, and location agreements are secured. There will be requirements specific to the production as well that reflect any special risks the production may pose. The letter of intent should include their fee as well. The cost of a completion bond ranges from approximately 3 percent to 6 percent of your budget. This is negotiable and is determined by degrees of risk, the size of the budget, and how frequent a client you are.

As all the legal documents get drawn up by the bond company, they will confirm that all your funds necessary to make the movie, as indicated by the budget, are in fact accessible to the production when the funds are needed. Not all the funds have to be dispersed to the production from the beginning. Some lenders and investors "cash-flow" the production, meaning on an "as-needed" basis, in regular intervals, the necessary funds will be made available to the production. A cash flow chart will be created and agreed on before the production begins, and it will be approved by the bond company. Investors generally like to hold on to their money until they absolutely have to let go of it. That money may be earning interest or at work in some other way. As a producer who borrows from a bank, you don't want to draw down any more money than you absolutely need, so you're not paying interest on money you aren't ready to spend. When large sums are being borrowed, that can add up.

The principal filmmakers will be asked to promise in writing that they will do their jobs competently and professionally to deliver the movie. The director will literally have to sign a legal document warranting that they have reviewed the schedule and can shoot the movie in accordance with that schedule. The producers will have to make similar contractual assurances. If the director or producer fails to deliver on that promise, the completion bond company has the right to take over the production and take whatever remedies they feel are necessary to successfully complete the movie as it was originally planned. Heads may roll. Directors and producers may be fired if they are found to be responsible for the delays or incapable of delivering the movie in a professional and timely way. In order to always be in a position to know when things are not going well, the bond company will assign one or more of their executives to monitor your production. They won't be breathing down your neck, questioning your decisions, unless your production starts to veer off course. They will require daily production reports that will be e-mailed to them as well as weekly cost reports. You might get a phone call from time to time and/or a visit to the set by one of the bond representatives just to see how things appear to be going. An experienced hand can often sense whether or not a production is going smoothly by just observing shooting for a short time. Their observation along with the reports will paint a pretty clear picture. They don't interfere with your plan. The plan has been set and agreed to as a condition of getting the completion guarantee. They will never question creative choices for sure. Their interests are the bottom line, namely a finished movie that has come in on budget and at a level of quality agreed to in advance.

I was connected with an indie production that required the help of the bond company. I was the executive producer. In this case, the title meant that I had secured the financing from a small studio on behalf of another, less experienced producer. The studio would finance and distribute the film. The studio asked me to be on set every day and protect their interests, making sure things were being done right. I was, by far, the more experienced of the producer and director. The studio and I had much to be concerned about. The director was unproven, and the producer had little hands on production experience. I knew from day one when I saw the director in action that he was not competent. He lacked an understanding of the process and protocols of making movies. His lack of knowledge was going to cost the production time and money through his lack of efficiency and indecisiveness. His reluctance to listen to more experienced voices added to my concerns. After week one, we were one day behind schedule. After week two, we were two days behind schedule. On a six-week schedule, this was an unacceptable trend. At that time, I advised the studio that they would be wise to fire the director and replace him. I warned that if they did not do so immediately, the production was on a downward spiral and would continue to lose time and money. It's not irrelevant to mention that the quality of the footage was not especially good either. It's not like anyone could say, "we may go over budget, but hey it'll be worth the extra exposure, the movie will be great!"

The situation did not escape the bond company's attention as they received their daily production reports and cost reports. They knew the production was behind schedule and over budget. It was time for an intervention. I volunteered to step in as the interim director until a new one could be found and prepped to take over. My experience would allow the production to continue without losing any more time and stop the bleeding. I knew how to turn things around; that's what I was there for. The director was lukewarm to my suggestions on how to turn things around, and the studio that had the power to force him to listen wouldn't assert its authority for reasons I can only guess. As the production limped forward, the bond company finally saw its interests were at stake. They called a meeting with the studio, the producer, and me. Everyone agreed, in order to put the production back on a strong footing, the production would be shut down. This was the best hope and the most economically feasible strategy to finish the movie in a way that would result in the quality of movie we originally thought we were going to get. The director, producer, and crew were released. The principal actors had to be compensated to honor the production's contractual obligations to them, and arrangements had to be made to bring them back at further expense and finish the movie. The extra costs incurred were borne by the bond company because they had guaranteed what did happen would be remedied. We then cut together all the footage that was shot and determined exactly what more needed to be shot to deliver the movie the studio thought they were buying. I assembled a new crew and I produced and directed two weeks of shooting to deliver all the elements necessary to finish the movie in a way the bond company had guaranteed it would be. We wrapped the two weeks of shooting on time and on budget, and cut and completed the movie, and it was successfully released. The bond company paid for all amounts over the original budget, which really wasn't all that much because they stopped the crippled production before it dragged on too long and become a more costly problem to resolve.

The bond company will want to know how you plan to manage the workflow during principal photography, whether you shoot on film or digitally. By workflow, I refer to the path that the images or content you have captured in a camera either on film or on a digital medium like a card or chip will travel. On that workflow path, a wide variety of film technicians and craftspersons with specific roles will come into contact with the media in order to archive, edit, color-correct, alter, or add visual effects. The smaller the production, the fewer the people will come in contact with and add something to your original media. The logistics of what has become a complex process will be assessed for security. In the digital world, there are numerous rabbit holes your digital media can fall into if not carefully and competently managed.

If your production is shooting on film, plenty of risks can present themselves as well. Rolls of exposed, unprocessed film have been left in a young camera assistant's car trunk in July, causing considerable losses. If you're on a distant location, how will the film be transported to a lab? How will your original negative and digital transfer be archived, protected, and conveyed to the editing room? The bond company wants to know everything that can jeopardize the production's successful completion, including the postproduction. The bond company also has experts in postproduction who will monitor the progress of the production's completion and delivery to whomsoever the producers are contractually obligated to deliver the completed movie to. They will continue to review cost reports until you reach the finish line.

To be clear, the bond company cannot guarantee how good the creative choices made by the filmmakers are. That's a matter of taste, which they don't guarantee. They guarantee that all the footage will be delivered to assemble a completed movie as written in the screenplay, for the amount of money indicated in the budget. Bond companies are not obligated or expected to bring their authority to bear on movies that are on budget but off message, meaning poorly crafted or without taste. There's no insurance against losses due to a movie being bad or not performing in the marketplace for any reason. There are financial strategies to soften the blow, but that's another subject.

It's worth noting that completion bonds are generally more associated with non-studio productions. Productions that are self-financed by the studios do not have completion bonds. The studio process of making movies has those safeguards built in. They have production departments that cost out and supervise every aspect of the production from the minute the studio agrees to finance it to its completion. Other departments determine how much and how money will be spent in the marketing and distribution of the movie. If budgets are exceeded for any reason, the studio has the resources to self-insure against those losses.

You may be saying to yourself, I'm the director of this movie. I can't and shouldn't be bothered or burdened with all the paperwork, business decisions, financial meetings, and bureaucratic tasks circling above my head. Insurance? Completion bonds? Take care of it; just tell me where to sign and let me get back to making my movie. You're only partly right in thinking that way. If you're the director, it's difficult to separate yourself from the business side. It's also not in your creative self-interest. Leaving all decisions of money and logistics to others such as your producer and placing yourself in a bubble of creative focus distances you from helping to make decisions about money and logistics that will support your creative goals. Participating in those decisions makes you an effective advocate for your creative vision and helps set priorities that are for the good of the movie as you see it, and not just the bottom line. That is the tension that always exists on movie productions: it's your resources versus your creative realization. As the director you want to participate in the management of that balance. Directors should not want to have their artistic vision modified solely by others who are not at the creative helm. It's collaboration. If you feel a certain stunt or stunt sequence is critical to the success of your vision for the movie, you must protect it. If your stunt coordinator tells you that they have a new and improved version of a stunt that will put the production over-budget in the stunt category and you love it because it will further elevate the quality of the movie, don't you want to be able to have a meaningful discussion with your producer to search for ways to afford this new and improved idea? You need to have a decent understanding of what things cost so that, when you are given the choice of taking money away from one scene to enhance another, you can make an informed decision.

So, to the extent you consider yourself an artiste and can't be bothered with learning about or dealing with the "paperwork," you are potentially limiting the realization of your vision. The best directors have both sides of the brain working. Having a developed business sense is really part of the director's job description. I would also point out that as a director you have numerous responsibilities. You are responsible for creative decisions and ethical choices and you're accountable for business practices as well. The first two of those responsibilities are pretty clear: you have the creative helm and you have the safety of your team always at the forefront of your mind. But you also have a responsibility to influence spending in a way that is fiscally responsible. We've all heard of directors who, according to some accounts, spend wildly and without regard to the limits set forth in the budget. This is a risky gambit. It risks the successful completion of your movie. It risks the hard-earned money of those who have placed big-time trust in you to make their very risky investment pay off. And it certainly risks your future career if you're labeled as someone who flagrantly ignores their financial duty.

It should be evident how intertwined the business and the creative sides of filmmaking are: how issues of finance, management, and administration can affect creative choices. So please put your creative hat back on, making sure not to let your business hat out of your reach. Let's explore one of the stunt world's staple gags.

Falls

One of the more psychologically interesting stunts employed in movies is the fall: the higher the better. The fluttery feeling we get in our stomachs when a character stands near the edge of a cliff or building is one of the visceral and palpable responses an audience can experience. This type of response is what storytellers work long and hard to arouse. Movies can cause not only an emotional reaction but, whenever possible, a physical one as well. As an audience member I want the story to make me feel some emotion and often along with those feelings come sweaty palms, a clenched jaw, light-headedness, or electrical shock waves radiating through my body … hopefully not all at once. Movies can do that to us. I don't know about you, but the very idea of standing on the narrow edge of a high cliff, traversing a shaky rope bridge stretched over a deep crevice or standing on the roof near the edge of a tall skyscraper, makes me weak in the knees. If you have the skill to make an audience feel weak in the knees or queasy in their stomachs, you're doing your job.

The high fall plays on that weakness many of us have. The uncomfortable feeling we get watching someone perilously close to the edge of any high place is a priceless moviegoing experience. I know when I see a character on screen getting close to that edge of doom, my body tenses and I feel the urge to move back away from that imagined precipice. There are camera positions and lenses directors and stunt people employ that amplify those responses. Point of view shots, in which we are put in the position of seeing what the character sees using wide-angle lenses that exaggerate distance and height, are examples of techniques used to heighten the experience for an audience. When the story demands that our worst fears for that character in peril are realized and they go over the edge, speeding toward a gruesome end, that feeling can be almost unbearable. We pay money to suffer through those exciting moments. As a filmmaker, you want to furnish those thrills to the viewers. You bring in the experts who know how to safely and convincingly stage such falls.

Depending on your resources, you will have a number of options to execute the high fall. Of course, the most straightforward is to have a stunt performer actually fall from a high place and, without cutting, watch him come to earth. That's not possible unless they land in deep water to cushion the blow. The camera can avert its attention to the landing to avoid revealing pads of all sorts that can make the landing a relatively safe one. A follow-up shot can show the actor drop to the ground, or if the fall is that high, we will only see the horrible aftermath of a body hitting hard ground from a high drop. Thanks to digital technology, these high falls can be passably realistic. Close-ups of a terrified victim and their point of view are now possible thanks to green screen technology or other computer-aided methods. Using a combination of wires that suspend an actor in front of a green screen and technology called "face replacement," a composite image of a character falling a limitless distance can be created. No need to risk a stunt performer's life or safety. But in some cases, the real fall is best. There's a level of reality that digital technology doesn't always capture.

> MARTIN CAMPBELL: *Nowadays, with face replacement and all the digital tools that we have, it just makes the lead actor look so much better.*

The cost of face replacement and digitally removing support wires or other devices used to recreate the illusion of falling or just being placed in extremely dangerous and precarious places may be prohibitive. For every year, every month that passes, technology utilized in visual effects not only gets more sophisticated and therefore realistic, but it gets less expensive as well. By the time you read this passage, you may be able to erase support wires and extraneous equipment on your laptop. It's certainly easy to composite images and create complex and convincing CGI shots using a combination of live action and digital imagery on your laptop today. The calculation as to the risk and cost of any given stunt is a fluid one based on current technology and ever-changing cost factors. Know that many movies relying heavily on CGI-enhanced or -created stunts have visual effects (VFX) budgets that equal the live action portion of the budget. It can be very expensive.

> JOHN BADHAM: *We're thinking that we want to chuck a guy off a building and see him fall down the building. We thought we'd get a guy to do a high fall off the building and the stunt guy looked at you and said, "No, we don't need to do that at all. We'll start him falling off the building and he'll fall into a net maybe 20 feet down and then we'll CGI him all the way down and it will be a safer landing." We ask him how much will that cost to do versus paying a stunt guy to do a 1,200 foot fall that I might have to do a couple of times at least? You hardly ever want to leave it to one time and every time you do that, you're going to pay your stunt guy for taking the risk a second or even third time.*

Someone has to do the math. You have numerous choices. Do the stunt live once with a dozen cameras, or do it three times with five cameras or do it once on location and do pickup shots in a studio and piece together the footage in a computer? There are all kinds of ways to go depending on the quality you desire, the cost you can afford, and the practicality of the stunt.

When working on low-height falls, it usually makes sense to perform them live. No tricks. Stunt performers will choose from a number of options to safely break their fall. We've all seen the classic scene where someone falls from a roof to the sidewalk, street, or alley below. Those locations are very friendly to camouflaging the padding. With cars, garbage bins, piles of rubbish, cardboard boxes, and any other naturally occurring items on a city landscape, you have perfect covers for materials used to break falls. Among those items are gym pads (tumbling), air-filled cushions (such as a fire department would use), or even empty cardboard boxes that will collapse and absorb the shock of a fall when a body hits it. The DIY (do it yourself) approach is the cardboard box. If you assemble the boxes, art-direct them to look old and used and stack them: you'll have a time-tested method of breaking a fall. Now of course it depends on how much weight is falling from what height. Sometimes the boxes are scored or weakened with a series of cuts to modulate the resistance the boxes offer the falling performer. These are calculations your stunt performer must make. This is also the case with more sophisticated and reliable materials such as pads and air-filled platforms. Your stunt team must be allowed to choose the right tool for the job, meaning they know best as to what level of protection they offer and by what means they can achieve it. This is not a decision a nonprofessional can decide.

If you're like me and know nothing about cars, you'll allow your mechanic to decide on which tools and parts to use to fix your car. Your mechanic will give you options based on cost and the relative need for the repair. My mechanic, Rudy, would say (in a German accent), "You can wait for the oil change. But the brakes, you need now. You can get the good ones, those are the ones I put on my wife's car or … you can go cheap. It's up to you." You can decide if you want the expensive brake shoes or the cheap ones, but you will most likely follow his professional advice to change your brakes to an acceptable standard of performance and safety. I have to trust Rudy will choose the right tools to do the job correctly and safely. I'm not about to tell him which wrench to use. Those of us who are not professional stunt performers also don't want to tell the pros how to do their job by imposing our idea of how something should be done when all that is probably motivating your thinking is saving money or time. Penny wise and pound foolish is the phrase that comes to mind in these situations (actually it came to Rudy's mind).

It's important to know that there are professionals who have made falls a specific area of expertise. If the fall carries enough risk and the stunt performer feels he or she feels they need specialized safety equipment, riggers will be employed to ensure the stunt is done safely and effectively. Not only do these experts own and operate safety equipment used for falls or anything that requires suspension of talent off the ground, but they often design and manufacture those devices. Straps, cables, harnesses, clamps, and turnbuckles are a few of the many pieces of hardware riggers utilize to ensure a safe stunt.

Sometimes safety mats, custom-designed for specific requirements of a movie, are utilized. One such example is the air-filled mat, which can be adjusted in its resistance using air pressure to perfectly respond to the force of the fall. That fall and its force will be mathematically calculated in order to employ the appropriate amount of resistance. Sometimes standard gymnastic mats are used as well.

Hydraulic lifts or air rams are also employed to enhance falls or to create the illusion of someone being catapulted through the air from an explosion. I'm constantly amazed at the aptitude in physics and math these pros display in the invention, building, or utilization of these devices. These stunt experts have to make precise calculations taking into account all physical factors that will affect the fall.

> DAN BRADLEY: *I'm very mechanically inclined. I laugh because I was one of those kids; I will sit in algebra class and think, "what am I ever going to need this for?" Two weeks ago, I was sitting down and doing calculus and trigonometry, trying to figure out what was going to happen or what should happen and where I needed to have things happen for a scene in my next movie.*

Whether they studied physics in school or most likely learned it instinctively from the understanding they have of the mechanics of a fall or stunt, the seasoned professional understands how to calculate and employ devices for maximum safety and entertainment value.

An important issue to consider when making the deal to employ stunt equipment companies performers is whether you should encourage them to use their own equipment or other equipment you arrange to rent or purchase. Maybe you have a friend or connection to free or discounted equipment your stunt and special effects pros require for your show. While this may be acceptable to your stunt people, in many cases it may not be acceptable or at least not advisable. The rental rates you will most likely be charged will be fair, market-driven rates that will be based on the value and sophistication of the equipment. The reason you should be willing to pay those rates and not look for the best deal is that these pros know their own equipment and the equipment's nuances intimately. They know how a specific device they own will react time after time. This consistency is critical to ensuring safety and reliability. If they actually designed and built the device, that's an even greater incentive to use their equipment. For instance, if hydraulic safety mats are used, the controls and settings have to be played with in order to gauge the device's performance: that's a margin for error you should not accept. In all likelihood, your professional will familiarize him or herself with the device before agreeing to use it on camera. But the time it takes to arrive at the point in which the stunt and special effects teams are confident the stunt will be safe and look good is not the best use of the very expensive minutes consumed. More study, more rehearsal, slower pace of work are all possible when stunt and special effects pros work with unfamiliar equipment. Actually this can apply to other departments as well. This is a prime example of how to spend your money wisely.

Anytime a dangerous or complicated stunt is performed, it's wise to deploy as many cameras to capture as many angles as possible. These stunts are very expensive. They can have substantial labor and equipment costs and are very time consuming. Depending on the requirements of the piece of action to be performed on camera, sets may have to be rebuilt or repaired. Extras will have to be repositioned along with anything else that may have moved during the take such as traffic. Safety precautions will have to be reinstalled or rechecked. Camera teams will have to reestablish and confirm their modes of communication, and the entire crew will have to analyze the previous take and make adjustments. This can take anywhere from fifteen minutes to the whole day. Not only do you want to be able to capture various facets of the fall for dramatic emphasis, but if a camera malfunctions or a camera operator misses a crucial moment in the fall, you want backup angles.

Editorial

The editor's primary function is to provide the heartbeat of the film, how it's paced and the information is disseminated.

DAN LEBENTAL

That's a big role. A picture editor who is experienced in cutting action can be an invaluable collaborator when planning your stunts and action sequences. No one on your team has a deeper understanding of the "moving parts" of an action sequence or stunt. Like no other filmmaker, they have identified, wrestled with, searched for all the pieces that, when cut together, become a believable action moment or sequence. As a director, you will of course be conceiving the moment or string of moments for the same result. If you lack experience in this specialized area, your editor can be a very valuable contributor. If you're a producer, this dynamic is an important one to appreciate, so you can support your director with every resource possible.

DAN LEBENTAL: *Everyone doing their best is how good films are made.*

Cutting an action sequence or a special effect, such as fire, wind, or explosions, is of course, in and of itself, not the ultimate objective. The ultimate objective is the same as any sequence is in any other genre of movie. The creative choices that go into cutting an action scene must be considered in the context of the overall story and how it is being told. The pace, tone, and style of the action should feel organic and cohesive to the complete movie. Your editor is a key contributor who implements choices that are in line with the overall story. How quick is too quick, or how measured and deliberate should the rollout of images and information be to achieve a desired effect? Will a shot's insertion into the movie's story arc be seamless, or will the audience feel the storytellers are stepping outside the narrative drive of the movie to offer a few moments of thrilling action? Both are legitimate choices depending on the overall vision. One approach is to design action sequences that serve to enhance or support the characters and their story objectives. Those objectives could be external, such as scaling a fortress to rescue a princess or driving through countless barriers to neutralize a criminal menace. Action often can serve as a metaphor for a character's inner drive to achieve a personal goal. The fight that proves one's courage, the race that validates one's skill, or the sacrifice that redeems one's honor: all are very familiar storytelling devices that are staples of the action genre. Action can be the roller-coaster ride or the revealing character device or both.

MARTIN CAMPBELL: *In that* Casino Royale *sequence with Bond, his heart is ruling his head. He's just got this fanatical obsession with this guy and he screws up. He chases this guy, he lands badly, he crashes down on things, he has an "elephant in a bathhouse" attitude, but he keeps going, which of course is the thing about Bond. It's pretty ugly stuff he does in the chase and the free runner does it like a bloody ballet dancer. The bad guy goes into the embassy and Bond makes the mistake of following him in to the embassy. Now anyone with half a brain would never have done that, because what you do is, you wait outside and when he comes back out, you nail him. But Bond, with his heart overruling his head, charges and creates this huge diplomatic incident, which is part of his character at this point. He's a rough diamond; he's not the Bond we know until the end of the movie. At this point in the movie, he screws up. He makes mistakes, but what he does have is determination and an obsession for getting his man. There's nothing graceful about his actions, he's as clumsy as hell. He's going on sheer guts and determination. That's what pushes him through, which clearly once refined becomes a terrific asset in the future.*

Set pieces work like the Michael Bay version of action, which are huge set pieces that are so spectacular because of hardware and everything else in the fast cutting effect. But they're meaningless in terms of character. They don't develop anybody. It's sort of a circus of action and pyrotechnics. I believe everything must relate to character and pushing the story forward as well. The opening sequence with the free running at the construction site is a good example of serving to both to develop character and advance the story.

Despite all the planning and dry runs filmmakers go through to avoid missing or miscalculating the pieces to the large narrative puzzle, omissions occur. They happen for a few reasons. Sometimes the holes in the story caused by missing scenes and shots are glaring, and the only explanation is, it happens. People can and do overlook what becomes obvious once the movie starts to be assembled in the editing room. The story and all its complexity becomes so ingrained in a director's mind in advance and during the shooting that it may, or actually *should*, feel totally familiar and complete … in their head. This is the way it should be. Every director should be so intimately familiar with all the nooks and crannies of their story that it feels like they've lived it themselves. The director must know the answer to every question about the story and the creative choices that address those questions.

> DAN LEBENTAL: *A great director is first and foremost a conductor. What I mean by that is a conductor tells an orchestra the way they want them to play the piece of music, but they don't play the instruments. A director is trying to get out the very best in all the different people that are going to work on this. They're the ones who are going to provide a lot of the direction and inspiration and knowledge. That doesn't mean that they're expected to know everything. This is where the young director always makes the mistake. They think they're supposed to have the solution or blueprint to everything. What they're supposed to be is more like a learned judge who decides from among the possibilities brought to them. And then through a give and take with the various departments, make it better.*

But what can happen as a result of this intense familiarity is the director may assume the audience knows a story point, understands some relevant aspect of a character's history, or has witnessed some event that is important to understanding the flow of the narrative, because the director has seen it in his or her mind's eye time and time again. So the director can be wrong in assuming or not thinking about what the audience knows and doesn't know from what they have actually seen and heard on screen. That assumption, if not challenged, can result in holes in the plot or sequence of events. It takes great discipline to avoid that trap. Long experience and thorough preparation such as storyboards and animatics can help, but not guarantee this from happening. It happens all the time. The editor can be the backstop, the omnipotent viewpoint of all the pieces to the puzzle the director has provided. That's a valuable perspective to have on the team. The editor must be able to spot those gaps and also be able to determine if performances are effective.

Another reason gaps can occur is because many movies, particularly less expensive or complex ones, take on a life of their own. Planning is important. But many directors working on character-driven stories prefer to leave the door open to inspiration while shooting. Others prefer to be locked down into a plan that they faithfully follow after much detailed and thorough planning and rehearsing. This is an efficient and methodical approach that makes sense on technically difficult stories or ones that emphasize "the ride" over character. However, other kinds of stories, ones that place a premium on behavior and character, can benefit from less precise planning, more going with the flow. This approach can result in fresh, vital, and exciting storytelling. But this approach also allows for the story to take on a shape and tone less predictable, arguably more organic and in the moment. Making movies this way makes the journey less predictable, more surprising. Some filmmakers prefer being surprised by how the movie turns out; others do all they can to eliminate the unforeseen.

So, once principal photography has commenced, the editor's early role will be to organize on a daily basis the material shot. When stunts or special effects have been shot, there is an urgency to seeing the raw footage of those scenes. While the production company may still be able to reshoot or add a needed shot to make an action sequence work better, the editor must closely comb through to assess all the footage as soon as possible to be able to notify the producer or director if there's a problem that must be addressed. If the company has one more day at the location where a fight was shot and the fight lacks a shot or in some way doesn't tell or sell the story, they may be able to reshoot or shoot the shot or shots before the company moves on to other locations. The sooner they can try and make plans to add this extra shooting to their already-busy schedule, the better. The editing team, knowing in advance the narrow window for correcting a potential mistake or omission, will make a special point of reviewing the footage quickly, possibly more quickly than their daily routine would call for. The director may be on the phone with the editor early in the day, asking how a stunt looked before the director has a chance to see it. The director will rely on the editor's judgment if there is no time to bring the footage in question to the set for the director to review. So it's a hard call to make but a completely necessary one, if the editor feels there's a problem that must be dealt with.

> DAN BRADLEY: *Those are calls that have to be made, they're very*
> *uncomfortable, but they do have to be made when things don't work*
> *out for whatever reason.*

The editor's goal in their first pass or assembly of all the material that has been shot is to come as close as possible to the original vision as laid out in the screenplay. Departing, improvising, rethinking, or reinventing the footage into a different version of the original vision comes in later iterations of the movie. You just also understand that the director is most often still making the movie when the editor begins the assembly. While the director may express preferences for certain takes either through script notes taken by the continuity person or by viewing dailies, the director's attention is more focused on the task at hand, shooting the movie. The objective perspective of the editor to look for the pieces that tell the story as described in the script is logical. Why depart from the plan before you haven't tried to make the original plan work? Going to Plan B before Plan A has been tried doesn't make a lot of sense. The editor should not take it upon themselves to decide they have a different and better vision for the movie and execute it in their first cut. That's not their role. Eventually, when the director has worked with the footage and determined it's time to go to Plan B, then the editor's input as to how to solve problems that may exist or how to best repurpose the story material on hand is a proper and valued role for the editor to fulfill. But the first pass must reflect a commitment to the script.

> DAN LEBENTAL: *If you know, if something was missed then the question becomes how front and center is this meant to be because generally if it's not as grand as, you know maybe somebody hoped, what we end up doing is we make it shorter. We make it less important and we make it as good as it can be without becoming silly because it doesn't work to the degree that we hoped. So we adapt to what we have.*

Editors can play a valuable role in evaluating performances in a character-driven piece. Where they are also very valuable is when they have cut together all the pieces of action and can see that it doesn't work as well as planned. The editor can examine every shot and diagnose where the problem is. Is there a missing shot? A gap in the flow of action? Or does a punch or hard landing not land hard enough to be persuasive or impactful?

> DAN LEBENTAL: *One of your primary functions is to report back and say we got what we need. Because if they think they have a marvelous stunt and it's not so marvelous, better to know it right away before they move on to something else.*

On character-driven, "walk and talk" movies, the editor is a very late addition to the creative team. However, many directors find the editor's lack of history with the production promotes a helpful, objective voice. The editor works with the material the director shot, not the material the director *wanted* to shoot but didn't. That objective perspective enables a good editor to view and evaluate the raw footage for its effective storytelling and finally to determine if any shots, beats, or even scenes are missing, in order to faithfully assemble the script's dialogue and action.

DAN LEBENTAL: *The editor is one of the director's chief advisors who they can trust because the old adage is "the editor sees the director naked." They see what they've shot in its totality. It's possible that much of it doesn't work but the world will never see what doesn't work. So as an editor, you have to be able to whisper in their ear about everything; the actress doesn't look good, there is something wrong, this isn't right… this performer is having trouble with this or that. So there's an advisory role that goes beyond the nuts and bolts.*

When you talk beginning, middle, and ends and editing what I said about entering and exiting frames also plays into that. We're very careful not to resolve things until we're ready to. This philosophy can go over a gamut of things, but certainly the stunt is one of them where until you're ready for the big resolve, never let anything else resolve. Always get out during… not after. They have to shoot everything like it has a full beginning, middle, and end and we'll always use it just after the beginning and before the end… until we get to the very end and then we'll let the scene have its major resolve and that way it will keep the story moving.

Dan Lebental describes below a scene in one of his recent movies in which the rapid action is assembled by eliminating the beginning and end of each shot until the scene's denouement.

DAN LEBENTAL: *On* Cowboys & Aliens, *I had a scene right at the beginning of the movie where a character is confronted and hoisted by three bad guys with guns and the good guy has nothing and he's on foot. He first takes out one bad guy. He stabs him, but before the bad guy ever hits the ground, you'd be into the next cut. You see our guy move in towards the other bad guy with his knife, but you don't finish the shot, you're already moving to the next part of the scene, you're never letting that action fully resolve. Then the other bad guy shoots, our guy moves, but before that bullet ever gets close to him, he's already dodging. Then you have the horse rear, before the horse ever gets to its height, you cut back and the good guy is moving on. And just as he starts to jump, you cut out, you don't go way into the shot and then you get into the next shot where he flies in and knocks the other bad guy off the horse. So again, you're giving enough to be able to answer one cut with the next cut, until you hit the very last thing, where you're going to take the bad guy out, then you give it its full resolution, the last guy standing kind of thing.*

Everybody has their own specific vision on how a story should be best told. That's called taste. Edit the movie crisply, clearly with attention to detail, or be scattered and impressionistic: a wild and dizzying ride. Each and every approach has an effect. The pacing can be deliberate and build, or be a race from start to finish. Each and every approach to telling a visual story is a reflection of very subjective as well as objective choices. Some filmmakers have taste that seems to produce the right formula for an audience to get the most out of the story being told. Other filmmakers are not as gifted, and their movies often fall short of that effective connection. Knowing when enough is enough or when it's not. That's taste. Your editor can be a great partner. Here's where all the planning and the theory are manifest. The footage, the material, is a product of all the planning and theory from preproduction. Directors and their creative team have made certain choices on how to tell the story. Those choices are reflected in storyboards, previz, shot lists, and, just in the moment, inspiration. The director has shot what he or she needs to shoot based on those choices. There are a few ways to work with the material. Some of it is meant to be utilized in its entirety, from when "action" called to "cut." Other shots are meant to be used in part.

> DAN LEBENTAL: *Now, there are those that as a style will actually cut things quickly to the point where you don't necessarily see the full stunt. One of the editor action tricks probably since the '80s is you'll never let something (or someone) enter a frame and you never let something exit a frame. You're always propelling motion forward. When one car smashes into the other, you get to the part you need to allude to and see what you need to see without resolving it and then you keep moving.*

The audience should see that the collision between two cars is inevitable and maybe they should see that they in fact do hit and start spinning. They don't need to see the energy of that action dissipate as they slow down and come to rest. Keep the tension in these moments.

The concept in editing high-energy, stunt-driven action is to allow the audience to imagine they've seen a shot resolve itself. It keeps things moving. It doesn't allow the audience to stop and take a breath or to think very much about what they are witnessing. It's more visceral, not intellectual. If you take this overall strategy of editing, the collective impact of that is a fast-paced movie that keeps an audience always "leaning forward." Not every scene can be cut in this breathtaking way. Not all scenes are designed like that. Even in the wildest of action movies, sometimes the characters have to just talk things out. But even then, you can adjust your editing technique to this approach. Even if characters just talk, we don't have to see them complete every action or enter or exit the frame.

> DAN LEBENTAL: *You'll get a character, you'll make the cut, a frame after they've entered and you'll cut out before they clear or exit the frame. And you're always doing that to propel a story. You want to answer one shot with a next shot, then answer that with a next shot after that. That's one of the major modern action editing tricks common in the industry today.*

If a character sits down, you don't have to actually include the part of the shot where they come to rest on the chair. The audience sees the character is moving to that inevitable conclusion. They don't need to actually see their butt hit the seat. If someone is to be punched or a car is to crash, if enough length of the shots leading up to the collision is sufficient, they will lead the audience to the inevitable conclusion that there's no way that anything but a collision can occur. So if they feel that way, you don't have to show the collision, or maybe you don't even have to shoot it. The audience will be participating in the giving out of information. The filmmakers offer up images and words, but the audience using their imagination, if properly prepared, will plug in the images not actually seen. Often we will swear we saw something happen that we didn't actually see happen. We imagined the culmination of an action or dynamic event. Remember my reference to *Jaws*. How much of the shark attacking do we ever actually see? Save the money because you don't need to see every detail of an action. Figure that out in prep with an editor.

> DAN LEBENTAL: *The audience will fill in the blanks, they will tell you if you ask them, oh I saw him hit the ground, I saw him take the knife out, I saw him come jump fly through the air and then fly into the other guy, and what they really saw was a lot of those things starting and almost finishing and then move on. They'll fill in the blanks and it'll keep it moving and audiences have a tremendous power to quickly absorb these days.*

Keeping in mind that well-constructed scenes have a beginning, middle, and end, just as stories do, it's worth considering how this approach to editing may apply to more micro-elements of a scene, the shot. A collection of well-arranged shots or moments create a scene. A collection of well-organized scenes add up to a story. As I stated, scenes and stories have arcs. Do shots? One could argue that stunt shots do. There is often in action scenes an inciting event that spurs the action. So the punch received will be countered with a punch delivered. A car rolling over and over does so after a collision with another object. We could demand to see every moment of that dynamic, but to do so might expose the less authentic moments. The actual moment of contact may be less impressive than what we can imagine it would be like and feel like. So you can edit the shots to keep the imagination of the audience active and participating in the action. The conclusion of an action moment or sequence may be best left out until a final and well-thought-out conclusion or resolution to the action can be designed and executed. The searing, flaming aftermath of a car wreck from which the hero crawls forms a collective sense of taste that reflects the director's perspective and enhances it with the objectivity the editor brings to the party. When it comes to stunts, this issue of how much to show and to what degree you push the action is critical.

DAN LEBENTAL: *You've got to know when it's too much, when to get out. I sat in a room with Spielberg and he said this to us. He said, don't play your 3s and 6s, just play your jacks, queens, and kings. Don't even bother ... the audience doesn't need it when you're showing lesser things with your ND [nondescript as in extras or peripheral players] characters, the people that you don't care about. Every bit of that you use just dilutes the story. His perspective was in movies, almost all fight scenes and action scenes are too long. You're almost always better off getting it tighter, shorter ... with just your very best stuff. It's not about how long you can keep the spectacle.*

That's Steven Spielberg's taste, which has been borne out in movie after movie, huge hit after huge hit. Hard to argue with his success, and why should we? But that's his taste. Other directors' tastes have been proved in the marketplace as well. Some directors also have the very distinct ability to sense what the audience wants to see and how they want to experience a story. I would place Spielberg in that category. His taste has garnered critical as well as commercial validation. We can all think of directors and producers who have a great feel for what the public wants to see, critics be damned.

DAN LEBENTAL: *Of course, I have had numerous discussions with producers and studio execs about overdoing the action. One exec cited their overseas audience that wants to be beaten down by our action scenes to the point of exhaustion.*

That's a reflection of an audience's perceived taste.

DAN LEBENTAL: *So you'll get five filmmakers together and you'll get six different answers. This whole world ends up being like everything else in film, a question of taste. Zach Staenberg cutting* Matrix *went for the pure spectacle of watching those guys enter that hallway, bullets flying and hitting the ground, like no one had seen before and it so worked. That was his taste and that of the Wachowskis.*

I use to work with the Hughes brothers. Their whole thing was action; real action is short and deadly. Indeed from that perspective, I always agreed that it's a disservice to the world to sometimes make violence a beautiful thing. And theirs was always meaner and nastier than everyone else had been, it was always short.

Storyboards and Previz

Astoryboard is the old school method of previsualizing a scene. Storyboards are a series of hand-drawn images that capture the important moments of action in a shot to convey a sense of how the action flows and what shots are necessary to put together a compelling action sequence. This is pretty much what comic books and graphic novels do.

This assemblage of images or the "moving parts" of a stunt or action is laid out on pages, each with a separate image, or the page can contain four to six separate frames that allow the viewer to track the action from frame to frame. The point of view is from that of the audience's eye or where the camera is placed using a specific lens. It's like a frame grab from the movie that is in your head. Storyboards may also flag any errors of omission or technical problems that may come up. Old school methods of hand-drawn storyboards, even if they're crudely drawn, are a very valuable planning tool. If you have no artistic abilities whatsoever, you have a couple of choices. You can draw stick figures: anyone can do that. Or you can take a little time and study or ask someone to teach you the basics of figure drawing and perspective. That's the level of art most of us learned in middle school. The lack of artistic ability should never prevent you from creating useful, classic storyboards. Also, they're quick and easy to revise. Computer-generated previz can be time consuming and expensive. It looks great and certainly has its place as a tool of choice.

If drawing is not for you, there are new ways of creating storyboards that use sophisticated software. Whichever technology you choose, you will find storyboarding to be a great help, if for no other reason than that it forces you to think about how you will approach shooting a scene. Even if circumstances change or you have a better idea that strays from your storyboards, the exercise of creating them helped you think clearly and completely about the scene. Because you went through the mental process, you are in a better position to deviate and make even better choices.

MARTIN CAMPBELL: *I do storyboards on paper. My problem with all the previz: the length of time it actually takes to produce the previz. Now if you're doing* Gravity, *of course you have to previz it. There's no other way to do it. But if you're doing something like the Bond foot chase or tank chase, I always had a problem with all the time it took to produce previz, and then it was never quite right. Then when you give notes and changes, it takes a while for that to happen. So I much prefer to do it on paper with storyboards, very specifically. I do them as edited sequences. Those storyboards are always the bible for the second unit. Often the stunt arranger himself will direct the second unit and it's always very specific, my instructions always the same so that he shoots the storyboards exactly how I want it. And then, do what the hell you like. If you can improve upon it, go ahead and do it.*

JEFF TUFANO: *The director on the second unit comes with a particular skill set. You can see that these kinds of guys have always done their homework. They bring in either storyboards or some sort of previz. A lot of people have programs on their iPads to create previz. Sometimes the visual effects team will create an animated version of the action that we are supposed to shoot. Sometimes they show it to us and we wonder why they just don't use it, it's so amazing.*

This planning tool enables filmmakers to anticipate problems and ensures that all the necessary parts to what is often a complex puzzle are identified. This process creates an open book of the detailed plan to shoot the movie. Each department can be prepared for those scenes if they can see what the director is planning. The camera team knows the shots, the AD can appreciate what's involved and plan accordingly and make sure everyone else does their jobs, sound can plan on what equipment they'll need, and so forth. It's a terrific means by which to communicate to all departments, so everyone has a common understanding. When everyone is pulling in the same direction, things go smoother, and you get the shots you want to get.

MARTIN CAMPBELL: *I do a lot of work on action in terms of the conception of action. This type of action-oriented filmmaking all comes down to planning. I storyboard all my action and the reason for that is, as an example, on the Bond films, you'll have a second unit and sometimes even a third unit who might do some model work or even some pickup shots. The only way to get everything you want is to storyboard the action. You sit down with your stunt arranger/coordinator, discuss it, and figure out what you want. Now if you have a very good stunt arranger, which I do, the two I work with mainly are Simon Crane and Gary Powell, they contribute an awful lot to it as well. In the case of Bond, Chris Corbould was the special effects guy, probably the best in the world in my opinion. He did Batman and Bond movies, he also contributes. For instance the tank chase in GoldenEye was Chris Corbould's idea. He came up with the idea and we ran with it. So it's a process where I lay down pretty specifically what I want to see in the action and sit down with my stunt arranger, who in my last Bond film was Gary Powell, and we'll talk about it. He'll add to that or conceive it a little differently, always to make it better and make it a little more spectacular.*

A perfect example of when and why storyboards are critically important, actually indispensable, when doing action sequences is described below. Action can be written into the script in very general ways. A collaboration of talent defines and designs the action and communicates those ideas through storyboards or previz.

MARTIN CAMPBELL: *In* Casino Royale, *the opening foot chase is six lines in the script. I think the script read something like, "and what follows is a foot chase, a 'parkour', a free running sequence. The best free running sequence ever made." That's about all that was written [in] the script. It was down for me to work it all out along with my stunt arranger and map it all out. As with all Bond films, you want a spectacular opening. But it was a foot chase on the page, fairly boring, but actually kind of exciting on the screen.*

RON SHELTON: *In* Dark Blue, *there's a four or five minutes scene where Kurt Russell is in the car and he's caught in a riot breaking out everywhere. That was a huge, huge sequence for a low-budget movie. We storyboarded it within an inch of our lives. We did like seven minutes of screen time in two days of shooting and it looked like a week's worth of work. We had the storyboards out and mounted and broken out into chapters for every department. We had a book printout of it.*

Also, the cinematographer, producer, screenwriter, AD, editor... *anyone* can examine the previz and determine from their perspective and in the context of their role in the production if the storyboards reveal holes, inconsistencies, or any other storytelling problems. It helps prevent unwelcome surprises when it's too late to do anything about them, or if there is, time and money are wasted to fix the problem caused by poor planning. Storyboards are a time-tested guard against problems due to lack of communication or appreciation of what's really going to happen on the day.

Sometimes the storyboards or previz are meant to be more of a guide than an exact blueprint.

JEFF TUFANO: *In the last couple of years, the bigger jobs like G.I. Joe and Twilight: Breaking Dawn always had previz on the set to refer to. They certainly don't run it past me and sometimes not even the cinematographer. But the visual effects people will of course be sharing their previz with the director and he usually shares it with the cinematographer. Even though they're so awesome, these computer-generated images are really meant to be a guideline. I've never been asked if we could precisely recreate them. But it's perfectly acceptable if they want us to get as close to them as is possible.*

Stunt coordinators or choreographers can rehearse how the action will flow in a scene they are preparing. Particularly among the guys who are always thinking how to tell the story through action, exact actions may be less important than the point or intentions of the action to tell the story. So directors and everyone else who are inclined to take the previz and shoot it may take certain liberties and not feel constrained by the visuals in the previz. They use previz as a foundation, not a prescription. It's like anything else; any form of rehearsal enables one to be free from constraints, not tied to them.

JEFF TUFANO: *Sometimes these teams like a dozen or two dozen guys work these things out and rehearse them. Everyone's got their iPhones or other devices. They don't come to the set without something to show. Again they're not asking you to do exactly as they did in rehearsal, they're asking you to understand the intentions of their work and to give it the best possible presentation.*

The editor can be a prime participant in this process. Because their job is to put the pieces of the story puzzle together, they understand storytelling from the inside out. An editor can be a very valuable collaborator before your movie is shot by not only pointing our potential problems but also suggesting shots that will make your movie better.

DAN LEBENTAL: *When it comes to who initiates ideas or concepts, it just depends. It can be any number of people, including the editor. Oftentimes if we're doing previz or even if we're deep in it, we'll say, well what we really need to tell the story is this and this. So editorial will literally suggest shots that we have to get or effects that we should do to enhance or bridge the story.*

Many sequences you dream up can be complex and need to be thought out and previsualized exactly how you see it in the final product, the movie. Deviation can be an invitation to miscalculations or omissions.

MARTIN CAMBELL: *You could look at my storyboards on something
like* Vertical Limit, *take the opening sequence where there's all these
people hanging off a cliff. It's pretty much identical to the storyboards,
because I make them as edited sequences. I had Simon Crane as
my stunt arranger and also it was the first time he had ever directed
second unit was on that show. I sat down with Simon, we talked
about it, I worked out these sequences and then Simon refined them
with me, all storyboarded. If you saw the storyboards for that opening
sequence, which was a pretty exciting sequence, it's almost edited
the same as the storyboards and the shots are virtually identical to the
storyboards plus there's second camera work and sometimes there's
three cameras. There's obviously extra footage due to multiple cameras
being used besides the storyboards. There were shots perhaps Simon
thought would work that were added in as well. It's all based on the
storyboards.*

Don't ever worry about who gets the credit for good ideas. If you're the
director or producer, the only way to get the most out of the team you have
assembled is to encourage them to contribute their best ideas without fear.
Providing a creatively "safe" environment as well as a physically safe one is
vital. Why go to the trouble of getting the best people on your team if they
can't operate in an environment where they can demonstrate or practice their
skills and talents to their greatest potential? You don't buy a Ferrari to drive at
30 mph. You don't hire great people to only give half their effort. Don't ever be
intimidated or jealous of your collaborators' creative gifts, because that's what
their contributions are to your movie, gifts: take them and use them as such.
It's about making the best movie possible, right?

DAN LEBENTAL: *This is a collaborative art and what you want is for
everyone to bring it ... that's how good films are made.*

Editors have a lot to "bring": insight, creativity, problem-solving skills, an
ability to see the big picture, objectively. That is their training and discipline.
Everyone on your team can have helpful ideas, but editors have good ideas
informed by structure, pace, and tone. When an editor tells me the blocking
I have planned for a scene may cause screen direction confusion, I listen.
The sound recordist may also note a potential problem with screen direction
or continuity, but the editor carries weight with their decisions unlike most
other creative member of your team. Directors should be proactive in their
pursuit of getting the most out of their resources. Ask questions, get opinions,
share plans with those who you feel are qualified to give you solid advice.

Few filmmakers have all the answers, at least informed ones. Moviemaking is too complex. It's very hard to be fully qualified or informed about the diverse areas of knowledge a movie must draw on. There's no real glory in claiming you made all the decisions that led to a well-received movie. Few people with any knowledge of how movies are made will believe you anyway. The glory is doing your best work that contributed to a well-received movie. Whatever it is you do, do it well and the glory will follow.

> DAN LEBENTAL: *There's not one person on a movie that knows everything that's going on in a movie, it's impossible. There's too much going on. There are so many moving things. Some people say to me, "you don't have final say" as if that's some sort of disgrace. I'm like, of course I don't have any final say. But you know what? If I haven't nailed 80 or 90% of the decisions right we don't even have a starting place to work with. I have to get us to the '80s or '90 s before they can even start giving me their notes.*

If you are editing a movie in which stunts and special effects will play a significant role, be proactive. Offer your help by showing your director and producer how you can be of extra value through your proactive participation. It's not that you necessarily know more than they do (maybe you do), but you are a bona fide, qualified filmmaker who is well versed in the sometimes complicated or obfuscated challenges that are common in movies with stunts and special effects.

> DAN LEBENTAL: *One of the things I do in prep, especially with the directors that I have a relationship and a trust with, I tend to give notes on the script. I have found the difference early in my career where I didn't want to do speak up and give my notes because I didn't want to rock the boat. But I saw that the problems I see in the script will follow us all the way down and will be the exact same problems that are going to exist when we're trying to finish the film. So I've learned that it's better to open my mouth in the beginning … everyone making the movie should have to answer to everything to really figure it out.*

The smart director or producer will have people around them who will challenge assumptions. Not only will this expose flaws in the plan, but it will also serve to reinforce, validate, or better explain the intentions of the filmmaker. I've heard so many times a young director lament, "I wish somebody had said something when I could do something about this problem. Now it's too late." As an editor, you may, for example, sense either a technical omission such as a necessary connecting shot between two pieces of action or a breach of logic and think, "Why would the hero walk under that ladder? I would never do that. It feels false." Speak up in such a way as to be perceived as a collaborator, not someone trying to make someone look bad by exposing their mistake. That's where you truly earn your pay, by seeing what others have not or cannot. Sometimes directors can just lose their bearings. It is so easy to get lost in the vast array of details and choices that one can understandably lose sight of the overall mission. Objectives get blurred or shift. Sometimes this is just the organic evolution of a movie, but sometimes it's trouble. The valuable editor might say, "wouldn't our hero walk *around* the ladder? And if he did, wouldn't that present *more* jeopardy? A new opportunity for an exciting or tense moment you didn't have when he walked under the ladder?" The good director will say, "Yes! Thank you!"

An experienced editor can look at storyboards or previz even if they are in the most primitive of forms. Stick figures on paper or animatics from a computer can validate the director's choices or enhance them with an editor's input. This is another area where an experienced pro on a critical part of your team can help elevate your project. Having the person in editorial who has wrestled with complicated or even perfunctory coverage over and over again to form a compelling action sequence or moment elevates the whole production. They have seen action sequences so many times that they can more readily spot gaps or gaffes. They can also have a favorable perspective in suggesting the narrative or editorial path less traveled to an inevitable conclusion.

Cars and Vehicles

The car chase is one of the true staples of the world's love affair with movies. Thrilling car chases in such modern movies as *The French Connection*, *Bullitt*, *To Live and Die in L.A.*, and *The Getaway* set a standard for gut-wrenching, heart-pounding speed and muscular horsepower. For that matter, car chases and vehicle mayhem of all sorts was an important storytelling tool in the silent era as well. If you haven't seen the car chases in Keystone Cops, Buster Keaton, or Laurel and Hardy movies, professional stunt drivers have. This is where the vocabulary of the car chase was created. It hasn't changed much; it's just faster and more violent. Of course in the silent era, just as today, filmmakers were not limited to automobiles. Trains, wagons, horses, and all other manner of speedy vehicles were used in exciting and astonishing ways to thrill audiences in the very same way they do today. The risks those early performers took seem unthinkable today. Car stunts are still a very dangerous business, but modern safety precautions and legal and industry protections make safe outcomes more reliable.

The *Fast and the Furious* series, *The Italian Job*, *Children of Men*, and, particularly, the astounding Jason Bourne series of movies have raised the bar to incredible heights. I won't spend too much time discussing everything that goes into these marvels of skill, logistics, engineering, and daring as few of us ever have the opportunity to pull off big-league car chases. They cost millions and employ dozens, if not hundreds, of top professionals. If you have that kind of money and access to the very best stunt coordinators, second unit directors, drivers, designers, mechanics, and engineers, you have a brain trust on board that knows what you need to know. For the rest of you who are planning something more modest or have more modest resources, it's instructive to understand how the big shows do it, to help you understand how the steps they take translate to the needs of your production. How can the protocols taken and lessons learned on bigger budget shows apply to your car chase that may only go around the block or from point A to point B in a few seconds? By understanding the support structure and their protocols that serve stunt driving at its most challenging, you can better understand and get a more complete view of the broad spectrum of their activities, planning, and execution.

In a well-funded and organized production, there are numerous departments that collaborate on a car stunt or chase. Assuming the cars are contemporary "street cars" or are mass-produced cars that may or may not be modified, the transportation department begins the process. On shows that utilize cars from the future or from the past or for whatever reason must be designed from the ground up, the production designer will begin the process of design and eventual manufacture. In fact, experienced production designers will know and recommend transportation and stunt pros whom they have collaborated with in the past on futuristic or highly designed shows. But on shows that use some version of production line cars, the ones that most often are involved in stunts, that is, General Motors, Ford, Toyota, BMW, Audi, Ferrari, Porsche, etc., the transportation department will acquire those cars as one of their initial responsibilities. Headed by the transportation captain, this department is responsible for the acquisition, maintenance, delivery, and often conversion of vehicles that appear on camera. Those are called picture cars. They also acquire and transport all vehicles that support the production such as equipment trucks, honeywagons, and makeup and wardrobe trailers.

On union productions, these drivers are members of the International Brotherhood of Teamsters as are the folks who operate the honeywagons (mobile trailers that primarily contain bathrooms and often feature makeup rooms, wardrobe, and office space) and catering vehicles. The drivers also deliver "above the line" talent (cast, director, and producers) to, from, and between the set(s) from their homes or hotels as required by Screen Actors Guild (SAG) or other union contracts. On locations where parking at the location is not practical, the drivers from the transportation department will acquire and drive vans or buses to shuttle cast and crew to the actual location from a designated parking area that a location manager has arranged for.

The "transpo" department often arranges for the rental or purchase of all the vehicles connected with the production no matter their function. As this pertains to cars and any other vehicles used in chases and crashes, experienced transportation captains (as do most experienced stunt drivers and coordinators) have their reliable sources to acquire them. One such company is Picture Car Warehouse in Los Angeles. Companies like them provide a one-stop shop where productions may choose to purchase their vehicles or rent them. This type of service company can also duplicate any car as many times as your show requires. If the cars are going to be wrecked beyond any reasonable effort to repair, it makes sense to buy the vehicle. If the car is the hero car or one of the vehicles that will be featured throughout the movie, it is common practice to purchase no less than two identical vehicles. Why? What if you're about to shoot a scene with your leading man's car and it won't start? What if one of the transpo drivers didn't notice that tree stump by the road and clips the bumper while delivering it to the set? Are you going to shut down your production until it gets fixed or reschedule the day to accommodate the loss or delay of your picture car? You can do all the above, but you've just spent lots of time and money to accommodate that mishap. What if take one of a car crash didn't work for some reason? The camera operator had an itch and lost the crash in his frame. You need to shoot it again. The hero car is now damaged and is useless. But, if you have a double or exact copy of the hero car, you won't miss a beat. If no damage or fixable damage is anticipated for shots that don't require the immediate use or reuse of that vehicle, you may rent that car from specialized providers of vehicles for the motion picture industry.

Another role companies or transportation departments provide is that of prepping cars for stunts in terms of safety and functionality. They install steel cages that protect the driver when or if it rolls over on its roof. They install or modify the braking system to enable the car to stop more safely or in a way that allows a particular action. Modifications to steering, suspension, or weight distribution can all be made in order to enable the stunt and make it safe. Often gas tanks are removed and replaced with gallon bottle that hold just enough gas to execute the stunt. That way if something unexpected happens, the car won't explode in a ball of flames fed by twenty gallons of gasoline.

One pretty interesting modification they make is called a cannon. A short length of telephone pole is installed inside the car and is attached to a detonator. The driver has a trigger that, when squeezed, activates an explosive force that shoots the pole downward onto the street, thereby violently tipping the car over. These modifications are critically important to make sure they are done professionally and with flawless care. The modifications should be double-checked by the stunt department and/or the transportation department, if they didn't do the work. It's standard procedure to make sure the modifications are checked with enough lead time to fix or rethink a modification that isn't up to par. I'd be nervous getting a car directly from whoever modified it without testing it first. Things go wrong. People make mistakes. Those facts of life must be factored into your way of doing business. The men and women who place their lives on the line, relying on the quality of work done by these people, will understandably want to make sure the work was done properly before going before the cameras.

Vehicles that are not be the "hero" or featured cars are called "ND" cars. ND cars are the ones you see parked on the sides of the street or in the parking lots. They may be cars used to recreate normal traffic or cars that you see being passed or running interference with the hero cars. They may be the unfortunate casualties of the chase car, getting side-swiped or crashed into during or at the conclusion of a chase. The ND cars don't require special equipment or preparation, as they usually are either stationary or are not required to maneuver in any extraordinary way. Once they exceed that demand, they become picture cars and will need the transportation department and driving team to inspect and ensure their readiness and safety to perform whatever is required of them on camera. It's not uncommon for the transportation team to install safety measures such as special tires, brakes, roll bars, or safety cages inside the vehicle. Often they will make these customized enhancements in collaboration with or under the supervision of the stunt coordinator and/ or driver of that vehicle. Many times they will collaborate with the special effects department, which may have to design and install specialized safety equipment necessary for the demands of a particular scene.

The car chase or piece of action involving one or more cars is called for in your script. It may say "Billy jumps in his car and chases Jimmy through a residential neighborhood ending in a fiery blast." That description leaves a lot to the imagination of the director and stunt team (remember the brief description written for the opening chase sequence to Casino Royale?). It could be designed to be shot in a day or a week. Or it may be very specific, taking a page or more of the script to describe exactly what will happen. This specificity could be because there are elements of the chase set piece that tell the story or because the writer has a vivid visual sense. In any case, at some point, whether it's all on the page or a mere suggestion, the sequence must be previsualized and planned. Much like a military campaign, all the objects in motion must be identified and their paths defined and the results of their actions articulated. The traditional manner of planning a car chase or stunt is done with small-scale model cars. Like a young boy playing on the floor of his room with his matchbox cars, the stunt coordinator and or second unit director will place small model cars on a surface meant to represent the picture cars and the environment in which the chase is to take place. Maneuvering the models around the surface meant to represent the location over and over again until all the moves and timing have been set is standard operating procedure for the proper planning of dangerous driving scenes.

Camera positions and coverage are determined once the choreography is set. Your cinematographer and production designer may also be helpful in this process if they are available and experienced. When the whole sequence has been mapped out, your stunt team or second unit director can demonstrate for all other relevant crew members, cast, stunt persons, and drivers, so everyone can clearly see how the shot or scene will work.

You may find that your stunt coordinator and driving team prefer this old school approach or your team may have moved into the latest phase of technology and will use software to construct storyboards in a computer. By selecting characters, locations, props, and vehicles that have been stored in the program, you can create a shot-by-shot version of your action sequence. You can take that to the next step and create an "animatic," which is a moving or animated version of your storyboards. Some directors who feel that action is not their strong suit may have a second unit director or stunt coordinator create the animatic based on what the script calls for and their input. That kind of realization of the storyboards is an advanced form of previz. It's like pre-shooting your sequence, thus enabling you to see how the sequence will play logistically and creatively. Either method affords the same comfort level a production needs to safely and effectively mount a complicated or even simple chase.

> JOHN BADHAM: *Storyboarding is an extremely wise idea because it's hard to describe action things verbally. A car comes down here and drives into the 7-Eleven store. Well, we may have 20 different visions of what that car driving into the 7-Eleven is going to look like. A storyboard artist working with the director and the stunt coordinator will create something that everybody will know we're hitting the window of the 7-Eleven store at this specific angle. We're going to knock over these counters. We're going to have smoke here. So everything is very clear. The pictures are very clear. In commercials, for years, they've done animatics which are very simple animation versions of hand-drawn storyboards because the client... the advertisers are so determined to know exactly what's going to happen, whereas in movies we have a tendency to put more faith in the director and the DP to work it out. The stunt coordinator will come up with a previz in some form, but the more detailed storyboards the director can show the coordinator the better. You can ask, "Do we have the right coverage or is what I'm shooting here only going to give me part of what I need?" And the truth is, in action sequences, you almost never have enough coverage.*

So preplanning and previsualization is particularly essential when planning car chases. The good news is that any sized production can afford to do it. Whether you use a software program, matchbox cars, or salt and pepper shakers, your stunt team and director (or second unit director if you have one) must meticulously demonstrate the movement of all the moving parts of your shot or sequence. This process will make evident that the vision in your head can be realized on-screen or not. You will move forward accordingly by either modifying your plan or confirming it.

On the production day when your stunt driving team is on set, in their cars and ready to drive, there will be a certain amount of rehearsal done at speeds well below the speeds the drivers will reach when the cameras are rolling. Your stunt team will have a process they go through. As a producer or director, be sure you understand that process and how much time your drivers require before they're ready to go for a take. This scenario is yet another example of how clear lines of communication between departments contribute to the ultimate quality of your production. If the production team is under the impression that a stunt takes one hour and it takes two, someone wasn't communicating. I'm not referring to a situation where the unexpected happens. I'm talking about a situation where the producer's blood pressure is zooming because lunch is in a half-hour and it doesn't seem likely that take one for the car stunt is anywhere close to being ready to shoot. The stunt coordinator explains he told the first assistant director it would take this long, so why all the tension? The 1st AD disputes the coordinator's story. It doesn't matter: there's been a miscommunication and here you are, waiting to shoot something that should be completed by lunch, but will not be finished until well after lunch. What happens to shots that were scheduled right after lunch? Good question. Productions are tightly planned and changes have domino effect results. Something yet to be shot may have to be eliminated or shortchanged or the car stunt will have to be simplified, all of which may compromise the entertainment value of your production.

One of many fundamental truths about stunts in general and car stunts specifically is that they take longer than you think. Stunts of any sort are a time-consuming process, due not only to their complexity and precision, but also to the precautions that must be taken to ensure safety. You cannot and must not ever, *ever* pressure a stunt person to hurry their process. Any competent first assistant director will not allow that to happen. When cars are involved, thousands of pounds of steel are moving at high speeds: your stunt team can never be too painstaking and meticulous. First assistant directors will not allow the shot to proceed unless they are fully confident that all reasonable precautions have been taken not only because as a human being, it's the right thing to do, but also because in California, they can be held legally liable for injuries on set due to negligence.

Precision Driving

The script calls for a car chase in which two cars must weave in and out of normal traffic flow. No collisions are called for: just fancy driving at high speeds. To begin with, the normal traffic flow is comprised of cars and drivers employed by the production, rehearsed in their speed and routes and fully aware of the speed and routes the chase cars have committed to. There is no such thing as mingling a stunt or driving sequence into uncontrolled settings. Every car, every pedestrian in the shot must be a professional if they are at risk in any way. If the stunt coordinator determines that certain drivers or pedestrians are totally in the clear, then extras without special skills may be used.

The drivers you might employ, with the consultation of your stunt coordinator, may not be stunt drivers. A separate category of skilled driver, known as a precision driver, may be used. These drivers can drive a car in extreme conditions such as great speed and unusual maneuvers. They are not trained to crash or roll the car. They just drive very skillfully. They may have been trained as race car drivers initially and integrated those skills with demands of driving on camera. Whatever their background, precision drivers are most often utilized in shots and scenes where cars drive fast and elusively but don't crash. An example of this is in a car chase sequence. The camera is often placed inside the car representing the driver's point of view. This camera position very effectively places the audience in the shoes of the driver, who is experiencing some harrowing, fast-paced near misses as he speeds through traffic. The character is weaving in and out of traffic, careening through intersections and barely avoiding crashing into stationary and moving obstacles. Exciting stuff. Camera positions on the outside of the car aimed toward the driver help sell the terror and danger. Further coverage from vantage points on the street, buildings, or other objective positions helps inform the audience of geography and help gauge the progress of the journey.

In the world of car stunts and precision driving, technology has made capturing authentic and real-time events in and around cars more exciting than ever. I will suggest that anytime you can capture a real event in the camera, you will be bringing that action to an audience in a more visceral, heart-pounding way that feels more real, because it is. A live action car stunt may not be as spectacular as one built partly in reality and partly in a computer, but if it's real, the audience can sense what is plausible and what is not. An audience will not be objectively assessing the relative degrees of plausibility or reality of any stunt, but they will feel in their gut how real something on screen is to them. And the gut is where you want the audience to experience your movie. Scenes in which cars roll out of control and become airborne just passing over the hero sound exciting. They look amazing. But how does that feel to an audience? Are they scared? Do they fear for the hero's imminent doom? Not like they do when they are given the perspective of a crash when it really happens.

The Director's Process

As I have stated before, a director's interests as they approach the job of making a movie are many. They can be divided more or less into three categories: creative, leadership, and financial. When the use of stunts and special effects becomes part of the plan, the directors must have a vision as to how a stunt or special effect will serve the story. There's that word again, vision: the approach, strategy, sensibility, guiding principles, upon which all choices are made. We know it when we see it on the screen.

> MARTIN CAMPBELL: *Of course there's always how the action itself looks. Take something as simple as a fistfight. We've seen fistfights 10 million times in every movie since movies were conceived, but how do you do it a differently. You can take the Bourne film for example, the ones that Paul Greengrass directed. That fight inside the house was absolutely incredible, albeit you never saw really what ever happened. It was cut so fast and the action was so quick that you really didn't see what happened. It was a very visceral and exciting sequence to watch.*

Leadership is a well-understood term, but in filmmaking it is very much defined by how one collaborates, not just gives orders. How does a director utilize the talents and energies of those around him? Directors must demonstrate a sense of maturity and drive that will set an example for the entire cast and crew.

> ROY WAGNER: *If you're the director, you're the boss, you can say no. You can say yes or maybe. How you manage your power is important. How you say yes or no has very powerful outcomes from you as the leader. It doesn't take a loud yes or a loud no when saying, "I'm the boss." Everyone understands the protocol and it's just allowing people to participate, to create a better environment for collaboration. I mean you can sit for hours and listen to everyone's vision or you can edit and manage that time whether you're the director or whoever and say that's terrific, but I'd really like to focus on this or that. Whether you're the key grip or gaffer or cameraman or assistant director; every*

one of us is a director in our own little part of that realm. I've always said, nothing ever fails from the top down, it fails from the bottom up. The truth is, if the director allows everybody to participate, then they ultimately get the credit.

Directors must act responsibly in the context of finite financial resources. Stunts and special effects make all these areas more fluid than most other aspects of filmmaking due to the relative uncertainty of their results. To be clear, the safe performance of a stunt or special effect when executed by experienced professionals is predictable, even in a business where bad things can happen no matter how well prepared you are. But the aesthetic outcome can widely vary. The punch that doesn't have the right velocity, the car that doesn't roll back onto its wheels, and the explosion that leaps out of frame, all reflect how uncertain results can look. For that reason and more, there will always be conversations about cost that a director and producer must have together. Can the budget as originally constructed before the director came on board afford the director's interpretation of the action? The producer always saw two cars in police chase and the director insists five cars are necessary to create the kind of tension and energy he feels is necessary to serve the story. And maybe the director is right. The extra three cars have a ripple effect on the budget. More rental cars, more repairs, more stunt or precision drivers, more transportation personnel, more car carrier trucks to get the added cars to and from the set, more gas, maybe another special effects tech to install safety equipment in the cars, more police and PAs to guard the expanded perimeters of the chase route, more time to shoot the larger scope of the chase … it goes on. So these choices have financial repercussions.

JOHN BADHAM: *One of the first things I have to do is to get on the same page as my producer. What do the producers really expect to see and talk about how I think it might work? I may have ideas that are way too expensive. So I have to go out after a simpler idea but sometimes the producer says no I want something bigger more elaborate.*

Managing a budget, particularly at the lower end, is a fluid exercise. As a producer, you make your best estimates as to what you think it will cost to make a movie from the script you have. A budget is usually created very early in a producer's path to production, because it is a necessary tool to attract investment, presales, or loans. As time passes, numbers can change. When photography begins, personnel may cost more than anticipated because of higher demand. Rental houses may have raised their prices. An oil refinery in California goes off line, sending gas prices through the roof. Costs in certain categories may decrease of course as well. A great stunt performer just became available because another job was canceled and they really need the work. Gas prices just dropped. It's fluid. These are cost fluctuations that are beyond control or anyone's ability to foresee and plan for. During the run-up to and production of a movie, daily choices present themselves. Certain spending decisions are elective. If you add three more cop cars to a chase, where's the money coming from? You can pull funds from the contingency budget (your emergency cookie jar), or you can take and spend the savings you may have made in another budget category and allocate it to the enhanced chase. The producer and hopefully the director will discuss these options together. Is this the best use of the money you can find in the budget? Sure, the bigger chase will bring added value to the movie, but is there another place to allocate those freed-up funds that may have a greater impact on the finished product? Maybe an actor with marquee value whose price was beyond the means of the production can now be made an offer they will accept. Maybe three or four cars instead of five would enable the production to allocate money to other areas that will bring greater added value to the production, at least as hoped for by the director or producer. Money is always being shuffled around on lower-budget movies to take advantage of any opportunity that may present itself and to deal with any contingency that may arise. On big-budget movies, these shifts in the tide are often less felt or easier to absorb due to a studio's more open wallet. The producer and director, needless to say, should have an open and free line of communication. With the relative uncertainty of stunts, contingent plans are especially necessary. Therefore, in the planning of stunts and special effects comes the decision as to how many times you think it may take to get it right. Is this an easy one you can get in one take using multiple cameras? Must it be only done once because of the complexity and expense? Or is this a shot where someone is thrown through a sliding glass door and must land on a particular mark? Do you allow for two takes? Three? Four? Your stunt coordinator will give you his estimate as to how many takes he feels will ensure success. Maybe he recommends you be ready for two takes because he feels he'll get it on the first take but wants one more for insurance. So have the extra glass door ready to install and allow the time in your schedule for two takes. The 1st AD will be on top of this bit of logistics, making sure the appropriate departments will be ready.

LINDA MONTANTI: *Going in, you always have a Plan B. How many windows should we get? How many windshields do we want to order? I ask the director, he says how many times does he think he might need to shoot something. I make sure the production has two windows standing by on the day. It's an ongoing conversation. If it's a huge thing with multiple cars, you only want to do that once. You've got to have an extra window there just in case. If the car is repairable, then you will have the glass right there and you'll have a mechanic there. I look to see what could go wrong and make sure they have stuff standing by to make sure that we're prepared to deal with it. You always go for another take. You always make sure you schedule enough time. If you get it done sooner, you can always pull something else out to shoot.*

This thought pattern applies to scenes in which special effects are significant elements to the scene. Explosions, for instance, quite possibly are events that propel a story forward. They are important and dramatic beats that change the dynamic of the narrative. You better be as sure as possible that a stunt is well planned or that an explosion is thoroughly ready. To that end, the director and DP must know as exactly as possible what to expect when something crashes or blows up. There should be an active exchange of ideas when setting up a shot between the director, the DP, the art director, and the stunt or special effects people.

ROY WAGNER: *I've often times gone to an effects person and said, where do you see the camera? Where do you think the camera should be, what film speed or lens should we have been there will be occasions where they say, I don't know. But I guarantee you that every stuntman and effects person previsualizes how they designed their effects and their stunts. And if you put the camera where you wanted in relation to where they wanted it, you may not have the best possible position. Every person who has the mandate to deliver to the film the perfect stunt, the perfect explosion, has previsualized where the camera should be. But I go to them and say where do you see the stunt? Often they'll show me and I'll say if I move the camera a foot and a half this direction or if I go this much lower or higher or if I use this lens, I think I can help you get what you're looking for. Oftentimes they'll say, "oh yeah, that's great that's exactly what I need." It's about being a good team member, a good servant. We're all good servants, we're all serving the material. We're serving the director, we're serving the film and there's nothing wrong with being that. Being a good servant is frankly being a good artist.*

You're not just catching a fireball rise to the clouds: you're also illustrating how that fireball is affecting the environment and its inhabitants. That's story. So all visual elements must be considered as to allow an audience to not only get a thrill but absorb its story implications.

> MARTIN CAMPBELL: *You have to decide when talking to your special effects department how big will the explosion be. How high will it go, how far will it come out? Where will the debris go? Those things determine the composition of the shot.*

The other consideration when planning in how many takes to attempt a complicated or dangerous stunt is once again the safety component.

> JOHN BADHAM: *You start thinking like a ten-year-old kid and suddenly the idea of the danger goes right out of your head because, "Oh, this is cool. It's a movie," and that's when things tend to go wrong. I call it the "take three rule" which is: get it right the first couple of takes because by take three or take four, people's minds start to wander off. They're totally focused on the stunt and I'm talking about all the crew and the actors and everybody involved. They're completely focused the first couple of times and then about the third or fourth take, they wander a little bit and something happens. Something goes wrong, something breaks … a fence, a piece of hardware, the front tire on a car … it goes to hell on you because you don't have the same intense focus that you have to have when you're doing these dangerous stunts. So I really work hard to get things right the first couple of times and not let it go to four or five. Some directors will want to print everything and just can't walk away from getting a special shot and that's when things, bad things, happen.*

Taking into consideration when certain kinds of scenes and shots are scheduled is a constant challenge to filmmakers. There are generally accepted notions of when it's best to shoot certain scenes. Intimate love scenes are probably best shot later in the shooting schedule as to allow the actors to get to know each other and gain a level of comfort that can help sensitive scenes achieve a high level of verisimilitude. It's easier to kiss someone you know, much less make love to them. While John Badham points out that repetition can dull the senses, so can working very long days or working in the wee hours of the night.

It stands to reason that dangerous stunts or special effects should be shot under ideal working conditions when everyone is alert, rested, and well fed. Shooting action is also done at a slower pace for reasons of safety and due to the complicated and, often, precise nature of the work.

JEFF TUFANO: *The amount of planning and preparation, and the pace of the shooting are the main differences when you're shooting action. When you're shooting, you have to take all the time that's necessary. You don't want to be on a shoot where people are saying we have to go, go, go; somebody's going to get hurt. Things go wrong. This is a job where you move slowly, you can't be stupid. It's like you don't run with scissors, you just don't. Something bad will happen.*

There's all kinds of different paces depending on the kind of work. In television there's a high page count and it's go, go, go. HBO maybe requires half the page count of episodic television, but they say, "Let's keep moving." If you're working with the studios, they don't necessarily work the day at rocket ship pace; they might do a couple of pages a day. But when it comes down to doing stunts, you might do an eighth of a page.

Bottom line is, it takes what it takes. You cannot compromise safety. The practical fact of the matter is that stunts are not only potentially dangerous, but they're often costly or uniquely available to be shot. For those reasons too, caution, methodical planning, and execution are essential.

MARTIN CAMPBELL: *You try not to do your biggest stunts towards the end of the evening when everyone is tired. But these big stunts take a lot of prepping. If it's a second unit type of shot, you may be spending five or six hours preparing to shoot an explosion. So everyone is getting wound up for the same moment. There's no particular time of day that's best, it's really as long as it's not rushed, as long as it's been prepared properly, as long as the safety precautions have all been mapped out; really the time of day doesn't matter.*

It's essential to understand the consequences of your decisions regarding the allocation of time.

DALE GIBSON: *The stuntman's lament is you do the stunts at the end of the day and you have no time left. So when I see people wasting the first half of the day, I know the second half of the day is going to be really tough on me.*

Most shooting schedules are a creation of innumerable factors that are processed, and the best compromise produces the schedule with the fewest headaches. Schedules strive for efficiency, cost-effectiveness, and creative compatibility. It's close to impossible to serve all those needs equally well. It makes sense not to have to blow things up or send a car flying over a precipice at 4:00 in the morning, after twelve grueling hours of shooting on some frigid distant location. But you don't always have any choice. The way movies are organized, how the days are organized has a deus ex machina aspect to it. It rolls forward, a behemoth that responds only to extreme prodding. Things will be shot when it's their turn to be shot, assuming lighting conditions are not in play, no matter what time of day it is. Of course there are exceptions: some productions spend the extra money it may take to reschedule things when conditions are more ideal.

> JOHN BADHAM: *I don't know how I can make any rule like that work because it always fits in with what else you're doing that day and when can you do it. The very end of the day when everyone's tired is not a good time do shoot stunts though I've done some very dangerous things at 5:30 in the morning with a guy falling out the 20th story of a building, smashing through glass and then parachuting down to the ground. I mean that's pretty dangerous stuff. And probably not the best idea at that time of the morning when our body is just in the worst shape it can possibly be. Probably for the stuntman who's going to do it, his adrenaline was going a mile a minute and he did fine but yeah, it didn't sound like a good idea.*

But you do it anyway after everyone has made their preparations and assessed the risk. You have pros who hopefully will exercise good judgment. There's always an accepted level of risk. Just be careful that no one exceeds that level. Working on difficult locations at all hours of the day and night is part of the deal. Just recognize that you and your cast and crew are not superhuman even if they do work in the movies. If someone looks tired and they might get hurt as a result, relieve them. That goes for a grip or a stunt performer. There are producers and directors, particularly in the low-budget arena, who are known for driving their crews into the ground, burning them out. There is a point of diminishing return that you have to reckon with. Excessive hours may produce more footage, but with less quality.

The director is the captain of the ship; he or she is the conductor of the symphony that is a movie crew and cast: merging, modulating, coaxing, motivating many disparate talents, shaping the story into a form of visual storytelling called a movie. They alone do not possess all the knowledge and craft to fulfill each and every function on a production. The concept of a crew is not simply to supply enough labor to alleviate the physics-defying strategy of one person creating every on-screen moment (see 1992's *Multiplicity* with

Michael Keaton), but it's to bring to the party the very best people with specific skills to enhance and elevate the movie through their participation. No one can know everything about everything. A director may be the most qualified person on the team to direct actors or to direct the camera, and some may be the most qualified in all areas specific to the craft of directing. They may come from another background such as stunts or cinematography, which can be of enormous value in the context of directing. But they most likely will not be the most capable production designer, electrician, sound recordist, actor, carpenter…and the list goes on. Directors who have recently moved over from a field such as stunts or cinematography may lack certain skills or knowledge that in their previous roles was not necessary to have expertise. The stunt supervisor turned director may have never had to consider visual design and a cinematographer turned director may not have had to delve too deeply into how to evoke a performance, although they may have picked some of that up from the directors they shot for.

So when it comes to any of these areas in which the director lacks the requisite amount of expertise necessary, the director should listen to, question, learn from, and engage in dialogue with his or her assembled crew. The stunt coordinator and special effects technicians are most certainly in this category of those on the team who have important knowledge to share. But some directors are very knowledgeable about stunts and special effects without knowing how to actually execute them. They've seen them performed countless times on their productions. They know what goes into their successful execution, because as conscientious directors, they've asked a lot of questions and have been taken through the process before. A director can have a working knowledge of stunts or special effects, and yet a significant gap in that knowledge between what the director knows and what they need to know probably still exists. To be charged with the responsibility of designing, supervising, and executing stunts and special effects demands a working knowledge, an understanding that comes from doing, not just theorizing.

Most directors just take it for granted that in any area where there is risk to life and limb, the best and wisest approach to planning and executing that stuff is to rely on the pros who specialize in stunts and special effects. Actually, this approach to the job of directing really applies to any genre. A wise director will employ people who are more experienced and knowledgeable than them in any and all of the fields of expertise utilized in a production. The director is too busy being a director. Why wear another hat when the one you're wearing demands so much time and energy? Even though you are the conductor, the leader of the orchestra, no one's asking you to play the violin or timpani. In fact, no one will let you and you shouldn't want to even if you can play each every instrument in the orchestra. It's not your role in the orchestra. Others who have been playing violin and timpani for many years will deliver to you, with your creative guidance, the music you want to hear. So knowledge is good. It allows you to contribute more to the planning and execution of stunts. But it's not required that you know anything; it's just required that you know what you want to see. Your team will make it happen.

The choosing of a stunt coordinator is one of the director's more important choices. The stunt coordinator is at the nexus of so many impactful streams of concentrated effort. It makes sense for the director to look at their coordinator as not only a department head, but as a manager of the efforts of the special effects, armorers, and the transportation department. Those other departments quite often exist in order to serve the stunt. The special effects people are making explosions and bullet hits that will be used by stunt performers. The transportation or special effects folks will be delivering and modifying cars used by the stunt team. The armorer will be providing weapons to be used by stunt people or actors trained by stunt performers. The stunt coordinator needs to be in the flow of decision-making and supervising these other departments, because what they all have in common is contributing to the successful execution of stunts. For this reason alone, the degree of responsibility and how pervasive these areas are in the final product of a movie with stunts and special effects, the choice of coordinator is a key one. Another reason it's so important is because the stunt coordinator is not only a manager, but also a creative partner.

> JOHN BADHAM: *Then you bring the professional stunt coordinator in and say not only how can we do this, but do it better. What would be more interesting or fun?*

The seasoned director and, therefore, those of you who are not should embrace collaboration. They feel secure in their role as band leader to be able to listen to ideas from their team and determine which, if any, should be used. The wise director doesn't feel threatened: he or she feels like there's a whole group of people working their butts off. Everyone's there for the same reason: to make the best movie possible.

> MARTIN CAMPBELL: *I personally work on most of the angles myself. I map it out through the storyboards and I work out the angles on the other cameras. But then, I'll have the DP work with me. I have a very specific idea of where I want the camera, but that doesn't mean I don't consult with my guys. The stunt arranger will often say to me, "Well how about an angle here or there": particularly with the placement of three or four cameras.*

ROY WAGNER: *You can get the very best cinematographer and the very best director, the very best stars and crew, but if they're not willing to collaborate you can have a disaster. There are many occasions where you've had those best people and come up with a complete failure. You cannot throw money at the screen and expect it to be the finest of everything. Look at* Star Wars, *for example, they had no money, no time and people with very little experience and when they became more experienced and they had all the money and time, I would suggest that the results were not as good as the original* Star Wars.

When it comes to stunt coordinators, their job description goes beyond figuring out how to execute a stunt safely and true to the vision of the director. It's absolutely within their role to offer ways to improve or increase the value of any particular stunt or stunt sequence. Being creative in the use of their skills and resources and being able to reckon those skills with their financial responsibilities is an important attribute of a good stunt coordinator. Not only should they be able to figure out how to pull off a stunt, but maybe how to add another layer to it all for the amount of money allocated in the budget or, better yet, for less than what was allocated. They should be adept at shuffling their resources, casting their stunt performers shrewdly, and driving hard deals with vendors and performers to bring the most entertainment value to the screen for the least amount of money possible. This is the credo of the stunt coordinator.

The stunt coordinator may have new ways to think about a scene described in the script. It's perfectly normal and should be welcomed for a coordinator to raise these issues at an early meeting between them and the director. Wouldn't you welcome someone coming in to meet you to interview for the job and suggest a way to make a cool scene cooler or a scene that is lacking in excitement exciting? You bet. That's music to the ears of any director who has his head screwed on straight. You suddenly see the quality of your movie jump a notch. Once on board, the coordinator is going to break down the script, cost out the stunts, and begin the process of working together with the director to refine, evolve, and, sometimes, reimagine the stunt work to be done.

In prep, the director begins his process by breaking down the script. He analyzes and makes numerous choices about how he sees the story when deconstructed into its parts. When an action occurs in the script that will require a stunt, the breakdown begins by mapping out on paper or in a computer all the beats of the action. This is no different than when breaking down a dramatic scene. In other words, this happens, then this happens, then this happens, until you have finally identified and separated the sum of the parts of the action described into its smallest units of action. In a simple fight between two characters, you must identify each movement that advances the sequence forward, such as a big punch or a big swing and a miss that leads to another moment that pushes the "story" of that fight, forward. That swing and a miss might lead to an opportunity for the other fighter to land a punch that sends his opponent over a precipice, thereby ending the action sequence and propelling the story forward. All of the beats or moments when the dynamic in the action shifts must be identified and described. The manner in which you describe and document this breakdown is up to you. That's where your choice of tools can be made that best fits your experience, artistic talents, or creative method. I'm not capable of doing much more than drawing stick figures, but I feel pretty confident writing out a detailed description of what the action should look like and in what environment.

Budget allowing, I could hire storyboard artists who can draw a series of images much like a comic book that will visually describe the scene with helpful captions. A professional storyboard artist or a motivated director can use one of the many software programs that have been designed to create storyboards and even replicate the figures in action: the animatic or animated version of a storyboard. This stage of preparation should be done before the stunt coordinator is brought onto your production. It's a clear way of communicating your vision. As I've said, words can too easily fail us when trying to describe what's in our heads. A high fall to me may mean a ten-story drop. To someone else it might mean fifty or a hundred stories. Always be mindful of the eternal directive in cinema: *show, don't tell.* It's always a more effective mode of communicating both to your collaborators and to an audience.

MARTIN CAMPBELL: *The thing is planning. Everything is planning. On the Bond pictures for* Casino Royale, *I had a model of the whole construction site where the running sequence took place. I remember coming in the office early one morning and looking at the models of the two 200 foot cranes and immediately I said, "Whatever happens, if they break through the fence at the construction site, they have to get to the top of those 200 foot cranes." Height is always a terrific, terrific thing to play with. Then you just start thinking, well, he's running, he's chasing this guy, how does he get on to the steel beams, the framework of these buildings? Well, he just runs up one of those cranes that happen to be moving and he utilizes that. Now how does he get off the crane? Well he's a free runner; the man's mad, so he jumps from one crane to another. Then Bond has to follow. There was no digital in that at all, the guy had a wire on and there's one shot where the guy jumps off one crane on to another. From that, he leaps on to the ground in only one shot. This was key for me. My stunt arranger said, yes it can be done. Just the preparation on the day was eight hours to get that to happen.*

Once you have shown your stunt breakdowns or any form of prep, to either a candidate for the coordinator job or the person you've hired, they will have the opportunity to get a good idea of what you're trying to do and how you see it looking once on the screen. The coordinator will go over every aspect of the breakdown with you to confirm his understanding and to identify each area of concern. One part might not be as clear an expression of your intentions as you thought. Another point in the scene might be very expensive to execute, and he wants you to be aware of that in case it exceeds the budget. Another moment you have in mind may inspire in the coordinator a better idea, one that takes your intentions to the next level without increasing the cost.

JOHN BADHAM: *Everybody can look at your storyboards and say, "Okay, we know what this shot is going to be, we'll be ready." You're having to coordinate many different departments who are not relying on verbal instructions to deliver what you need to shoot a stunt or special effect. Visual instructions are just much more powerful, infinitely more powerful.*

The coordinator often has the advantage of having vastly more experience and knowledge about stunts, which informs their imagination as to what is possible and what is not. Their knowledge and experience focus their creative energy toward the possible. This can be a very productive and creative process in which ideas are raised and tested. No idea should be withheld. Your idea may not work as you originally conceived it, but it may initiate a version of that idea that will be terrific or better. Don't hold back.

DAN BRADLEY: *You really want to find somebody you can work with and who will give you valuable advice. I like to work with people who have really strong opinions because I have strong opinions and I don't mind debating ideas back and forth. You have to find somebody who will tell you the truth and who you feel comfortable debating with.*

The next step in this process is for the stunt coordinator to create a revised draft of the director's previz (in whatever form that takes): one that reflects a refined plan that can be re-budgeted and planned for in preproduction. The plan if revised will reflect some or all of the issues I mentioned in the paragraph above, that is, adjustments for cost, practicality, and creativity.

BUDDY JOE HOOKER: *I've been doing this since* To Live and Die in
L.A., *even way before… when we're setting this huge massive car
chase scenes Friedkin had in mind, I had to figure how to capture what
he wanted. It had never been done before. I made these big diagrams
of it, every move, the director wanted was there. I took out the
matchbook cars too and plotted the chase with these little model cars.
I showed it the director, he gave me some ideas and I finalized the
plan. That way if he wanted to edit it, or change it, we had something
to work from.*

Stunt coordinators will often take their team out to a separate location and
shoot a version of the scene yet to be shot. It will have all the angles and
camera positions and will be cut together. It will be a rough approximation
of how they suggest the director approach shooting the scene. It's a form of
previz that allows the director to see the scene so he can approve or revise it.

MARTIN CAMPBELL: *Gary Powell added a huge amount to that chase.
Both Gary Powell and Simon Crane are the only two I've ever worked
with in my movies and the only two I want. There's two things they
do that are extremely important: first is rehearsal, they rehearsed
the hell out of it. They also work it all out for the camera. Nowadays
they'll work out all the movements on video and they'll have an edited
sequence to show me. They'll show it practically to me with stunt
people. I'll see the whole action. He's actually done a cut for me. I'll
look at the cut, make all my notes on it, discuss it with him, and that's
obviously a terrific plus.*

The director may now be forced to rethink their plans in part or totally.
Assuming a draft of the budget reflected a decent estimate of the costs
associated with a stunt or special effect, it's unlikely that you would have
to totally abandon your original vision. Hopefully, just a modest adjustment
of the action would bring the scene in line with what had been budgeted.
There's always the possibility that your producer may encourage you to think
bigger, understanding that a big infusion of energy and excitement at a key
point in the movie would be helpful. Don't laugh: it happens. Endings can be
the movie's main selling point, its commercial "hook." Sometimes rethinking a
key piece of action or how the end of your story resolves can be the difference
between a movie that leaves little impression and one that leaves a lasting
impression. Your audience can walk out of the movie wondering where to
grab a bite to eat or wondering how in the hell the filmmakers created such an
incredibly exciting and memorable moment. The folks who control the purse
strings are not oblivious to this.

JOHN BADHAM: *The dream is for the producer to call you and say, "This scene is kind of a boring ending to the movie. Can't you guys do something more exciting?" And that's happened to me on* Stakeout *with Richard Dreyfuss and Emilio Estevez. Jeffery Katzenberg, the head of the studio, called up and said, "You know, this looks kind of dull, this fight in a boathouse at the end of the movie," and I just said to Jeffrey, "This is the ending that you said you could afford. If you want to contribute some more money to it, we can absolutely do something more fun," and he said, "Okay, here's $300,000 more. Go do something more fun." Now the stunt coordinator goes out and comes back and says, "I found a lumber mill that's out of business and we can now go in there and can get the machinery revived and working so it looks like saws are coming down and logs are rolling." It was money well spent because it's way more exciting than the simpler kind of thing we had planned before we had the $300,000.*

After a director has thoroughly planned and replanned stunts and special effects with his team, the more practical phase begins. As I've mentioned, if the budget allows and there is the time, stunts and special effects that have been specifically designed for your production should be tested and rehearsed. Many stunts and special effects gags are frankly routine and don't need to be rehearsed before they're shot. But if there is a significantly challenging element added to what might otherwise be considered routine, rehearsals are advisable. If a car has to roll over onto its roof, that's pretty routine. Those stunts usually are written in the script and performed in relatively open spaces for reasons of safety. If, however, you decide to increase the level of excitement and place that stunt in a confined location such as a tunnel, your stunt team will want to do some homework. They might get out their calculators and dust off their physics books to calculate speed and distances and any other factors that will help them make the stunt as predictable as possible. If possible, they will apply those calculations and try the stunt at the actual location or a close replication of it. If they feel confident, the director may be invited to observe to make sure it's what he or she has in mind. Suffice to say: when it comes to dangerous work in movies, surprises are to be avoided. The "happy surprises" a director gets from a dramatic scene in which an actor reveals something spontaneously truthful about their character because they accidentally dropped a prop or spilled their drink in the scene are not desirable when big hunks of metal are launched and people are squarely in harm's way. Anytime a director can get a preview of a stunt or special effect, it's a chance to confirm an understanding between them and their team who are preparing to execute an important and often expensive part of the story. It may be the last opportunity for final revisions or even rethinking. Sometimes when you see something that's only been in your head, it doesn't live up to the fantasy. Seeing an event, experiencing it, is a far superior perspective to be making decisions from. I can tell you, my most cogent and creative thinking takes place when I'm shooting the scene. That's when you find out how thorough your prep was. Did you think of every possibility? Did you run down every creative option available before you committed in preproduction? It's often too late once on the set and shooting to change plans. So, it's good to get a real live preview of a stunt or special effect gag whenever possible. A next best scenario is for the stunt or effects team to record their tests and rehearsals and present that to their director. This is not uncommon when it comes to previewing the choreography of a fight. Stunt doubles can be used to demonstrate the beats of a fight. Arguably it's a step up from watching an animatic, which still has an artificiality about it that reduces its effectiveness (but better than nothing). Often there's no good substitute for a real human demonstrating their movements for the camera.

Another time and place for a preview to be shown to a director is on or just off the set before the stunt is scheduled to be shot or is ready to be shot. All kinds of practical considerations go into when that preview takes place, but it mostly boils down to time and money. There often isn't the budget to bring stunt and special effects crews on too far in advance of the shoot. The cost of providing the space to rehearse a stunt or effect prior to the shoot is also costly. So sometimes a director previews the stunt: sees it played out at full or partial speed just before it's scheduled to be shot. But there should be an opportunity for a director to adjust a stunt to make sure it will serve the story, someway, somehow.

> JEFF TUFANO: *If it's a car stunt you may get a quarter speed rehearsal. It might be just a drive-by where the car drives right up to a ramp or place where something happens you can't do that in rehearsal. You may get [to] rehearse the scene where three guys are coming out with automatic weapons, they jump out of the van and we'll watch them without firing, cold weapons. Or you might get no rehearsal at all. I've been on certain types of stunts where everybody is supposed to get behind their predetermined camera positions, put our finger on the trigger, and we go. It's a one-time big event.*

Now it's time to shoot the stunt or special effect gag. This part of the protocol is unlike shooting a dramatic scene. It is a slow and meticulous process in which total attention and concentration are absolutely required. You may remember that John Badham indicated his preference for shooting at a time when everyone is at their most alert, most likely meaning not at the end of a twelve-hour day. Linda Montanti, the 1st AD, echoed that opinion. That portion of the cast and crew who will be involved in shooting the gag will be present while the director, stunt coordinator, fight choreographer, 1st AD, and director of photography will demonstrate what is about to be photographed in as much detail as possible. It's your last chance to make sure the shot will tell the story you want to tell.

> MARTIN CAMPBELL: *Often you set your angles based on how the special effects are being done. You have to collaborate with the special effects team. It may be that each explosion will have a one-second delay or there may be a certain amount of time between explosions. We're usually running the camera at 96 or 120 frames per second knowing I can bring it back to normal speed if I need to. The same goes for the stunt team as well. If the crowd's running out of the house before the whole thing explodes, where they're going to be, where are they going to run to? Our angles have to take advantage of that because hopefully, you'll get the thing in one take with six cameras and six different angles. There will be people running out and explosions happening and buildings collapsing. You want to relate the people to the destruction happening behind them. So obviously your angles are critical. You'll probably only get one take on a big shot because the preparation time could be another day or two if you had to go again.*

The demonstration will often be performed at a speed a little or a lot slower than it will actually take place, so everyone will understand everything that will be happening during the take. By demonstrating the shot, every department will clearly see the scene in the context of their duties. The camera team will see where the action or pyrotechnics will take place so they don't miss the whole reason the shot exists. The art department will see what area the action will take place in, how much of the set will be seen by the camera, and that all set decorations and design will be properly placed. The sound team will need to know where it will be appropriate to place their microphones. It goes on and on: department by department must be fully aware of what will take place. It's possible that everyone will only get one chance to do their job perfectly, as the high fall through a series of skylights or the detonation of a tractor trailer may not be repeatable.

Many of you are thinking, quite properly, "Forget all those 'tentpole'-level stunts; I can't afford to repeat any stunt. I only have enough in my budget for a car crash, a fall out of a third-story window, and a man set on fire, and

I can only shoot them once." Do the math. Either figure out a way to shoot with multiple cameras or find a way to budget in another take for insurance. It's really taking a big risk to rely on the hope that you will get a stunt right, the way you want it, on the first try. Not that that can't happen: it can. I could usually only afford to shoot stunts and special effects once. I had to get it right the first time or learn to live with what I got on film. I lived with a number of painfully inadequate stunts.

I had a very complicated scene that required the utmost coordination and communication between multiple departments. The scene had the hero and heroine driving in an open Jeep down a dusty main street of an African township. Shops of all sorts were on either side of the street, over which we had spread a layer of dirt to add to the feeling that our characters were in a primitive, remote area. Suddenly the characters in the Jeep are attacked by a helicopter approaching from the opposite direction, firing a machine gun into the street, straight toward the Jeep. Before the stream of bullets reaches the Jeep, the hero swerves off the street and crashes through a beauty salon filled with customers. So we have a moving Jeep, a flying helicopter with a machine gun firing visible bursts, bullet hits planted in the dirt in the street, and a crash through a building (we built the beauty parlor in an open space between two shops) filled with extras and actors. We had about five cameras covering this in a master. We would go back for close-ups after all the fireworks. This shot took some careful planning. The 1st AD's role in this operation is to coordinate everyone's efforts in such a way as to ensure a successful shot. Lines of communication are established and confirmed by all. Who will say "action"? This isn't always an obvious decision. Directors under normal circumstances of course call "action." In situations such as I've just described, many directors wisely choose to hand that chore off to the stunt coordinator or someone else who is at the very nexus of all those moving parts. That could be the AD, but often the stunt coordinator, who may also be the second unit director, is central in planning complicated and dangerous shots. They have probably been involved in the planning on a much deeper and more detailed level than the director, who often relies on the other pros to work out the small details of execution. So it makes sense for the coordinator to be the one and *only* person who should have their "hand on the controls" and say "action." Unambiguous and decisive communication is critical. One clear voice. Confusion or the potential for any confusion must be addressed and eliminated from the realm of possibility.

JEFF TUFANO: *Unless it's a director with a very large ego, which there are a few of them, the assistant director is running the set and will call action on multi-camera shots.*

It's a tough job because things can go wrong even if you know what you're doing, and timing is everything. That's why I have the stunt coordinator do the timing. I have them give the cues. I don't do it. Or the director, but very often depending on what they're doing, will just say, "OK, you do it."

> LINDA MONTANTI: *Sometimes the director wants to call action; sometimes the director doesn't want to do it, he doesn't care; sometimes, it's better for the stunt coordinator to do it because they have to coordinate with the effects guy, the camera teams, and everybody else. They have to have visual contact between all of them as well, so that the effects don't go off before the stunt guy is on the right spot and the camera operators keep the shot in frame.*

Any crew member who is part of the chain of people with a task to perform when shooting a stunt should feel free to abort the shot if they experience a problem or even a potential problem that may affect the shot. This is very important for obvious reasons. You don't want to hear someone say after you've blown up a building or even a trash can, "my camera was making funny sounds. I'm not sure if it's ok. But I didn't want to hold everything up just because of me." In the meeting before the shot is taken, anyone who is designated as a key camera can call "abort" or some other cue that will immediately shut down the shot before it goes past the point of no return. Every camera operator should understand before the shot whether or not they are designated to call off the shot; not everyone always has that choice.

> LINDA MONTANTI: *In the pre-meetings you agree among everyone. You say…once we're rolling, nobody is on the air, nobody is on the radio. Very often, you have to turn them off if there's explosions anyway. If there is something wrong with the camera, if something jams or whatever, abort…Just say loudly, "cut."*

With all that being said, stuff happens. Mistakes are made. In my Jeep-versus-helicopter shot, the copters came in too early. The master shot would show how the timing was off. I knew it when we shot it. But the sun was going down and a monster rainstorm with lightning was minutes away. So my big wide shot that showed all this great action and special pyrotechnics could never be used. I had to use all the coverage from my secondary cameras and close-ups I shot some other day. To stay on schedule, we had to leave that location that night and drive back to our base of operations over two hours away. No second takes for that one.

JEFF TUFANO: *On* Enemy of the State, *directed by Tony Scott, they brought 8 or 10 operators for a shot. They were going to collapse the Dr. Pepper plant in Baltimore in a shot. It was a seven-story building. There were 14 cameras, some of them were operated, some of them were locked off. It was a fun day because I can remember they brought all of these guys who I had heard of and really looked up to. A couple of the guys operated and did Steadicam for Steven Spielberg and Tony Scott's regular operator was on board ... all of these great guys. We get in our camera positions, everything is set up. We had our safety meeting. We talked out the shot. In this case, there is no rehearsal or dry run. You get behind the camera, you're told what to expect, and you wait for it to happen. This particular stunt had many components. It probably ran for 2 miles over a winding road. There's a train involved, there's helicopters ... Everybody has their camera positions; everyone has their own assistant director by their side. It was just as simple as each assistant director by a camera position had to shout out in order, "Camera A rolling, camera B rolling," and so forth. Each assistant listened for their turn to tell their operator to roll camera. If anybody has a problem, certain cameras have been told "That's life, sorry." Other cameras are told if you have a problem, you have the power to call off the shot. Call "abort!" There's certain things you can't do. You can't back a train up. So we go through this whole process to make sure everybody is ready and doing what they're supposed to. It can take up to five minutes on a big shot like this for everybody to be up and running.*

One of the cameras, actually the most distant camera, was a Photo-Sonics camera, which is a high-speed camera that runs film at 400 or 500 frames per second [for extreme slow motion]. The film is really moving fast through the camera and there's only so much film. So that camera is going to be cued last. Everybody's ready, everything's good, and nobody is saying abort. Everything is safe, there's quiet on the walkie-talkies and there's one voice, the assistant director. He calls out the sequence of events and he calls action. We're all hearing things like explosions and cars roaring closer, and all of a sudden I have this great shot: the car's coming right at me. He's coming right at my lens. I'm behind a sheet of plywood for protection and I'm shooting the cars coming straight at me and behind them, perfectly framed, the buildings are collapsing right behind them! So I get my great shot, everybody gets their shot. It was one of those unbelievable shots. Everybody is cheering and whooping. It's hard to describe. So we go back to the monitor and there's Tony Scott and the other operators. They had video playback for all 14 cameras. We're just about to start when someone says wait a second, where's Scott? He's not back yet. He had the high-speed camera. So out of respect, we're going to wait for him. A few minutes later, the van rolls up and Scott hops out and Tony asks him, how was it? Scott shakes his head and looks at him and says "it's not good." Apparently what happened was, the assistant director by Scott's side with the walkie-talkie to queue Scott to shoot, cued him too early. Since the film moves at a very high speed, it ran completely through the camera before the building ever imploded and went down. It was a big money shot that was never to be found. This very experienced operator had to come back and deliver the bad news. Do you think Tony Scott screamed and yelled? He said something to the effect, "Well that's why we ran 14 cameras." So we proceeded to watch all the video playback. Everybody did their best. This shot was as big as they come, it was very carefully planned. It was storyboarded. It was very carefully choreographed. But the flaw in the plan was an inexperienced assistant who was actually only a PA who miscommunicated the all-important cue. Any other camera would not have mattered so much.

There are also protocols for safety during the actual filming or capturing of a shot. The camera team is completely concentrating on their jobs. The operator is concerned with getting the shot, making sure the shot is well composed, is in focus, and captures all the images necessary to tell the story. The camera assistants are there to support the operator with focus and keeping an eye on how much film has been expended or data have been captured. They cannot be distracted by whatever is going on around them: total concentration. When there's a risk of the action spilling off course and endangering the crew, in particular the camera team, a spotter is assigned to stand next to the camera. If a picture car careens off course and is headed toward a collision with the camera, the team is vulnerable. By the time they realize they're in harm's way, it'll be too late. A grip or preferably an experienced crew person is best to serve as a warning and escape system.

JEFF TUFANO: *We have a system on the set where those perceived to be even remotely in danger have been assigned safety person right next to them. Because of my job description, I'm often in line with whatever action is happening. It's not unusual for one of my grip buddies or stunt guy to stand by my side, put his hand on my belt and spot me while we make the shot. That particular system where a person alongside me yells, "get out!" is really important. I'm looking through a camera, not even in the world that everybody else's in. I'm in a completely different place. I have no concept of time and space.*

*I have absolutely been in that situation where that person saved me.
I mean obviously through the lens I have a sense of what was going
on, but when he said "go go go!" I hit the lock on that head and I
ran ran ran. That car ran over the top of my camera. The director and
everyone in the video village were 500 feet away in a tent. They all
thought I was dead. But that was a situation where there is a system
that we count on that worked.*

You can almost predict that something unpredictable will happen at some
point in your career. By practicing safe protocols, you dramatically increase
your chances of escaping injury or worse.

JEFF TUFANO: *In that particular situation, the car was going over a
guard rail, down a hillside in the rain. All the experienced people gave
their best estimates where that car was going, but while they weren't
far off in their estimate, the difference was significant. After a while,
you develop your own instincts about these sorts of things. In this case
maybe was the rain: the X factor. On that particular shot I operated
with my feet pointed in the direction I was going to leave if I had to.
That particular night I just had an inkling. I thought I had to be just a
little extra prepared. As much as I knew that guy driving and I felt good
about him, I also feel good about myself, my future. But I did get the
shot. Interestingly enough the shot is in the movie. It's in slow motion
and goes right up until the car runs over the camera.*

It should be mentioned that whenever a stunt or special effect with some
degree of heightened risk is executed, the protocol is for every cast and
crew person to remain in their positions or stations when they hear cut. The
coordinator and sometimes and *only sometimes* the director will quickly go
to the stunt performers in the shot and make sure they were not injured. The
stunt people sometimes need help extricating themselves from whatever they
were driving or involved with. They may be trapped or tangled up in a vehicle
or set construction. No one should interfere with this part of the process
unless they are instructed to do so by the coordinator. It's important to keep
quiet and calm after a dangerous stunt to ensure safety.

So the big crash or explosion is done. Hopefully, it looked great and you don't
have to shoot it again. The director confers with his team asking if it worked
as planned from their perspective, that is, camera, stunts, effects … anything.
If you have video playback, that of course is a very helpful tool when shooting
difficult things such as these. The team will carefully watch the playback to
make sure everything looks good. After all is reviewed, the AD will check with
the director for marching orders. Are we going again or are we moving on?

Ethical Responsibilities
of a Director

The added elements of stunts and special effects bring a heightened sense of responsibility for the well-being of everyone who works on the production and may be exposed to any danger or unusual risk. Just like any other workplace environment, the producer has a fiduciary responsibility to ensure a safe set, as they run the business of producing a movie or any screen entertainment, and employees are in their care. The first assistant director has a prescribed role as the person who runs the set and is also the first safety officer with an ethical *and* legal (in California) responsibility for the safety and welfare of the cast and crew. Numerous other department heads who participate directly and indirectly in a stunt or a dangerous special effect must exercise all necessary safety measures in their areas of direct responsibility. These areas of responsibility are in some cases codified, but in all cases are parts of the culture of moviemaking. This is the way we all think and hope you do too. Whether or not the AD has legal liability in the jurisdiction in which you're in production would be missing an important point. In the litigious world in which we live, anyone can be sued. I'm not saying that I think these types of lawsuits are necessarily frivolous. Some may and some may not be perfectly justified. However, anyone who is in a supervisory capacity in a workplace where risk is abundant or even remotely possible is vulnerable to civil or criminal consequences if they fail to exercise reasonable caution. The AD who crosses his or her fingers hoping that a poorly designed stunt will go well is flirting with disaster on many levels. It will be a disaster if someone is hurt trying to execute that stunt. It can be a disaster for that AD as they possibly face criminal negligence-related charges arising from their lack of will or knowledge to prevent a reckless stunt or special effect from being attempted, no matter what state of the union it occurs in. So when a young, wrong-headed director pushes the safety envelope, demonstrating a lack of ethical awareness, someone has to step up and prevent a potential mishap. Normally, that's the 1st AD.

While the director is not the last word or the highest authority on a set when it comes to safety, their proper role is one of setting the tone, leading by example when planning and executing anything that poses an unusual safety risk. Not only must directors always include in their calculations and decision-making the storytelling and entertainment value of a stunt or special effect, but the risk versus reward must also be a part of their deliberations or creative brainstorming. And, knowing when enough is enough, because stunt performers want to do a great job. Their reputations and livelihoods depend on that reputation for perfection and a can-do attitude.

> MARTIN CAMPBELL: *Safety's a huge element in all of this. Stunt performers are obsessed with safety and quite rightly too. I've had one or two accidents. I learned my lesson on the first Zorro where I had a scene at the end at the gold mine and there's this huge scaffold. The big sword fight takes place and the whole place is in flames. There's a point where Zorro is standing on a beam above the bad guy and he leaps off and does a flip in the air. He does the flip and he lands. We did it in one take and I thought it was perfect. Let's move on. And the stuntman said to me, "no, no, no. I can do it better!" I told him I was quite happy. And he begged me. So we did it again and this time, he mistimed it and crashed into the wooden fence posts that were next to what he was supposed to jump on. He smashed his knee in 14 places. He was in the hospital for eight months! So I learned my lesson on that. If you're happy, move on. Under no circumstances should you do it again, if it's not necessary.*

Stunt guys want the adrenaline rush as much as anyone: they just want it to be safe. The risk/reward calculation is always in play. The director should be at the very top of the production pyramid setting the tone for behavior and a mode of thinking that informs the production: the ultimate moral and ethical leader. The standards they set should serve as a guide for everyone working on the production. Leading by example is a very accurate description of the dynamic of leadership a director must display on a production.

> MARTIN CAMPBELL: *A director has a moral responsibility to listen to a stunt arranger and be guided by him and if the arranger says "No, we cannot do this or you have four takes, you can't do anymore," you absolutely have to listen to him.*

The director, who might be perceived as willing to take unnecessary risks to be the biggest and baddest action director around, sets another tone as well. The one who declares, "it would be amazing if Mel could drive his motorcycle *upside down* across the Grand Canyon. Everyone would be blown away. I'd make cinema history!" needs to be supervised by level-headed, responsible adults. The ones with tunnel vision, who see little but *the shot* and with insufficient regard for the risks, should not serve as anyone's model or leader. There are moral and ethical components to stunts and special effects that must be respected if legalities are not a sufficient motivator in any decision.

> MARTIN CAMPELL: *When your stunt arranger says no, you personally have a responsibility as a director not to do that. You have to listen to him. If he says no, you don't do it. As long as you've got what you want, even if it's only 90% there, if it's too dangerous you get into the* Twilight Zone *situation.*

I once heard a story that a particular movie star with big action credits framed a safety concern to a director like this; standing beside a specially rigged car he was being asked to drive, he asked, "would you put your two-year-old kid in this thing?" The director thought about it, conferred with his stunt and special effects team, and decided to have a particular feature on the car modified before he asked his star to step in and operate it for the shot. I would argue that that conversation should've taken place before the director ever asked his actor to get in the car and risk his safety. I would further argue that the most important conversation that should've taken place is the one where the team responsible for that picture car explained to the director how it was going to work and what precautions had been taken. I imagine the actor thought the same thing and never felt completely safe or trusting again in the hands of that director. That scenario is not desirable for a great collaboration of talented filmmakers. A misjudgment such as this could affect the quality and/or cost of the film, because a breakdown of trust and weakening of the bond that comes from close and complete teamwork can only take away from the best environment in which people do their finest work.

This question of ethical responsibility doesn't just pertain to a director. They aren't the only responsible adults on a set, as I've previously described. The 1st AD can shut down a set if they feel safety is being compromised, but anyone can voice their concern or objection if they believe they or anyone is being asked to risk their safety. For some reason, some people (producers and directors) don't always view actors as deserving the same rights and protections. Is it because in some cases (not many) they are highly paid and should bear more risk? Or is it because risk is part of the gig? No and no. Almost everyone recognizes everyone's safety is an inalienable right, be you a grip, set decorator, stunt performer, or actor. I'll grant the possibility that some directors just aren't thinking clearly when they ask an actor to take an unreasonable risk; they have bought into the Hollywood mythology of swashbuckling, hard-charging actors. They just need to be made aware of their oversight. I could also be cynical and suggest that actors are vulnerable in so many ways and directors and producers know it. Their job demands openness and self-awareness, making them vulnerable emotionally. Many actors are thinking in the back of their minds that the job they're on will certainly be their last. That makes actors in that category insecure and, therefore, vulnerable to pressure in order to please their master (director). The actor who is told to jump over that fire pit or roll down that hill makes a calculation. "If I say no, Mr. Director will never hire me again. He won't think I have the right stuff or confidence in his judgment. If I say yes, he'll love and respect me … but I may end up in the emergency room … mmmm. Maybe …"

> DAN SPEAKER: *We've heard a lot of stories where an actor has been handed a weapon that if he didn't use it, he was a wuss. We don't understand why actors are put in that position and it happens often. Actors want to do the job. They feel if they say no, they're going to lose their job. As an actor you have to decide is it really worth doing something that could affect the rest of your life.*

On an indie feature a friend of mine recently produced, his first-time director was overtaken by an inspired idea for a scene that had already been planned and rehearsed. He suggested a totally new choreography to a driving gag, but didn't fully appreciate what it would take to execute and didn't really care. He just had to do it this new and improved way, not factoring in or raising the question as to whether it posed an extra risk to his cast and crew. Kicking around in the motion picture ether is the romantic notion of the swashbuckling director leading his cast and crew into the jaws of hell in the name of making the best movie ever. Risking personal harm and possibly risking harm to others, these directors have to get *the* shot: the one that will send shocks of electricity coursing through the collective veins of the audience. Why not? Bad things rarely happen. This director was willing to take those long odds. Besides, this is a simple shot, he'd seen it done in movies many times before. It couldn't be that difficult. In movie production, ignorance is not bliss: it's potential disaster. Arrogance, the belief that nothing really matters except that which sheds the light of fame and fortune on a filmmaker, is arguably a worse sin.

> JEFF TUFANO: *You're more likely to run into those guys in the lower-end budget spectrum. Those are the guys who are looking to make a name for themselves. Those are the guys who were looking to shoot in a place where there's nobody around, where there is no one around to tell them what they can and cannot do.*

Here's the scene. A muscle car rockets down a dusty country road heading straight toward the camera. The hero suddenly slams on the brakes and skids sideways to a stop just close enough to the camera so that when he emerges, he rises into a powerful, low-angle close-up that will show the audience his steely resolve and cool demeanor...all in a swirling cloud of dust. Certainly a version of this shot could've been pulled off with great stunt drivers, but it's highly unlikely the lead actor could control the car so precisely that it would come to rest in just the right angle and distance from the camera to allow the actor to step out of the car and into a heroic close-up. The director however, thought it was absolutely doable: wishful thinking. If you will it, it will happen: which, by the way, is a way of thinking that has its place in the business side of our industry, but not when safety is at stake. Everyone agreed it's a cool shot. However, with a nonpro driver at the wheel, chances of hitting the mark were remote and the chances of something unsafe happening were all too plausible. If the car slid too far or overshot the mark, it could slide into the camera, which would be a disaster.

The director ordered the actor into the car, instructed him on how he wanted the actor to "come in hot," slam on the brakes, and slide the car to a stop, just kissing a crushed beer can (symbolic of the hero's damaged life) that was strategically placed in the gravel. Once the car came to rest (but just barely), he was to immediately jump out of the car, "feel the lens" (sense where it is in relation to your body), and look off into the distance, as if in search of a clue to the mystery that haunts his character. Beautiful.

The 1st AD told the director that he was not going to allow the shot. No way. The director's response was, "I'm the director!" The AD's response was, "I'm the AD and responsible for safety on this set. This is not safe." The director marched over to the actor and ordered him into the car. As I mentioned, actors' allegiance is always to their director, the person who has their likeness and image in their capable hands during the shoot and in the editing room (and possible future employment). The poor young actor was being pulled in both directions and didn't know what to do.

> ROY WAGNER: *I find most of the time, young filmmakers are more eager to protect their ego than to protect themselves. They'll come and draw a line in the sand, not even knowing what they're doing is really ego driven. They've observed other people who are saying, "it's either my way or the highway" and they figure they have to do the same thing. I contend that that is unacceptable.*

The AD wisely called in the stunt coordinator, veteran of a thousand shots like this and asked his opinion. The stunt coordinator looked incredulous. "When did we decide to do this?," he asked. "Just now," replied the director with great authority. "I'm afraid I can't allow that," the stunt guy said respectfully and calmly. It may have been his calmness and confidence that drove the director over the edge. A fit of screaming and chest thumping followed, during which time the stunt coordinator and AD instructed the transportation guys to drive the car away. The director sensed which way this thing was going and took a deep breath. "I can't do that?" "Nope," said the stunt guy, "but here's what we *can* do. Bring back that car." They couldn't do it in one shot, but they could use a stunt driver to slide the car to the mark, but at a safer distance with a longer lens. Cut. Then have the actor emerge from the car. By making sure a healthy cloud of dust was churned up, neither the greater distance or the cut will be noticed by the audience. The director learned a few things. He learned who's really in charge when issues of safety are raised. He learned that he has valuable collaborators who may have solutions to problems and can figure out ways to make shots exciting *and* safe.

JOHN BADHAM: *It's a difficult position to be in as a director because on the one hand, you're supposedly responsible for everything that goes on the screen and there's a tendency, like with royalty, to make people believe that they don't need to put their pants on one leg at a time and that all of their ideas are wonderful. It's a common, common thing to happen with any level of director. So being able to be grown up enough to listen to people whose ideas don't match yours is a very difficult step, especially for a beginning director who's already feeling insecure and feeling like people are going to believe he doesn't know what he's doing.*

Directors, who are nervous and keep to themselves, set one tone. Directors, who are loud and abusive, set another.

JOHN BADHAM: *The young directors will tend to be extremely argumentative and say, "No, this is the way we're going to do it." And people will try to, you know, try to talk to them. So at a certain point, somebody's going to blink. But this can be documented forever, because I think every beginning director has probably had this phenomenon happen and has been able to say to yourself, "What if they're right?" in terms of something risky. Being willing to have a discussion, is critically important and especially in low-budget situations where producers are often pushing to, "Let's just get it done." So they may doing something for the wrong reasons and that's not as safe. So the person who's pushing for the safer approach is probably in a difficult position.*

ROY WAGNER: *Fear can destroy a talent quicker than anything.*

Directors with all the best of intentions want their work to be the best: for themselves and for everyone else whose reputations are staked to their production. A trait widely regarded as essential to a top director is a dogged pursuit of excellence. Settling for something that you know is not up to your standards is "death by a thousand cuts." Compromise is arguably a slippery slope to mediocrity.

> MARTIN CAMPBELL: *The other safety issue that both Simon and Gary have is, we had a very tricky scene in the opening of* Vertical Limit *where five people, all at once, drop off the mountain and they're all roped together, hanging there, all sort of brought to a halt by the rope. They're all hanging one under the other. We built this 110-foot wall in the Alps of New Zealand. We did three takes of this and I wasn't quite happy with what I was getting. Simon said to me, "that's it, no more." Now when I hear that, I know that's it. I don't push it. What I got was very good, but directors tend to be perfectionists sometimes. But he just said to me, "that's it. You've had three, no more." If anybody gets injured or badly hurt, it's on me.*

Of course, arrogance or the admirable drive for perfection are not the only reasons directors take unreasonable risks. Sometimes they just don't know any better.

> JEFF TUFANO: *I don't think these people are inherently evil, it usually means they're just not thinking. And they may not be thinking because they just don't know any better. Or they may not be thinking because they're so excited about being on a movie set…We've got this star and this exciting thing we're shooting, this is going to be great, this is going to make me somebody, it's going to make a ton of money.*
>
> DAVID WARD: *I think many young filmmakers tend to feel invincible because they're young, they haven't seen things go wrong. So it's not on their mind, because it's not in their experience. So they have to be mentored and have somebody around who can tell them "look this may not be part of your experience, but I can give you several examples of things that have happened because there were some chances taken that didn't need to be taken." So you have to think about it.*

Directors will plan to shoot a gag a certain way that poses a risk they just never thought of. It happens. But the pros surrounding and supporting that director will catch the flaw in planning and point it out to the director. The reasonable director will thank them profusely and figure something else out that serves their purpose.

> JOHN BADHAM: *In* Blue Thunder, *I was in downtown Los Angeles in a big parking lot surrounded by high-rise buildings and two helicopters are supposed to come down the street, turn into this parking lot, one flips around 180 degrees and fires at the other one, flips around again and exits the parking lot. I get my big 30-foot Chapman crane down in the parking lot to shoot up at the helicopter and get a good angle on it and we're ready to go and the helicopters don't show up. "Where are they? Where are they?" And I get the stunt pilot, Jim Gavin, on the phone and he says, "You can't have that Chapman crane in the parking lot." "Why not?" "Well, if we hit something, it's going to take out the crane and the people sitting on top of it, the guy standing below watching it and you're probably standing there too." I said, "Well, Jim, we need this crane here. We need to get this particular angle." He said, "I will come in there when you have Chapman crane taken out of the parking lot." And by now, I knew him well enough to know that his next statement would be, "I'm sure someone will be happy to do this. It just won't be me or any of my guys. We're going to go park our helicopters and you do what you have to do." So I had to swallow my pride and my arrogance and say, "Let's get the crane out of here because we can't shoot until he does that." So after the* Twilight Zone *accident happened, I called up Jim Gavin and I said, "I'm calling to thank you for being such a wonderful asshole and protecting me from myself so many times." Because if the* Twilight Zone *guys had done the same thing and been willing to stand up like that, then that accident might not have happened.*

So what this means in practical terms for many of you who have yet to feel at home on a set and are not sure of all the protocols attached to a production is that your approach to planning and executing each and every event on your set that poses a degree of added risk should be participatory, actively engaged in bringing together everyone involved in making reasonably sure these events will be safe.

> JOHN BADHAM: *My first principle is there is no stunt in any movie worth hurting anybody for. That has to enter into all decisions. Risk is an ethical part of my calculation.*

Having produced many feature films, I felt ready to try directing. I had watched directors on my productions work. I was a very actively engaged producer, in part because I had been involved in the writing of the screenplay as well. But my partner and I wanted to know anything and everything that went into the making of our movies. We were in most preproduction meetings and were always on set at all times. There wasn't much we weren't aware of on one of our movies (although I was always the last one to know about on-set romances). We knew what had been shot as well as the director: the coverage, the takes…all of it. I felt I understood what was required of a director. I had seen stunts and special effects planned and executed many times. I pretty much knew the drill.

When it came time to finally direct my first movie, *Jake Speed*, it had plenty of action and special effects. This was a low-budget action comedy shot in Zimbabwe, Paris, and Los Angeles. We got a lotta bang for our buck, but believe me, it was very low budget. We had a world-renowned stunt coordinator with some very impressive credits. We had car chases, planes and combat helicopters, fights, explosions, gunplay…the whole playbook. Somewhere toward the end of the schedule, we had a very big stunt to shoot: at least it was big for our modestly budgeted production. We had built a giant set that served as an opulent and large-scale entry and living room to a mansion, the villain's lair. A wide set of stairs led up to the front door from outside. In the script, a car driven by our hero would drive through the mansion's mammoth double front doors and drive around the hallways in search of the damsel in distress, guns blazing. Two of the bad guy's hapless guards make a futile effort to stop the car's advance by slamming the doors shut and bracing themselves against them. The choreography had to be carefully calculated to pull the two stuntmen out of harm's way before the car was launched from the stairs and through the doors, which they were standing next to. The doors were connected to wires and were to be pulled open just as the car reached them. This was a precisely drawn plan designed by the stunt coordinator with the assistance and very important cooperation of the special effects team. On the day of the shoot, we walked through this chain of events in the shot many times. As the director, I understood the weight of what we were about to undertake. I asked every question I possibly could think of about how every phase of the stunt was going to work. I often asked, "what if this part doesn't work or that action doesn't happen on cue?" I inspected and asked for explanations of how various timing devices worked that controlled various parts of this complicated stunt. How do we stop the stunt if something goes wrong for any reason? All was explained to me, my producing partner, and my 1st AD in a way that sounded well thought out and reasonably safe. It wasn't. The car crashed through the doors before the stunt guys had been fully pulled out of harm's way. The timing was off: human error. They were both seriously hurt and were rushed to the hospital where, thankfully, they recovered from broken bones and internal injuries. One of the stuntmen had actually stopped breathing. But for the heroic intervention of our key grip using CPR to get him breathing normally again, we would have had a horrible tragedy on our hands.

This is a cautionary tale for which there isn't a direct or specific thing you in your role as director or producer can do to prevent a stunt from going wrong. There are many things you and your team will do, protocols to go through, that are intended to prevent bad things from happening. But this tale raises many issues. Is the stunt safe? How do you know? Have you and your team studied the plan and are satisfied to the best of your knowledge that the best thinking has gone into it? Are all communications and channels of command clear to everyone? What does your gut tell you about the stunt or effect? All of these questions were raised and answered to everyone's satisfaction, including me, yet the stunt did not have a good outcome. I had great confidence in my stunt and special effects team. Their safety record was spotless. We did a lot of other things that were challenging on that show and everything came off flawlessly.

MARTIN CAMPBELL: *On the second Zorro, there's a scene on a train and Zorro drops through the skylight in the train. The sword fight starts, a very straightforward thing. But the drop was about 13 feet and I said, "Have we rehearsed this?" They told me they had, that they had practiced the drop. But then I learned that he hadn't actually practiced the drop through the glass. I asked about that and they said, "No no no. It's fine, don't worry about it." I was really worried about it. The stuntman insisted that it was all fine. He did the drop and he broke his ankle. That put him out of commission for a long time. I just knew in the back of my mind, having done a lot of action, that jumping through a skylight of candy glass and balsa wood is different than jumping through a hole. It can change the direction of the fall. He was even on a wire. And even though he rehearsed it a number of times, things go wrong. When we reshot it, I insisted they use a descender cable which has much more control. I probably should have insisted they rehearse going through the glass and balsa wood and use a descender cable in the first place. I could have said, "I'm not shooting this until you've done that." But we listen to everyone's opinion, the stuntman's opinion, everybody's; you just sort of make that decision as best you can. I've done enough to instinctively know things could be a problem. I could've insisted they put him on a safer wire and say, "to hell with it, let's shoot." At least we'd know we had a safe jump.*

Things happen despite being thorough and competent. As the director, the one who often dreams up these wild things, don't ever forget and factor into your thinking that there is always risk, even though experienced stunt and effects pros are managing them. Their fundamental principle is safety first. You won't find a stunt or special effects pro who won't mention that from the get go. If you meet one who doesn't feel that way, steer clear.

The protocols are fairly uniform in the movie industry and are observed and practiced by almost everyone working in the business. Although they have evolved, many of them have been in place for generations. Things are pretty much done the same way, in the same order, using the same language, from production to production. This uniformity is meant to make communication efficient. When communication is efficient, free flowing, and comprehendible, there is a reduced risk of something going wrong whether it affects safety, reduces efficiency, or wastes resources. In my section about the use of firearms, for instance, the protocols are identical or *virtually* identical from set to set, no matter who is practicing them or what the scene's narrative entails. That way everyone understands what's going on. No one is reinventing or making up language and actions that may be misinterpreted. Anyone on a set, who has experience on productions where firearms were used, has seen and heard the same ritual used by the armorer or prop master. No one wonders what the armorer means when he announces "fire in the hole!" The lack of understanding of these protocols and the nomenclature can lead to accidents. Protocols are a good thing. There is little, if any, demand to reinvent the protocols by which movies are made. Improvements? Yes. New technologies or storytelling techniques? Please, yes.

Second Units

The second unit or a second and smaller crew is assembled to shoot any interstitial or detailed shots that do not require the cast. The "first team" actors always shoot with the first unit. The second unit always works with stunt performers, doubles, or other players who have no spoken lines. This unit, therefore, shoots without the need to record dialogue, since the material they record does not include scenes where actors talk or interact with each other.

When it comes to action scenes, a second unit makes a lot of sense to employ. Action takes a long time to shoot compared to scenes that are dialogue driven. They can be complicated and dense, meaning a lot of shots are often necessary to comprise even the briefest moments on screen. Remember that stunts are creating the illusion of a violent event. Shooting the real deal is usually not practical due to the risk of injury or death or even how doable the stunt would be to execute in a real setting. The person most qualified and who is usually designated to be the second unit director is the stunt coordinator. They're wearing two hats when a second unit is needed: specifically, they are the stunt coordinator/second unit director. If their services are required with the main unit and they are at another location shooting with the second unit, they will most likely appoint a trusted stunt performer who has the experience and know-how to supervise the stunts on that day. The planning has most likely already taken place and all that is left is the actual stunt to be performed. As long as the substitute coordinator has been fully briefed (they may have participated in the planning), you should trust your stunt coordinator's judgment that the stunt will be in good hands with his replacement.

Typical kinds of shots that are assigned to second units are scenic beauty shots used for establishing shots or for transitions between scenes, "inserts" or "cutaways," such as a shot of the clock on the wall or extreme close-up of a watch. The very nature of creating compelling action scenes requires many "moving parts" or shots, which, when cut together, create not only a depiction of an action or event but its energy as well. Not all the images are meant to be objective or identifiable "puzzle pieces" that lead an audience to an objective understanding of an action. Borrowing language from the world of painting, both representational and impressionistic images can be used together to effectively present an action or event. Some shots are very tight or close up. Others may be shaky or blurred in order to convey the energy. A clinched fist mid-flight, a spinning rubber burning tire, or a pair of nimble feet dancing away from an opponent are the meat and potatoes of a good action second unit.

The bar has indeed been set very high for action on the screen. Scenarios are complex, and in many cases, they defy nature's physical laws. The styles and methods of creating exciting and convincing action may vary among filmmakers, but as with any other specialized talent, it takes experience, creativity, technical know-how, and ingenuity to succeed.

When to utilize a second unit instead of the main unit is an option determined by the director and stunt coordinator. Some shots that may not reveal the identity of the actor may be important to capture with the main unit as a part of the rest of the sequence of shots for a few reasons. The location may only be available that day and cannot be reproduced somewhere else. A certain amount of momentum is built as an action scene is being shot. Plugging in a shot captured by another unit at various points in the action may not match in energy or in other subtle ways. Even though a shot may not reveal the actor who is being shot (it could be the principal or a double), sometimes it makes more sense and it is more efficient to just get the shot while you're there shooting the rest of it. You can't separate out every shot that can conceivably be done with a second unit. Common sense and experience will dictate how to parcel out those shots that make sense for a second unit and the ones that don't.

The advantage of a second unit is that all the time the main unit has allocated to it can be dedicated to its cast at the original locations or on a soundstage. The costs of an actor's time and of a location or soundstage are relatively high. So if certain shots can be captured without taking away from finite time with the cast or at a location or stage, that can be an economically wise choice. Taking the time for instance to set up a shot of your star's watch, because in the story the audience needs to know what time it is, is arguably not an efficient use of resources. There's lots of expensive talent in front of and behind the camera whose talents are not necessarily required for those kinds of shots. Isn't your A team better utilized setting up for the next scene in which the actors are featured? There may be so many of the kind of shots such as sunsets, skylines, text, or anything that requires close scrutiny by the audience (but without the actors) that the time necessary to shoot them can add up to days' worth of work. If the math works out, you may find that it would be less expensive and/or a better use of important and valuable time with your principal cast and crew to hand those shots off to a second unit.

Sometimes these shots include the characters in action. They run, fight, jump…do all kinds of actions. Do you need the actual principal cast to be in those shots? Not always. The simple solution is the use of doubles. Just as the use of stunt doubles to replace an actor with a stunt performer is common to eliminate the risk of your actor getting hurt, the double or stand-in will be used to take the actor's place when the shot is composed in such a way as the audience can't tell and have no reason to suspect that the actor they've been watching up till this point is not still being photographed. We'll see in the final movie the wristwatch from the principal actor's point of view that's been photographed on the wrist of their double. We may see quickly moving feet that are needed to indicate the character's need to hurry, but in reality we will be seeing the feet of the double before cutting back to the wider shot that reassures us we're still with our protagonist. After all, a foot is a foot, a hand is a hand, and if the shot is wide enough, a body is a body. Now you're probably thinking of the obvious caveat: the double's feet hands and body must approximate the features of the actor they are doubling. You can't have a very thin person double for a very heavy one, at least not easily. If the shot is very close, then it becomes more important to match an actor's hands or other physical feature as to not raise suspicion in the audience. Hands in particular can be very telling. Another feature that demands a good match is complexion. A double with fair skin won't do when you see their skin tone doesn't come close to matching the principal actor's. Blondes can't double for brunettes for shots where the audience will see the disparity. So there are reasonable tolerances you must observe.

When stunt doubles are chosen, other factors besides physical resemblances are important. The first consideration is: Are they qualified to do the stunt? So you start with a group of stunt performers who can do the job. Then you narrow your choices down to physical resemblances such as gender, weight, and height. If you can, you can identify more specific traits that will make the switch out to the double that much easier and more convincing, such as gait or posture.

Addressing any disparity in the physical characteristics of a double and the principal cast member, certain traits can be made to match using wardrobe and makeup. Padding, wigs, makeup, and all other applicable layers to alter appearance are used all the time to contribute to the seamless illusion that we never take our eyes off the actor. No reason to suspect a switch has been made should ever occur to an audience. If and when it does, you have broken the trust you as a storyteller have earned from your audience. Your movie becomes just that, an artificial version of the world you're depicting.

Martial Arts

Martial arts used to be a separate kind of movie. Unfortunately, they were usually low budget. They weren't studio movies. The Matrix *was a good reason that changed. It helped move those movies to the mainstream. Martial arts has become a pretty big part of major movies. They're no longer the "you killed my teacher" story. You have Liam Neeson with a whole new action career with* Taken. *The moves he makes in that movie definitely come from a few different martial arts disciplines. Those are not street fights. The same with Matt Damon in the Bourne movies.*

JAMES LEW, MARTIAL ARTS EXPERT AND CHOREOGRAPHER

What was once a specialized and specific form of fighting has morphed into and become part of the fabric of new general audience action movies. Martial arts used to be confined to movies in which the stories lived in the world of Asian culture. The stories took place in the worlds of warlords, Triad gangsters, and young avengers seeking justice for their venerated teacher's senseless murder at the hands of their bad apple student. Martial arts, in its many forms, has transcended the specialty or B-movie market and has seamlessly been infused into studio-style action flicks. So, like many other directors and producers, you should know a little bit about this school of combat.

Like any other form of combat, it requires experts trained in a martial arts discipline: people who have experience not only in martial arts, but in choreographing it for the screen. As a general rule, any and every expert you are considering working with on your movie to plan and execute stunts needs to know more than just how to perform the stunt and perform it safely. They must have a thorough understanding of how the stunt needs to be photographed to be believable. Don't hire your kid's judo teacher: he's only partially qualified. For that matter, don't hire a national champion unless they understand the difference between a live performance and one that has to be believable and exciting on screen. You can conceivably work with a stunt coordinator who is not a martial arts expert. A martial arts expert and a stunt coordinator can combine their talents, knowledge, and experience to deliver what you need for the story. Not all stunt coordinators know every style of fighting or can drive a car or do a high fall. The coordinator will bring onto your show the specialist who can do what you require; that's why they're called coordinators. Also, if you're not in a major market where experienced motion picture craftspeople are available, combining various attributes to have all your bases covered (safety, reliability, and understanding of the camera) makes sense.

For martial arts fight coordinator or designer, expertise in the practice of martial arts is, of course, essential. The question as to whether they're qualified to coordinate a fight for a camera is actually no different than in any other form of combat. Just because the style of fighting is specific doesn't call for any special approach to covering the action. A fight is a fight in terms of how to shoot it.

> JAMES LEW: *As far as making a punch work or a kick, the principles are all the same as in other forms of fighting. Whether it's a stick, a knife, or a sword, you still have to stay with the correct camera angles. It's all similar. It's really the same as when you're shooting dialogue scenes; you have a choice of drama or comedy where you do the basic coverage. That doesn't change.*

There are issues of tone that apply to any kind of fight. Is this an edgy piece in which an audience should feel real jeopardy for the characters, or is it more along the lines of a comedy, where it doesn't occur to us that anyone is going to be seriously hurt in the story: vanquished, yes, but not maimed or killed?

Most Hong Kong-style martial arts movies approach combat as a choreographed event much like a dance number in an MGM musical. The defeats are symbolically represented by combatants lying motionless or limping away from the fight. There's little, if any, blood or mangled bodies as there would be in a real fight. The aesthetics and narrative elements are the currency of these set pieces. When those fight techniques are adopted by Hollywood-style movies, bones crunch, blood flies, and firearms often get added to the mix. These fights are more edgy and realistic; they're short and deadly. Efficiency trumps beauty.

> JAMES LEW: *Jackie Chan's movies are very stylized. The moves, the beats create a very specific feel through the timing of his movements. The fights aren't very deadly. They're very stylized, which goes back to the older Chinese movies, the classic kung fu movies. I compare them*

*to dance movies where every step has an exact place, one foot goes
here and the other goes there, as opposed to a street fight which is
a little looser. The footwork on street fights is not as accurate. You
can shuffle your feet or stumble, which gives it a more realistic and
intense feel.*

Jackie Chan is one of the greatest examples of the lighter tone in martial
arts movies. His choreography and structure to fight sequences is as much
a ballet as it is a fight. His fights are very much about style. They express his
characters' "who am I" through the style of action. His characters laugh in the
face of danger. They play with their opponents. They seek to humiliate or show
up a foe, not destroy them. Hollywood "superhero" movies have arguably
adopted that sensibility. The body count in those movies is enormous, but
somehow it's not as horrifying as it should be considering the mayhem that's
going on in those action sequences.

JAMES LEW: *It's very important to understand the tone of the
movie. Is the director looking for a very intense, realistic approach
or a lighter, fantasy, tone to the story? For example, in* The Matrix,
*those movies worked very well for that tone which was a little over
the top. Another example is* Romeo Must Die *starring Jet Li, which
is a pure urban, modern-day, street movie. You don't suddenly fly
and have wire work in a movie like that. That would take you out of
the story. Where did you establish that he can jump like that? He's
a regular person. It's the same with dialogue, even if it's good, if
doesn't fit the movie, it doesn't work. So it's the same with style of
fighting. The wrong choice could take you out of the movie. That's
why it's important to understand the tone of the movie and design
choreography that stays within that tone.*

When a producer or director meets with a candidate to choreograph or
oversee martial arts in their shows, it's not unlike the meetings interviewing
guys who do car chases. They should come in having read the material and
having formulated some ideas.

JAMES LEW: *I don't ever take a meeting unless I have read the script
and taken the time to read it again. I make notes on what I think I
can do with the material. I even jot down a few beats with specific
techniques for a few scenes, so I can pitch my ideas. So when I go into
meet the director, I've done my homework. I try to let the director talk
so he can tell me what his vision is.*

The best coordinators will bring great creative ideas to your story as well. The good ones are always thinking how to apply their craft to improving the story. I love it when anyone on my productions comes up with an idea that elevates the script. Not all ideas that come from your team will be gems. But I'll take the one that is.

> JAMES LEW: *I try to dig and dig into the characters. I try to find in the writing little setups and payoffs. I look for the specific bits of behavior that they tend to do, set that up and then in another scene later, pay it off through a final fight scene. It could be some odd thing they do that saves the day. I did* Get Smart *with Steve Carell. There's a big scene towards the beginning where the bad guy is falling through the air, skydiving with Steve Carell and Anne Hathaway in each of his hands. Anne's character gets an idea how to distract the guy so they can escape. She gives him a great big smooch on the lips. He so stunned, they're able to break away from him and open up their parachutes to escape. In the final scene with The Rock, they're on this SUV. The script says Carell's character is supposed to say to The Rock, "Hey, look over there!" The Rock falls for it and turns around, allowing Carell to get in a little cheap punch. I thought about that beat and keeping in mind that it was a comedy, came up with an idea where Carell would give The Rock a big smooch on the lips that stuns him and let's Carell get the upper hand. So I pitched it to the director, who loved the idea. He said he had to pitch it to Carell and The Rock. They came back and said they loved it. It got in the movie!*

Invite ideas. Create an environment in which all your collaborators, at all levels of the production hierarchy, will feel safe to offer their ideas. No one should feel they're just a set designer or dolly grip, so that their ideas on how a character might negotiate a tough situation won't be valued. Making movies is not exactly a democracy. But all ideas should be heard. Professionals understand that every day is not a brainstorming session in which the director must listen to everyone's thoughts for the day. Pros know that when they have an idea that really feels worthy, they will be heard. You should understand that the free flow of ideas manifests in the work of the people you've paid to make the creative choices that will tell your story.

The same broad questions arise when talking about a James Bond movie as when discussing a martial arts flick. You will discuss how you, as the storyteller, want the style of fighting to function. Do you see set pieces that evoke beauty or even a spectacular and visceral detour from an otherwise straightforward melodrama? Many fight choreographers, whether from the martial arts world or not, see fights as an expression of character. *How* they fight is a reflection of character.

> JAMES LEW: *Creating character through the fights I design is absolutely the most important thing to me. Without that, you don't care for the characters. Once you don't care for the characters, your movie is lost. It just becomes a series of cool moves. When I see those movies with special effects and explosions, after a while, I really don't care about the characters. Within a fight scene, if you consider the moves as dialogue, each punch or kick can say, "I want to kill you" or "I just want to mess with you." All of those elements add up to a story or the story point within a scene. We might have a bad guy steal a purse or something very different, the guy killed your wife; you're going after him with different techniques and different intentions.*

These introductory meetings should result in a meeting of the minds regarding the overall vision and a strong feeling on the part of the director and the fight coordinator that they can do good work together and that the coordinator can make the action look great.

> JAMES LEW: *The first thing that's important about hiring a coordinator is there has to be a chemistry. It's such a collaborative business that if you don't feel comfortable with each other or there's a difference of opinion, there's going to be conflict. That's not going to work. If you meet someone just because they're martial artists, that doesn't make them a good fight choreographer. There is a distinct difference between the real stuff and the movie stuff. You have to know how to sell it a little bit bigger. You have to know the better angles, to have the right body positioning. There's a lot of little things that are different.*

By the way, there's a whole world of young devoted martial arts fighters out there who are dedicated to this art form. They practice among themselves, often shooting choreographed fights with digital cameras or smartphones. They edit the fights together and share these short movies with each other and on the World Wide Web. They learn by doing. Trial and error. I've seen some of these "home movies," and they're pretty good. They may lack production value or quality acting, but they definitely showcase some good martial arts fights and are sometimes shot well. If I were making a very-low-budget movie with martial arts, I'd definitely consider working with guys like these, assuming they had a safety in mind. So if you meet a martial arts expert who tries to sell you on his ability to bring his expertise to the screen and he's never done it before, I'd steer clear. There's plenty of enthusiasts out there who love it so much that they've gone out and shot tons of martial arts fights.

JAMES LEW: *If someone doesn't have the credits to get a job and they're serious, they can get a bunch of friends and go shoot something themselves and cut it together. They can show that and if it's good, get a job. There is no reason for anyone not to have something to show.*

Once again, not all directors know how to stage fights or even care.

JAMES LEW: *I'm thrilled when the director isn't familiar with or is not experienced in fights and martial arts. I get to be more creatively involved. But either way, whether they know what they want or not, they hire a fight coordinator for their experience and knowledge. They have to trust that you're going to bring them something they like.*

Designing and executing a fight using martial arts techniques will sound familiar to you. Everyone agrees on the goals and style. The choreographer either interprets the director's vision or what the script describes…or both. The choreographer designs a fight, works it out with martial arts stunt performers, and, hopefully, gets to present it to the director for their approval.

JAMES LEW: *These days, a lot of coordinators and choreographers are shooting rehearsals as a form of previz. You get the stunt guys together and you choreograph the scene and you shoot it. Sometimes go a little crazy and really shoot it like a full-on scene with every bit of coverage. I loosely do between that extreme and just a simple recording of the fight. I do shoot the basic coverage with 2-shots and over the shoulders. I tried to stay away from too many little insert shots like the fists in the stomach or those type of shots that are real tight. I don't want it to look too much like a finished product. I used to do storyboards. But it's really great being able to use digital technology to record the rehearsals because I was a really bad drawer. By doing this, someone can get a good feel for the tone and pacing and editing. You have to be careful, because sometimes the director or DP can get offended; they think you're doing their job. I just try to make sure they can see the moves rather than trying to create the drama. That's become a handy tool. But that's enough for them to say, "yeah I like it, let's go with that" or they can offer some suggestions.*

Interestingly enough, the hierarchy is quite different for the fight choreographers and directors in Hong Kong and mainland China. The choreographers are considered the action directors. A lot of times, the first unit director just goes home or just sits back. The "action director" runs the show completely, from where the camera goes to the actors' performances. In the 2013 movie *The Grandmaster*, the world-renowned director Wong Kar-wai beautifully tells the life story of legendary Wing Chun master and teacher of Bruce Lee, Ip Man. The Action Choreographer on that movie, Woo-ping Yuen, is afforded a main title credit placed just before the stars', whose credits are followed only by the director's "Directed by Wong Kar-wai" credit. In other words, that position is afforded the highest regard, other than that traditionally given to the director. It bears repeating that there are directors from all corners of the globe who will similarly step back and have people who have the expertise in shooting action, which they lack. It's a wise delegation of duties.

Once shooting has begun, your choreographer/coordinator's job is not done by a long shot. Their understanding of the relationship between the action and the camera is part of the expertise you really need. When you do a take, if you're not experienced in fights on camera, give a look over to your choreographer, who should be looking at a monitor to make sure the hits look like they landed and the illusion of a fight where no one gets hit is not broken. Someone should be watching the action who knows these things. Discovering a hit is a miss in the editing room, is too late.

JAMES LEW: *Every coordinator needs to know where to put the camera. It's absolutely crucial. Shooting we're shooting, my job is to be behind the camera or by the monitors watching, to make sure that the camera's in the right places to make the hits work the best. Maybe a hit can work in two different places, but there's definitely a sweet spot. It has to be pretty accurate to really make it good. So sometimes if the cameraman is going handheld, the operator might be a little too much to the left. Or he may need to stay a little more still to capture it. And sometimes you'll see a tiny bit of air between the fist and its target and you know it's a miss. I can spot those things quickly on the monitor.*

Some fights go on for a long stretch of time and cover a lot of ground. It helps to have a shooting strategy when working with fight sequences. Divide up the scenes into sections and shoot out (shoot all shots that make up that span of action) each section, and then the next. This way, with fewer shots to account for, you don't leave any coverage behind and it's easier to maintain continuity. Storyboards and previz are a big, if not required, aid in making sure you have captured all the necessary coverage. You go down the list or pages of storyboards, shooting them one by one and checking them off. So each section, or, as Jackie Chan refers to them as, "mini-masters," is a unit or portion of the story that is covered completely, as if it were a stand-alone scene. In order to make the editorial breakpoints between units invisible, Chan reshoots the last beat of the previous unit and lets it run into the next unit, thereby creating overlapping action that hides the seams (edit points). It's a pretty standard concept of matching action that applies to any movement that is covered from different angles and where editorial breaks are anticipated.

> JAMES LEW: *Jackie Chan's entire approach is to shoot these fights in "mini-masters." A lot of people like to shoot one big master just to have it in the can. But there's always something that's not right partway through and you always have to go back to the beginning. You actually spend too much time shooting the precious master, which you're going to cut up anyway. It's also better for actors because they just can't remember all 50 moves. It's safer too. They might forget and kick instead of punch and somebody gets smacked and hurt. Then you're shut down for the day. And it's so tiring to shoot a master. When you're tired, you're not thinking. You can get too close and someone gets hurt. So I'm a strong proponent of mini-masters.*

You may be wondering where you find stunt performers who are martial arts experts for the screen. Not that hard. Most stunt coordinators and choreographers who work regularly work with a group of stunt performers they're familiar with. They know their talents and work habits. This is true among cowboys, drivers, fight specialists of all sorts, and any other specialized skill set you can think of. Martial arts choreographers have a group of performers they like to work with too: men and women they can count on to do the job. They know that just being a good fighter is not the same as being a good stunt performer. Fighters from the live arenas have different approaches to their work. Their moves are designed to do damage. They aren't the ones you hire.

> JAMES LEW: *I've worked with a lot of MMA [mixed martial arts] fighters like Randy Couture. They would absolutely kill me in a fight. But for some reason, on the screen, they didn't look powerful. They're not what we call "telegraphing" their punches. It's almost the opposite of what they're trained to do. If an actor or stunt performer doesn't telegraph a punch or kick enough on-screen, you really can't tell what they're doing. They're going so fast with the punches that are so short, we really can't appreciate the power. Watching a live event is*

so different than watching it as we do on the screen, which is a two-dimensional image. Even 3-D is seen on a flat surface. It's still not quite live. That's why strikes have to be telegraphed. They have to be a little bit bigger. Also, these guys aren't used to throwing punches in movies. For Randy's entire life, he's been used to throwing punches that are real. So he's not that comfortable pulling up short. I tried to un-train him to keep it safe. He's trained to step in to striking distance, but that's too close for movies. I'd have to keep asking him to back off. Backing off is not his natural instinct. That was scary. Also, actors who don't know anything about fighting or fighting for movies have the same instinct to move in close. They think they're too far away, but there's a reason for that, safety, and it's just not necessary.

Firearms

Using weapons on your show is when you really have to pay attention to long-established protocols. Firearms in particular demand the closest attention to detail and professionalism. Many, if not most, actors are not familiar with the intricacies of how guns and ammunition work. Most of us are not familiar with the mechanics of how a gun fires and what it is firing. Just looking at a gun and not seeing a bullet inside a chamber is not an indication of whether or not a bullet is situated elsewhere inside the weapon, ready to be fired. All you have to do is read newspapers or watch the news on TV to know that accidental deaths and horrible injuries happen every year in households where untrained people are killed or injured, *unaware* the weapon they were handling could be fired. Presuming the gun is locked or unloaded is an all too common and fatal mistake to make.

Arguably as dangerous is the actor or crew member who thinks they know all about firearms. I know this may come as a shock, but there's an inordinate amount of outsized egos in the filmmaking community. Actors who want to maintain their airs of cool, directors who must confirm their macho authority, low-profile crew members who seek validation or elevation of their status, all may be motivated to show off their "expertise" with a gun or rifle. A tragic accident can cruelly reveal how poor their knowledge of firearms was.

Jon-Erik Hexum and Brandon Lee are tragic and fatal examples of what can happen if weapons used on a movie set are not supervised and used expertly and in a completely conscientious way. Both actors fell victim to improper safety precautions, poor supervision, and ignorance of how a "prop" gun might prove dangerous.

MIKE TRISTANO: *In any of these incidents such as what happened with Brandon Lee or Jon-Erik Hexum, there were no safety precautions taken. The person handling the weapons didn't know how to take care of them. I don't think it was ever maliciously done of course, it was just negligence. These people were not armorers at all. They were just prop people who were handling guns and were not familiar enough with how they worked. And I'm not saying most prop people who have licenses don't know how to handle them, but there are a lot of people who come into the business without having the experience of working with a master prop master or being around weapons. They don't really know all the safety procedures to go through or generally how to handle a gun on a set.*

It's not an incorrect assumption to make that if a firearm is present and being used on a set, it is safe and presents no threat to anyone in the company. Who in their right mind would allow something as potentially deadly as a firearm on a movie set where reality is an illusion? No one. Real, fully functioning firearms are not allowed on a union set. But that does not mean firearms used in movies are not dangerous.

If they are the genuine article, they are always modified to prevent them from being used as they were originally designed to, but they can still pose a danger because of the blanks they use. With today's strict protocols in place and if they are fastidiously followed, the set is a safe workplace. But please note my caveat: "If today's strict protocols are in place and are fastidiously followed." Those cautionary words can never be regarded casually.

If you have a position of authority in a movie production, you have the very serious responsibility of following protocols, making sure everyone on set follows those protocols, and being certain that you have hired experienced armorers (firearms experts) to work with and control the firearms, and that an environment of awareness and caution pervades your set.

MIKE TRISTANO: *Some people call us weapons handlers, weapons experts, weapons wranglers. I've heard all kinds of different terms. A master armorer is someone who's been doing it for an awful long time. He has other armorers that work under him on his team. He's also the person who most likely owns all of the weapons being used on the production.*

The current safety protocols that are now in place are, in part, a result of tragic experiences such as with Brandon Lee and Jon-Erik Hexum. If employed conscientiously, the protocols will most likely eliminate the chance of a ruinous mistake. Do you know that paper or plastic is sometimes used to hold gunpowder in the brass casing used for blanks? Do you know that that material, called "wadding," is propelled out of the gun at an explosive rate of speed? If fired close to a person, it can have and has had fatal consequences.

There are specific gun props that are designed for specific uses in movies. If a scene requires that a gun must be fired and a muzzle flash seen, that may suggest a slightly modified gun that will only shoot blanks.

MIKE TRISTANO: *We have the real firearms of course, but they are "blank adapted," meaning they only fire blanks. But we have to be on set with those, because they are real firearms. We call them either the real gun or the hero weapon. And they may have the replica versions which are totally non-firing versions of those guns. They look exactly like the hero guns or sometimes when they don't have to fire they actually are the hero guns. That's when the hero can be termed differently.*

Blanks can kill people. So there's a lot that goes into setting up the shot safely knowing what types of blanks to use, and this comes with experience. Anybody who works for me has to intern with me for a year before we send them out on a show whether they have licenses or not. There is just so much to know in terms of safety, in terms of setting up things for the director so he'll be happy with the look of what's being done, working with the actors.

If the gun does not have to be fired, and the scene only requires that it be displayed to withstand the scrutiny of an audience, a fully detailed facsimile or a modified, but genuine firearm may be the right choice. These "function guns" will have a blocked barrel, so nothing can ever escape it.

Still other options for prop guns are made of rubber. Although greatly detailed, they aren't usually suitable for close-ups, but are very useful when used in fights or on any situation where a metal replica can hurt someone. Getting whacked with a real metal gun can do real damage. Rubber guns are cheap to make and they can look pretty real. In scenes where they need to be disposed of and can't be recovered, as in a body of water, they are a great option as well.

MIKE TRISTANO: *If they're doing a fight or the stuntman is doing a fall with a weapon and we don't want him to get hurt, we go with the rubber gun. You have to consider that even with replicas, they can be broken. If a stunt performer hits himself with the replica by accident, that can really hurt. If they are doing a fight scene, we always want to use a rubber weapon. And even within the rubber weapon category we have grades of rubber weapons. If we have a scene where a guy can possibly really get hit by someone using a gun, we have a very soft foamy weapon. Other times we'll have a weapon that's made of a harder rubber. They often have armatures inside so they don't wiggle around and look fake. We try to have as many options as possible to make sure whatever the scene is, the weapon looks good.*

I do all the painting on our weapons to make sure they all look as photo-real, weathered, and aged to look the best they can possibly look on camera. Nothing is going to look as good as the real weapon, but no matter what it is, we try and make it look as real as possible. Sometimes I've had actors pick up the rubber gun or the replicas thinking they're picking up the real gun. It looks that good.

Of course when you do inserts or cutaways to a gun safe skittering across the floor you can use the real weapon. Remember nothing looks as good as the real thing. If we are on set that's something we would make a recommendation about as to when to use the real gun and when to use the replica. But if the production can't afford to have an armorer on set at all times that would be the role of the prop person. They would be handling all the rubber guns and the replicas. Remember only licensed armorers can handle live weapons. The prop master would be working along with us where real guns are concerned. On a day where there's no actual gunfire, we would just have the replicas for the close-up and use the rubber gun if the actor had to make a fall or there was a safety issue.

But be aware: prop masters may or may not be properly licensed or experienced in handling live firearms. If you're in a position of authority on a production, it's your job to know if the people handling weapons and dangerous materials are licensed to do that. Be thorough in your investigation of an armorer's references. Make contact with those references to be certain the people you are considering are safe, collaborative, and reliable.

MIKE TRISTANO: *If there's ever gunfire on a set or real weapon being used we have to be there. Even if the real weapon is not being fired it's still a real weapon and by law there still has to be a licensed handler to be with that firearm.*

The Entertainment Firearms Permit is issued by the California Department of Justice, which allows people in the motion picture industry to be able to possess or rent certain firearms to be used on a set.

MIKE TRISTANO: *All of my crew and I are fully licensed armorers. A prop master also has to have a permit if they're going to handle or rent live firearms. But that doesn't mean that he or she has any real experience using firearms.*

The introduction of the Entertainment Firearms Permit in California came about because the Department of Justice and ATF felt that guns were just being handed out to people who didn't really have criminal background checks or the experience. While the permit process doesn't really check people out for experience, it does weed out anyone who has a criminal record who tries to rent a gun. That still didn't compensate for how you check for experience.

> MIKE TRISTANO: *When I hire someone onto my crew I am so particular about who I hire. I may get 50 applications and hire one person because I'm very particular about [how] people handle their weapons, their knowledge of weapons, how meticulous they are about safety, and how they interact with other people on the set. You're not just an armorer, sometimes you're also a politician because you're dealing with strong personalities regarding something that involves not only safety, but making things look good for the actors and the director.*

Any and all firearms that are used in making movies should be acquired through professional, experienced movie armorers or master armorers. In the major markets, there are many to choose from. Most have vast inventories of a wide variety of firearms (and other weapons as well). Their firearms have been checked and rechecked, cleaned, and maintained. Their owners know them intimately, allowing them to anticipate how they perform. You will arrange to "rent" them for use in your movie. If your licensed armorer doesn't have the weapon you're looking for, it's very likely they can acquire it through other trusted armorers, purchase and modify it, or even manufacture it.

> MIKE TRISTANO: *I generally try to avoid using firearms that are not mine or that haven't been in my control. Every weapon that goes out of our shop is meticulously cleaned and checked for functionality and reliability. If I'm working with someone else's weapons, I don't know what the history of those weapons is; if they've been damaged, if they've been checked or cleaned properly, if they're reliable…That's why I try to avoid situations like that. It doesn't happen very often, but once in a while you get a director or a star who wants to use a personal gun. In that case, I say okay. I'll take the gun and I'll check it out thoroughly. From then on, it will be our weapon to bring to set. We try to be accommodating in those kinds of situations as long as safety isn't compromised.*

Your armorer is fully versed and properly respectful of the seriousness of using a firearm, albeit modified on a movie set. They know and follow the protocols (and in California, certain laws) that have been established as industry standards. Even the most experienced and knowledgeable gun owners do not know safety protocols specifically created for movie sets. Your *expert* duck hunter Uncle Fred, for instance, does not. So please don't consider hiring people who claim to be qualified just because they've been around guns all their lives. A qualified weapons handler will not only have long experience with weapons, but experience of handling them on movie sets. If your production is located outside of California, be certain of the laws and all legal requirements required in the jurisdiction you're working in. Federal, state, and local laws pertaining to firearms and explosives are serious.

Imagine it's a big day in your shooting schedule. It's the climactic shootout in the story. There's a lot of coverage to get. Everyone has to be on their game to finish the day's work. If on his way to set, your pyro-technician or weapons handler is stopped because they rolled through a stop sign and the police officer discovers a box of detonators or a trunk full of shotguns, they may be delayed in getting to your set *if* they don't have the proper permits to possess and transport those items. It will be time consuming and expensive to deal with that screw-up.

Assuming your licensed armorer makes it to set without incident, they will demonstrate and practice a uniform safety protocol. It starts with the handling and possession of a firearm. If anyone, including the talent, *ever* picks up an operational or live firearm, it's either when they are being instructed by the armorer in its use or when the scene is being shot. There should be a run-through or rehearsal when a live weapon will be used to make sure the actors know exactly what they'll be doing with the firearm that will be loaded with blanks. So, in the words of one of Hollywood's most experienced armorers, here is what takes place.

> MIKE TRISTANO: *First of all, the guns are in the hands of anyone but us as little as possible. We will do the rehearsals or the walk-throughs and setting up the shot with a rubber gun or a replica gun. Then when we're actually ready to film the scene I walk on the set with the gun that's going to fire the blanks. The gun will be open if it's a revolver, meaning the cylinder will be out. If it's a semiautomatic or automatic, the slide will be back. So it has to be obvious to everyone that there's nothing in the gun. I walk up to the first AD and show him or her that there's nothing in the gun. Then I'll hold up the blanks and say "here are the blanks we're using, does anybody want to look at them?" If so, they can.*

I've never seen anyone actually take the armorer up on their offer, but a point is made. There's more.

> MIKE TRISTANO: *All the blanks we use are crimped, meaning that there is no paper or wax wadding in them except for shotguns. The*

only thing that's coming out of that blank is powder. That can still be dangerous because you can always get a powder burn, but there's no projectile. So I'll explain that to everybody on set.

So now there'll be another rehearsal with a real gun but empty for the actor to do a final check of everything. And only then when everybody is all set, the lighting is ready, the camera is ready, the actors' movements are set; then were going hot with a weapon.

I tell everybody how many of blanks I'm loading up. I'll tell everybody what size loads I'm using such as full load, half load, or quarter load blank, because that's going to dictate the sound everyone hears from the round and also how much flash is going to come out from the muzzle. Then I'll say, "The weapon is hot," and hand it to the actor. I'll ask him or her if he or she is comfortable with a weapon and if they have any questions about anything.

Assuming everyone feels comfortable and ready to go, you're ready to go for a take. The only other thing I would mention that pertains to safety protocol is that whenever a weapon will be discharged on a set and particularly in an indoor location or soundstage, the prop department should hand out foam earplugs for everyone on that set. The 1st AD may also announce loudly, "fire in the hole!" This is a traditional warning, with military origins, announced before any explosion to make sure everyone is aware, both near and far, to expect a loud noise. That way, no one will panic or interrupt the shot in any way because they weren't aware of what was being done on set. You don't want to hear someone scream or be startled, ruining a take because they were somehow unaware of the gun shot or explosion.

MIKE TRISTANO: *Generally any accident that has ever happened in the industry where people have been hurt or killed with blank weapons is because there was not a licensed armorer on the set. Of course we have the famous incident with Brandon Lee which was a horrific incident where they died, because the person who was handling the weapons didn't know the difference between a dummy round and a blank and how to check the cylinders and make sure everything was clear. I mean we check everything about every gun before it goes on set, while it's on set, and before we ever hand it to an actor to be used.*

One of the critical things an armorer will make sure the talent understands and executes is where to aim their firearm and from what distance that is safe. A live firearm is never aimed at another actor or crew member. It's always aimed just off-axis away from the camera and at a safe distance.

MIKE TRISTANO: *While we're setting up a shot even though it may look to an audience like the gun is pointed at another actor, it never is. It's always off angle, never pointed directly at the other actor. So that if anything was ever to come out of a gun such as a piece from a blank, which I've never seen happen, but in theory it could, it would never be pointed at the talent or the crew. The most common mistakes actors make are they point their weapon at one another or they get too close to another actor with a weapon. We've blocked out the scene, we've tried to be very meticulous about how the scene is going to play. But sometimes actors can get into a mode where they're not thinking, they're so concentrated on their performance. You find this particularly true with new actors. Veteran actors will have it down to a science.*

If the armorer sees an actor or anyone doing anything with a weapon they are concerned about, they can call cut. This is a rare event, but if there's an imminent threat due to someone mishandling a firearm, it's their duty to stop everything in its tracks to prevent a disaster.

MIKE TRISTANO: *If I see the actor doesn't have the gun in the right place, meaning it's pointed at another actor or at the crew, I will stop the scene. That very rarely happens but I could step in and call "cut." Of course I let people know in advance that I can do that, but it rarely happens. We are very meticulous about this. I can't say what the experience is for other armorers in terms of how often they have to step in and stop a shot because of safety. We run through the drill to make sure everybody knows what's going to happen. We always leave a certain amount of leeway. We might tell an actor they have a range of about a foot where they can aim, but it might really be three. I always leave room for error.*

So the director calls action and the scene is played out. When the director calls "cut," everyone on set should freeze while the armorer steps onto the set and takes possession of the weapons. The firearm is checked by the armorer to make sure there are no blanks still in it and he will then declare, "Okay, the weapon's clear." When the weapon is called for again, the protocol is repeated. Firearms should never be out of the possession of the armorer when not being filmed. They are literally placed in locked containers when not in use in a scene.

MIKE TRISTANO: *After a take with a real weapon I step in and I take the weapon from the actor. It's never left on the set. It never goes to a dressing room or anywhere else. The weapon always comes to set and leaves the set with us. Not so with the rubbers or the replicas, but the real guns, yes. Before an actor leaves a set usually the prop master will take the replica weapon from the actor. They won't go to lunch with it. There are a few rare times when I have let actors leave the set with replicas such as in Westerns. They like to keep the guns in their holsters and get the feel of the weapon. But I make an announcement. I say "the actors have replica weapons, beware!" You don't want anybody to ever feel uncomfortable on a set or have any possible safety issue.*

Unsupervised firearms in the hands of bored, agitated, or untrained actors or crew members have led to disaster. No shortcuts. No unlicensed or inexperienced gun handlers should ever, ever be allowed near your set to perform the duties of a licensed and experienced movie armorer. When a replica firearm is all that is required, the prop master on your production can be designated to be in charge of the weapon, if they are experienced and qualified.

While safety can't be stressed enough, there are a few other very vital roles armorers play. They are historical authorities on the weapons they work with. It's an important part of their job to know the history of weapons whether they be firearms or other types of weapons. Armorers are historical authorities as well as technical consultants. Not only is historical accuracy a point of personal pride, but armorers are keenly aware that there are many in the audience who know the difference between accurate and bogus.

MIKE TRISTANO: *I work on a lot of productions where it's important to know which firearms are appropriate for the time. For example I do a lot of Westerns or movies that take place in the flintlock era like the American Revolution or French and Indian War. The weapons have to be accurate for the times.*

To those people who recognize historical correctness, any misstep can diminish the whole entertainment value of the movie. It sends the message that the filmmakers aren't really serious about telling a story in a truthful way.

MIKE TRISTANO: *Everything we do is period correct. If someone wants to use a Colt Peacemaker in the Civil War I'm going to tell them they weren't around then. If we do that and there's people who have knowledge of these things, they're going to know no one did their homework. So I'm a real stickler when it comes to historical accuracy.*

Most directors, particularly the ones who have a particular passion for stories in which weapons are common, will insist on historical accuracy. But any director or actor who's passionate about doing their best work need not be knowledgeable about weapons or for that matter any special activity. That's why there are technical consultants aplenty who bring their expertise to bear on a movie's authenticity. Armorers have the background and knowledge to educate, consult, and serve as historical references for directors and actors. They are a wealth of valuable information that will support the efforts of the filmmakers.

> MIKE TRISTANO:　*Most directors really appreciate it when you stick to the historical accuracy. Sometimes when directors don't care, I will mention it to the actor, because the actors are even more sticklers for accuracy. This is true especially if it's a name. They want to be historically accurate. They care about how they look and that everything is correct. Most directors are of course concerned with historical accuracy, but the ones that aren't, usually can be brought around by me telling them what's going to look best for camera.*

So not only do the weapons have to be historically accurate, but the way in which they're portrayed must also reflect authenticity. The actor has to be able to "sell" an audience that they are using a firearm as it was actually used back in the day. Actors quite properly take this very seriously. So, since most actors are not familiar with the use of firearms and particularly unfamiliar with historical pieces, they must be trained by experts such as your armorer. Depending on your budget, the armorer can spend a great deal of time before principal photography begins with your talent. They can go to a gun range and get the feel of the real thing.

> MIKE TRISTANO:　*I love to get the actors out and train them on the weaponry especially when there's a role where the weapons are a significant part of what they're doing. What you'll find when you're doing Westerns or a movie from the colonial period is that weapons played a big part in the lives of those characters. I start the actors .off by doing live fire with them. That way they know what it's like to fire a real weapon with a real round in it. The difference that makes is tremendous because on set we're using blanks and blanks don't have any recoil. So the actor has to compensate for that. If he's firing a musket or an 1873 Trapdoor Springfield that was the weapon of choice for the US cavalry, those weapons had a big kick and of course with blanks, they don't. But an actor can and should have the feel for that*

because they fired the real rounds in prep. Another commonly used firearm is the lever-action Winchester that you've seen in so many Westerns. If an actor isn't used to that lever action, it's important that they get trained on it. There's a very specific action when you're firing and reloading that rifle.

As you will always be advised by seasoned professionals, rely on your team. Surround yourself with filmmakers who can elevate your vision. You can't do it all or know it all. In this challenging area of firearms, that goes double.

MIKE TRISTANO: *I always say to young filmmakers, "Don't be a control freak." When I was directing low-budget features, at first I wanted to control everything, but I had some experience in other areas of production and I let the experts do their job. If you hire a DP, you're not going to tell him how to shoot the movie. You may tell him what you're looking for, but then he's going to get it for you. Same with us. If you want a gunfight, I'll sit down with you and tell you how to make it good.*

Just for the record, and this doesn't come up very often, the only time an actor cannot work with a live firearm is if they're a convicted felon. Although this is a relatively uncommon situation, don't be surprised if it comes up or is revealed. But it's worth mentioning in case it ever comes up. Armorers are well aware of this fact. The only option for them is to use replicas.

I hope I've conveyed the seriousness of everything described in this book regarding most stunts and special effects. But the gun thing poses special challenges. This comes under the heading of "if you can't do it right, don't do it at all." The stakes are too high. To someone who hasn't had the experience of using weapons on set and dealing with these professionals, you might feel the use of firearms is beyond your reach. But there are usually terrific and experienced pros who can help you within your means, depending on your location. Do your homework. You can find them using the methods described often in this book. The culture in many segments of the movie industry, particularly stunts, special effects, and weapons, is to be generous with young filmmakers and those who have limited resources, whenever possible.

MIKE TRISTANO: *We get involved with low-budget filmmakers more often than not. There's times when I get involved and if only to help tell people what kind of permitting they need. We help filmmakers figure out how to save money, we even help them figure out how to save money when working with us. We also work with them by giving them a lot of free stuff. When people work with us, they get the same quality of work they could get at any level of the business, so it elevates the production value of what they're doing. If you're [a] young producer or director and have the right person there to handle them, there's nothing to be afraid of. They will give you an immense amount of production value.*

If you're wondering why this industry seems unusually generous by nature, I'll tell you it has a practical side as well. Many experienced technicians and craftsmen in the business wisely think long term. The filmmaker just out of school with a few bucks to make a movie may someday be the major director making blockbusters for studios. It's a wise investment.

MIKE TRISTANO: *The best advice I can give to any young filmmaker who needs to use weapons in their movie is to give us a call, then sit down with us, and let's talk it through. You may be able to do more than you think. All the guys like me in stunts weaponry and other specialties feel the same way to just sit down with you and try to help you figure it out see if they can help to give you the most bang for the buck. Sometimes you'll be amazed at how much you can really put up on the screen. I have so many people I've met when they were just film students or doing the first feature or even a short film. And now that they're working on big features, they're still working with us.*

There is a very obvious question we all ask when it comes to how to capture the excitement and danger of firearms. There is the digital option. Anyone can find online how-to videos that instruct filmmakers how to recreate muzzle flashes, smoke that comes out of a gun barrel, and explosions exclusively generated in a computer. You've all probably seen Robert Rodriguez's "Ten Minute Film School," where he demonstrates various movie production and postproduction techniques on the cheap. You can judge for yourself how well those methods work in his movies. Other filmmakers and TV producers utilize those methods as well with varying degrees of success, depending on your standards of realism. Sometimes CGI is used to enhance live fire and smoke, rather than replace it. This may be your only option because you simply can't afford to do it the traditional way, no matter how big a break you get from experienced weapons experts. This of course is a reality that many of you who are starting out making micro- and low-budget movies must deal with. Hopefully on your next production you can go with the real deal.

There are, by the way, a few low-cost ways of creating some effects that armorers can create sometimes, such as dust hits and blood hits that are non-pyrotechnic. Dust hits are when puffs of dust kick up on the ground to suggest that bullets are tearing into the ground. They are actually capsules filled with Fuller's earth that are shot from a compressed-air gun. Blood hits that were developed by Mike Tristano are also a non-pyrotechnic blood effect. They're also fired from a compressed-air pellet gun. They're almost like a paintball. They put a protective plate under the wardrobe of the talent, and then from right off-camera they fire the little capsule from a distance of about ten feet. It hits the actor so they can react to something like an explosive squib does. It breaks on the plate and it looks like they've been shot. It's fast and it's non-pyrotechnic, so there's no requirement for a special effects permit to be pulled and all the other things the state of California insists on, such as a licensed pyro-technician, fire marshal, water trucks, and various other safety measures that cost a lot of money.

It's understandable if you have really made the effort to see if you can afford the services of an armorer and you just don't have the funds. If that's the way it has to be, then that's the way it has to be. But know what you're getting. Understand the results you can expect before committing to that approach.

It may sound odd to say "there ain't nothing like the real thing," because an armor dramatically brings the illusion of a very dangerous event to the screen. This isn't to say creating the illusion is not without its risk, but in the hands of the professional, it is a relatively safe process. But there are some small but important details that contribute to the authenticity and excitement of firearms that the digital options are challenged to deliver. There is the matter of an actor's performance and of the realistic way in which a weapon operates that provides for the accurate recreation of a weapon firing. There is a kick or recoil to a gun that is loaded with blanks. The benefit to the actor is clear. There's the cascade of casings that fly from a semiautomatic rifle and clang to the ground, another realistic touch that contributes to the realism of the scene. These touches can enhance an actor's performance.

MIKE TRISTANO: *There are shows that specifically use only replica weapons. They feel they can put the flash in in postproduction. I think that's a naïve opinion, because there's a lot more going on with a weapon than the flash coming out of the muzzle. Let's say, for instance, a semiautomatic weapon fires. When it fires the slide goes back. The shell ejects out the right side and the slide goes back. So there's a lot of action with the weapon itself. There's a lot of moving parts. I think most people can tell when the gunfire is fake, when the flash is put in in post. But that's the way some people do it and we have no problem supplying them with replica weapons if that's the way they want to go. You get a lot of actors who won't go along with that at all. They want no part of that. To them, it's hindering their performance when they're not using a real firearm. I can always tell the difference between a real and digital discharge of a gun. But I'm not the average audience, maybe to some people there's no difference.*

If you have a project where the actors are not that into the guns, they'll be accepting of it. But I've been called on shows and an actor will show up on set, the prop guy hands him a replica gun, and they'll say, "What the hell is this? I'm not going to work with this!" I've had that happen many times. There's a lot of actors who know a lot about weaponry.

It's all about reconstructing dangerous or exciting events in the most convincing ways possible that keep an audience riveted to their seats. The accumulation of choices, techniques, approaches, and applications of detail adds up to an overall sense of truthfulness and therefore effective storytelling. A weak decision or poor choice here or there can undermine the overall authenticity of a movie or may not do much damage after all, but the collection of choices does add up to profoundly impressing an audience. A filmmaker must always strive to make each and every decision as if it were the only one that matters.

Swords and Knives

All the precautions I have described in the previous section on firearms should, without reservation, be followed when using sharp objects such as knives and swords. Here too, these sharp metal objects can do a lot of damage if not used carefully. Sword masters carry a wide assortment of replicas and rubber or plastic duplications of knives, swords, or even more exotic weapons about which they have a deep historical knowledge.

> DAN SPEAKER: *Sometimes people think sword masters are just teaching but sword master is traditionally the term that is used for the person who oversees the use of swords and knives on set and in a production.*

Sometimes they just need to watch all the sharp objects to ensure that they are used properly and appropriately. That is part of their job unless a prop person is on set to handle that assignment. Weapons on a set can cause the most horrific accidents or relatively minor ones. They must always be controlled and their use supervised by qualified crew members. The director Martha Coolidge recalls an accident on the set of her movie *The Prince & Me*, which was shot on location in Europe. She was rehearsing a scene that called for the actor to make a sandwich. The prop man, a local hire, gave the actor a real knife to cut the sandwich in half for the rehearsal. It was an emotional scene, and the actor was distracted and nearly cut his own finger off cutting the sandwich! The shoot was delayed six hours while the actor was taken to a hospital. The fact that he returned with a big bandage on his hand didn't help matters either. It wasn't the actor's fault. It was the inexperienced prop man who made a mistake.

Even though you might find armorers who have an inventory as well, the specialists are the sword masters. They've dedicated their careers to bringing swords, knives, and their many uses to the screen realistically and accurately. Like armorers, these pros not only know their weapons but also are great sources of accurate historical information on those weapons. They know which weapons belong in which time period and geographic location. They often know the chronology of their development and use as well as their place of importance in history. They know how they were used and in what situations. These guys are seriously educated about their weapons. Filmmakers often rely on their advice and knowledge to ensure the authenticity of their movie.

> DAN SPEAKER: *Screenwriters will call us for a consultation just for the writing of some action scene. That doesn't necessarily get us the job later when they make the movie, but sometimes it does.*

The kind of weapons expert you want to work with is the one who takes the word "expert" seriously: the ones who have done exhaustive research and have deep reservoirs of knowledge. They bring a realistic perspective to your story and add a patina of authenticity that serves to transport an audience to the world you are depicting. Truth and realism do that, and combined with inventive and exciting action using swords and knives, can create memorable movie moments.

> DAN SPEAKER: *You don't just take fencing technique and make it bigger, you actually look at these historical texts which are still available. You can go to the woodcuts or reproductions of hand drawings from historical times and get an understanding of what sword fighting might've looked like. So often I go through the texts that sometimes I have to get translated. You can actually figure out where and how those techniques I read about came into modern fencing and how that could give a flavor of the time period you're trying to depict.*

Along with your stunt coordinator or fight choreographer, your sword master will help plan the appropriate use and mix of real and fake weapons to ensure that the audience experiences the seamless execution of what appears to be the very dangerous use of a knife or sword. As with other members of the action team, your sword master has to be on board with the vision. He has to be making the same movie as the rest of the team.

> DAN SPEAKER: *So when we get to work with an actor, the first thing we look at is what is the vision of the writer and director? What is it they want? Do they want an authentic flavor of history or do they want something that's out there, less tied to realism? Are they going to do a* Three Musketeers *with really traditional rapiers and daggers or they going to do sort of vaudeville Hollywood swashbuckling? We did a "brat pack"* Three Musketeers *with Charlie Sheen and Keifer Sutherland that wasn't historical at all. But they have things they call rapiers and they're waving them around in the air and it's kind of fun.*

A sword master is also qualified to design a combat situation in which their weapons are to be used, such as a sword fight or any confrontation that uses blades exclusively or in part. They are coordinators, choreographers, stunt performers, historical authorities, and so much more. They understand how swords or blades were or are used with historical accuracy. Unless otherwise requested by the director, they will design a fight or incident in which a weapon with a blade is used that reflects how people fought when the story takes place.

> JAN BRYANT: *We did* Master and Commander *with Russell Crowe. We designed all the fights, trained all the people, we created all of the action in all the scenes where there were battles. A lot of people said, "We didn't see your work. Where was the sword fight?"*

Sometimes the best work from your action specialists is invisible or at least unobtrusive. Often, that means your story is working so well, the action so organic, that the audience isn't taken out of the movie.

> DAN SPEAKER: *That whole battle scene had cutlasses, dagger, and pistols. There were head-butts. We hit somebody with a bucket. We figured out how all of those elements came together in a single fight. That's why sometimes we use the term fight coordinator or fight choreographer because our job goes beyond just the use of weapons specifically. We design and supervise the use of various weapons as a part of a more general kind of fight. But in my capacity as sword master, those fights will contain swords or knives.*

Training

Some actors come to the job with a little experience and training in stage combat, which includes fencing and swordplay. It's part of a classical acting training regime. Whether actors are exposed to swordplay in college or beyond, it's not unusual to see that skill listed on the bottom of a resume along with other specialized areas of training and skill. Whether they have acquired enough skill from that training is a big question: usually not. But it's a place to start. If an actor's character requires any specialized skill, whether it be hitting a baseball or engaging in a duel with sabers, intensive training over a period of time is required. Call it a boot camp or extended rehearsals: you're asking an actor to appear to be proficient, superior even, in the use of a pretty esoteric exercise. That takes time and skill on the part of the director and his team to create the illusion of mastery.

DAN SPEAKER: *Training really focuses on making sure people understand that they have enough training in their muscles so that when they get into that wonderful adrenaline rush when the director says action, they don't lose control and really hurt someone.*

Like any physical task or skill, practice makes perfect. Muscle memory, or the body's ability to enable the reiteration of an action without conscious thought by repetition over time, is heavily relied on to train actors in a specific and limited action. If someone repeats an action hundreds of times, it sticks. It's like "they" say, it's like riding a bike: you never forget. Teaching actors to use a sword or knife relies heavily on this principle.

DAN SPEAKER: *We worked with a young actor on Spielberg's* Hook *a long time ago. He was one of the Lost Boys. We hadn't seen him for 20 years and we got back together with him on a new project. Because we had trained him so much on Hook, he was able to pick up a sword and go through the same choreography we did 20 years ago without too much rehearsal.*

Learning the fundamentals in any skilled action is a sensible approach to teaching and training. Time will dictate how much of the fundamentals you have time to teach. The best trainers and teachers greatly value fundamentals. A strong foundation is a boost to more nuanced learning. We learn the scales before we play melodies on a musical instrument. Depending on the tone of your story, authenticity may be of varying importance. The use of martial arts-style moves in *Master and Commander* would've been ridiculous and taken us out of the movie. But approaching sword fights or the use of knives without being restricted by historical issues can make for pretty cool or groundbreaking fights. It's all about what's appropriate for your specific story.

DAN SPEAKER: *A lot of people get trained in a method we call "cool move." They learned some cool moves and some choreography. But that's all they know. That's their little thing they learned by rote. It's a very limited way of approaching their training. They can extrapolate a whole sequence out of those few little tricks. But when we train actors our way, it allows us to see what their bodies look good doing. So then we can organically make the choreography work for their scenes not imposing what they're not comfortable with and won't look good doing.*

Cool moves have their place, but what Dan Speaker is referring to and reminding us of is that cool moves can be fun and entertaining, but limited, if not informed, by a strong foundation of the art and practice of swordsmanship. Ideas that have little foundation tend to get repetitive and contrived looking. It's hard to be creative and go outside the box if you were never in the box. It can become a random series of moves or an expression of sheer energy, without the style that comes from the basics. After all, as visual storytellers, aren't we concerned with style?

Choreographing on set

DAN SPEAKER: *There's an old saying, "They hire you for your expertise to do the job and defy you to accomplish it."*

Long rehearsal periods are often unaffordable or impossible to schedule. If an actor is wrapping a job two days before they're to start work on yours, how do you prepare them to look good in a sword fight? How do you have the time to teach the basics? You may not think you can afford to dedicate any time to anything but the choreography. It's like other protocols in filmmaking: sometimes you have to take a reasonable amount of time to prepare to shoot a shot that counts. When you don't block a scene for the camera and the shot is out of focus, you've wasted time and resources. Maybe you should've taken the time to block and rehearse the shot for the camera, so the assistant could be sure of his focus marks. Maybe your actor with a sword in his hand should understand a few of the principles behind fighting with a sword before trying to imitate their version of a sword fight. When something is not authentic or real, and I've said this repeatedly I know, and it's expected to look real, you lose your audience for at least a moment, maybe longer. Maybe for good.

DAN SPEAKER: *When we get onto a TV show, we may only have an hour for the entire job. Once we were called in by a really big-name stunt coordinator he said, "Ok, I've got this pilot I'm doing and I want you choreograph this big fight. I'm letting you have doubles, but I'm having you choreograph this big fight with the lead actress and another guy. She's never done anything like this before, so just come in here and we'll put together a fight. Ok?" We can do this, but we always start with showing people the basics. When the stunt coordinator asked if we couldn't just show them a piece of choreography? I said, "Well I could, but give me 15 minutes to show her the basics and I swear it'll make everything so much easier in the long run." After 15 minutes, she was able to do enough of the routine that on the day, she was able to go with it or any of changes that had been made, because she understood the basics behind the specific choreography. So when there are changes in choreography, if an actor understands the theory behind it, it makes the them ready to adapt to any changes that might be thrown their way.*

When it comes to a physical action your talent is not comfortable with, do yourself and your story a favor: find a way to give them some amount of training and practice for as long as possible before the shots go before the camera. It will pay big dividends. If you can't afford it or it's practically impossible, understand the challenges you will face with an unprepared actor.

Another benefit of lead time for an actor to prepare a sword fight is not only teaching moves and technique, but also teaching those things in the context of the actors' specific physical capabilities and proclivities. Some actors are more flexible than others, and that can be used in the imagining of a fight. One of Hollywood's biggest stars, Burt Lancaster (look him up if you've never heard of him), known for his athleticism, played many roles that took advantage of that. Lancaster's pre-Hollywood years included being a gymnast and a circus acrobat. Guess what kind of roles he was asked to play. One example was the *Crimson Pirate* (1952), where Lancaster's action sequences were choreographed to utilize his acrobatic skills and way of moving. His sword fights were high energy and gravity defying. Many other roles in his career, and, let's face it, many, many other actors' careers, capitalized on their specific physical abilities and unique physical manner.

JAN BRYANT: *We've seen choreographers come in with their list and try to give it to the actors and the actors can't do it the way they want him to and then they get mad at the actors! That's a real clue when you're teaching people about what to look for in a fight choreographer if they can't work with their actors or their director, then that's a problem with the choreographer and not so much with anyone else. Choreographers should be flexible enough to go with whatever looks good for the actors and their special abilities and not be stuck on their list of moves they've come up with on their own. That's if they have the methodology. We've come across the situation quite a bit.*

DAN SPEAKER: *All too often coordinators want to see it right then, right there, right now. So under that kind of pressure the coordinators will sometimes take their lists of moves, composed in their head or even with previz that they did with other expert stunt people doing it. They want to put that on top of the actors and they've never even met these actors and they will blame the actors if they can't do it. In those cases you'll find sometimes they have to take those actors' faces*

using green screen and put them on the bodies of stunt performers.
Sometimes coordinators will come on set and say, "This is my cool
move and I want the actors to perform it." It may not look good on
those actors. That's why sometimes you see a scene with quick
cutting and you only see shoulders because someone has come in
and said this is my idea for the fight and if it doesn't work out, they
have to shoot it so tight and cut so quickly, you can't really see the
fight itself. It hides a very bad action. We like to pull back. It's the
whole Fred Astaire way of seeing them head to foot you. Let's see the
action, because it's telling the story, it's dialogue without words. It's
"movement dialogue." All the good people in the business we know
work that way.

When a knife or sword has to be used in a scene, you have to be concerned
with it doing damage. This is really no different than the precautions and
protocols used when firearms are part of the story. Depending on the shot,
you may have to use a gun that fires or you may need to use a rubber replica
so you don't knock your star's expensive bridgework into the next county
when struck by the butt of a rifle. Weapons that in real life have sharp edges
need to be respected as well. A sword made of a lightweight alloy can do
damage. It may cut, or the sheer weight of it can cause bodily harm. When it
comes to swordplay, as with other forms of stunt work, there will be risk, but
the word *risk* should always be accompanied by the word *reasonable*. Sword
masters understand how to lessen risk by using the right instruments.

When a sword is being shot in wider angles or is being used in a way that
can hurt someone, safe replicas are often substituted. When close-ups are
being shot, the real thing or at least the more authentic-looking replica may
replace the safer version.

> JAN BRYANT: *A sharp weapon should never be used in my opinion,*
> *unless in an insert shot. It's my overall policy. It's not an industry-wide*
> *rule, but I think it's a good one. There's no reason to have a sharp*
> *weapon on set. Maybe if you're doing an insert shot such as when you*
> *need to feature the edge of the blade to show how sharp it is or to*
> *show it cutting something, you can justify it.*

There always comes the time to decide whether to use your principal cast
or stunt doubles to shoot a scene using swords or knives. Coverage and
camera angles are designed to feature an actor who can deliver a great
performance using a sword or hide the fact that he can't. Also, coverage and
camera angles are chosen when there are two or more versions of the same

weapon, one being substituted for the other at appropriate times to create the illusion of reality while keeping things safe. When you constantly cut back and forth between shots that feature the principal actor and their stunt double or between the more accurate weapon and the rubber one, that illusion is perfected.

Dan Speaker makes a few good points that will help inform sword masters or directors as to when to use doubles and when to go with your cast. Safety is of course paramount. Competence, believability, all are critically important. But there're a few other issues, such as avoiding a competitive dynamic between your cast members, that must also be considered.

DAN SPEAKER: *Of course we use stunt doubles when the principal actor can't do the action convincingly. We also like to use stunt doubles pointing the camera, over their shoulder, towards the real actor, in order to give them the comfort factor of working with someone who's better than they are at using the weapon. And then we turn around and use a double for that actor and shoot over their shoulder, towards the other actor in the combat scene. That also avoids a competition from arising between the two actors. The two actors are never actually fighting each other in the intense coverage, but instead are fighting a stunt double who is more in control of the scene. If you have two actors who are the leads and they get into a competitive situation, it can actually destroy the look of a fight completely. We like to have the two leads who are fighting in the scenes, to rehearse and feel comfortable with each other, but for the close intense shots, we like them to be able to hack away at the stunt guy; that looks great in a shot.*

I've detailed the step-by-step protocols for firearms that are industry-wide. Interestingly enough, and without much in the way of a good reason why, no such protocols exist when it comes to swords and knives. I'm not saying caution is not observed or that crews on a particular production don't have their own protocols when sharp weapons are being used. But a standard has not been adopted by the industry. Hopefully, common sense prevails when sharp objects are being used, but we all know, that can't be counted on.

Many productions don't hire sword masters simply because a sword or knife is being used on a set. This isn't automatically a wrong-headed thing. Sword masters are a must when it comes to combat using those weapons. Stunt coordinators, in their capacity as the central, responsible person on a production for action scenes, know they need that specific skill set to pull off a good sword fight. But if a sword or knife plays a passive part in the story, if it's seen but not used against another character, the prop master is trained and able to acquire and maintain swords and knives, viewing them simply as props. Even when sword masters are used, prop masters are often appointed to acquire or even manufacture the weapons. If a knife is used in a story to depict a simple stabbing or slashing, the prop master may be all you need to handle the situation. The well-trained prop master will have a healthy respect for anything that can cut or puncture. The less experienced ones can cause a high level of risk than is necessary by not taking proper safety precautions, controlling a sharp weapon, or choosing a weapon that is inappropriately dangerous in the hands of inexperienced cast members.

> DAN SPEAKER: *I've done some big productions where a prop person has handed me a very sharp weapon to use and I asked where the ones I made up were. Mine would not cut anyone.*
>
> *People tend to regard weapons such as swords and knives as sort of quaint and not that dangerous. So there really is no formal protocol in the handling of those type weapons on a set. The protocol in which a weapon is immediately returned to the prop table when not being shot is supposed to be enforced. But sometimes we've heard of prop people who would give an actor a weapon that are personal props, to hold onto or carry around at all times. Sadly, there's no protocol as to when you can use a sharp or blunted weapon.*

There are numerous versions and functions of prop knives. For instance, there is the retractable knife. The blade is spring-loaded into the handle, so that when it's pressed against a body, it appears to penetrate the skin but has actually retracted into the handle. There are knives that have small reservoirs of stage blood on one side of the blade (the side hidden from the camera) that can be drawn across an actor's throat or any surface, leaving a trail of "blood." Prop masters are very familiar with and are qualified to use these kinds of prop weapons.

The main idea when using weapons with sharp edges or at least that appear to have sharp edges is, once again, to get an expert to consult and supervise their use on your production. Martial arts weapons and other exotic arms are certainly as formidable as knives and swords. Take nothing for granted when it comes to safety.

Horses and Livestock

Making a cowboy movie? The hero is introduced when his gallant steed gallops into frame, rears up on its hind legs as he doffs his Stetson to the sheriff's lovely daughter. That's a signature moment of the classic cowboy move. How about a drama with the rodeo as its backdrop? You'll need a bull or two to give your character the roughest ride of his life. I mentioned early in this book that the origins of stunt work lie in its connection to our Wild West history. America's expansion West gave birth to a breed of pioneers and settlers that learned and perfected horseback riding and herding skills as a means of survival. Cows and sheep were raised in vast numbers to feed and clothe a rapidly expanding nation. Horses were raised to facilitate the management of livestock. Horses could carry their riders great distances to accompany and direct huge herds or could be nimble enough to chase errant cattle and redirect them to rejoin the herd. The skills horsemen gained from these necessary activities eventually transcended into entertainment. As part of traveling Wild West shows and rodeos, riders displayed the skill and derring-do working cowboys had acquired in their line of work. Technology pushed this form of entertainment onto early movie screens when the Western genre of movies was nascent. Real cowboys came to Hollywoodland, excited by this new medium, sensing its importance in the world and their potential importance to this expanding industry. There were jobs aplenty for horseback riders. Even today, many of the cowboys who perform in movies as stunt performers and actors are drawn to Hollywood by the excitement of performing dangerous feats of horseback riding skill, for some pretty good money.

> DALE GIBSON: *We left Kentucky and came West. My mother was a trick rider. I grew up with horses and I began performing in rodeos when I was 11.*

Quite a few horseback riders are second- and third-generation cowboys who grew up riding on ranches their families worked or in rodeos. The skills they acquired they didn't learn in any school. They learned from doing, in real-life situations and/or by competing for many years with other riders whose lives were all about horses and cattle. Not unlike most of us who grew up playing football in Pop Warner and Little League before moving on to high school and college sports, many riders grew up competing in junior rodeos and then college rodeos. Their experience runs deep. Their skills are developed at a very young age.

The best stunt drivers grew up in Chevys and Dodges. Cowboys grew up around mustangs and bulls. The people who put their lives on the line steering fast cars or riding powerful animals rarely pick those skills up later in life. It's a lifestyle they grow up in. The cowboys are truly a special breed. Rough and ready. They are known to be the ones who volunteer to do the stunts many of their compadres consider foolhardy.

> DALE GIBSON: *We're called cowboys. Most of us came from a rodeoing background. It's a good background, the rodeo thing. You know when it's time to go and step up to the line. You can't overthink it too much. When they yell action, it's time to go.*

Try galloping full speed on a horse and backflip off, hitting the hard ground with a giant thud. It's one of the most spectacular and dangerous stunts there is. Not many are qualified to try it. But to many of these horsemen and women, it's what gets them up in the morning.

> DALE GIBSON: *We hit the ground pretty hard, but after you've been riding bulls for all those years, to hit the ground without something about to come back and kill you, makes stunts pretty easy.*

It's the cowboy credo to be ready, willing, and able. Directors know they can count on the cowboy stunt person to take the greatest risk.

> DALE GIBSON: *My trick riding experience came in very handy on Hidalgo. Viggo Mortensen's character had to shoot two Bedouins off their horses and I was one of those two guys. They wanted us to do backflips. They're called back-overs. We had to ride full blast at Viggo and fall backwards off our horses. There were 15 or 20 stunt guys standing around and the producers asked, does anybody want to do this? It was something that I did all the time but nobody else really volunteered.*

If your production calls for horses and other livestock, choosing the right stunt coordinator is as important a decision as any you'll make. Of course this is also true if your show has such specific action dominating the story such as cars or martial arts. You need the right person for the job. They will intuitively understand not only the mechanics of the genre but also the spirit or ethos of it. This informs your story with authenticity, which every good movie strives for and achieves to a great degree. It gotta look real for the audience to connect. If it looks phony or untruthful in any way, your audience may be lost and never come back from the refreshment stand. Your cowboy stunt coordinator is your key creative partner if your movie is predominantly a Western or utilizes horses or livestock. Same rules apply to hiring the cowboy coordinator as the car and fight guys. You look at their resumes and their reels and check on their references. Assuming those all check out, it then becomes a matter of chemistry. Do your personalities mesh? Is it easy to communicate? Does the coordinator seem ready to go the extra mile to deliver your vision? Does he have creative tendencies, able to come up with workable solutions to production challenges?

Your cowboy coordinator knows all the other cowboys in the movie business. The top ones know who specializes in what kind of stunts, allowing the cast of riders to perfectly fulfill the needs of your story. You need someone to do the back-over or get dragged behind a horse? Maybe you need someone who can take a tumble with a 1000-pound horse? There are stunt riders who can do many things or specialize in a few actions that they may actually be famous for. Your coordinator is your guide through this world that, to many of us, is quite foreign.

One of the important members of the team is the wrangler. We've all heard that word, but do we really understand what a wrangler does? It's pretty straightforward. The wrangler is the person who brings and cares for the horses or other animals on your show. The wrangler may own horses or steers or be able to resource them from other wranglers and trainers who are in the business of supplying animals to the movie industry.

DALE GIBSON: *On features, your stunt coordinator and your wrangler work very closely together. Stunt people depend on the horses so much, hoping the wrangler brings in the best horses there are. If you're the director and you hire me and there's a lot of horse work, my question to you would be, who's the animal wrangler? If you have somebody in mind, I want to sit down and talk with him. Or they may ask who I like to use.*

There is no shortage of trained animals for any and all purposes in the production of movies and television. Furthermore, if there is an action an animal must perform on camera that is specific to the story, the trainer/owners of those animals will teach them that action in advance of the shooting. Wranglers know all these folks and their stables. They know which horses are trained to rear up on their hind legs or which ones will gallop through a burning building.

> DALE GIBSON: *There are movie horses out there who know where the camera is. I rode horses on* Natural Born Killers *where Oliver Stone used a dust machine. It was so smoky and dusty that I couldn't see, but I knew my horse could. I literally ran him towards camera and reared him up and fell off my horse. When they yelled "cut" and the dust cleared, I was on my mark.*

The wrangler will be responsible for getting the animals to the set or location and then feeding and housing them. They will prepare a budget that identifies all those costs.

> DALE GIBSON: *Horses cost about $75 a day for standard horse just for walking around. The "cast" horse that your lead actors will use is going to be about $150 a day, rearing horse will be around $300 a day. It cracks me up because people say Westerns are so hard to do. Those prices aren't really much. If you have a show with 10 cars, you pay the same price as you pay for 10 horses. You have wrangler, sure. But you also have people who have to handle the cars.*

Horses and other animals are actually cast for specific abilities. They are trained to do amazingly specific actions. Directors are often very surprised that they can have a bucking bronco or bull perform a particular action, take after take, with consistency.

> DALE GIBSON: *Leslie Dektor, who won a lot of commercial awards, wanted me to do a Dr. Pepper commercial with bull riding. I said, "What do you want the bull to do?" He looked at me and said, "Do? I just want him to buck." I said, "Do you want him to buck left or do you want him to buck to the right? How do you want to set up your shot?" It never occurred to him that I would bring him a bull that I would know what it will do. I got two bulls that matched each other that when they came out of the gate, they would circle to the left. I would ride them for four or five jumps and then jump off. If I didn't know what he wanted, if I had gotten bulls that circled to the right, when they were set up on the left, we would have been chasing shots all day. You really need to know what your animal counterparts are going to do. You bring in the right ones.*

>   *On* The Client List, *I brought in five bulls. They had a casting session and picked out the one they wanted. The director just wanted a bull he thought looked right. He didn't care about anything else. I said, "You want a bull that does this, this, or this?" He said he had no idea he had those options. I said, "That's what you pay me for."*

There are so many good wranglers out there who have horses that can do anything. If you need someone to ride up and rear a horse for a hero shot like the Lone Ranger, but you want the horse to be black, we'll go find one. They're out there. A good wrangler can find anything. If you want a pinto that walks backward or a palomino that can stop on a dime, they can be found. Just communicate that requirement through your script and directly with your stunt coordinator. Let them tell you that that horse can't be found. Odds are, it can. The wrangler will set up the casting session in which you can see the animals and see what they can do. There's always the option of training a horse to perform specific actions that matches any physical requirements, if given enough time in advance.

>   DALE GIBSON: *There's a lot of great horses with great reputations in the movie business. You can rely on them and their expertise. Some of the great falling horses, like Twister, are famous for what they do. And they will do it. I got cast on a commercial one time. They said, "Wow you can ride a rearing horse." I said, "Yes and I have a great rearing horse and we can use him." They said they had a horse guy and wanted me to ride his rearing horse. "He's a great horse. Don't worry." I got there on the day and it wasn't a rearing horse at all. It was some guy's white horse that had no idea how to rear up. They were looking at me and asking why couldn't I make it rear up? I said, "I don't know. Why can't I make you pole vault?" We had to redo the scene.*

The wrangler is responsible for that part of your budget that pertains to the animals needed for your show. Your coordinator will figure out the human side of the budget related to horse and animal work. The wrangler will cost out and make sure the animals are transported to and from the set, housed, and fed. Horses and animals all have their rates: day or weekly. They are of course determined by the specificity and degree of difficulty of the actions they can perform. Interestingly enough, the cost of horses is not much different than the cost of cars. You just have horses instead of cars. You have riders instead of drivers, wranglers instead of transportation and special effects personnel. The comparisons are pretty accurate. Approximate rates for the services of a walking-around horse are about $75 a day, a specific horse cast for a featured part in the movie is about $150 a day, and horses who do tricks or have special training, maybe $300 a day.

As I've made abundantly clear, when you have big, fast-moving objects working in front of the camera such as a car or a horse, there's a significant degree of danger that must be respected. Experts are required to not only execute but also maintain safe working conditions. Cars can be dangerous, so can horses and cattle. But the difference between the animate and inanimate is the living character: the 1000-pound horse or steer has a brain. They may not be all that smart, but they have a mind of their own, and that poses an extra dimension of risk than does a car that only reacts when and how a human controls it. Cars don't decide to balk at a stunt. Horses might. Horses used in movies are trained not only to perform certain actions or tricks but also to do so in a production environment surrounded by lots of people, vehicles, equipment, bright lights, etc. This adds to their reliability and safety, particularly compared to horses with no on-camera experience.

Lots of actors think they're pretty good at driving a car fast and maneuvering it in exciting ways, and maybe they are. Often, however, in their passion and commitment to their craft, actors overestimate their abilities to control a powerful car at high speeds. The men and women who are stunt and precision drivers live in and have grown up in that world of fast cars. It's not often that a great stunt driver picked up their skills later in life. So when your lead actors tell you they can ride with the best cowboys around or at least well enough to look authentic, take that with a large grain of salt. Have the actor tested by the professional riders or coordinator. They not only have to ride well and safely, but may also be required to act as they ride. It's very likely that your actors can perform some basic riding or they may be able to get there with some advance training by one of your cowboys' stunt performers. Depending on the movie and the degree of proficiency the actor needs to achieve, the training can take anywhere from a couple of weeks to a couple of months. But even a few months can never result in the kind of on-camera authenticity a lifelong cowboy can bring to the party.

When you have an ensemble of riders required by your story such as the posse or the cattle drivers, it's always worth trying to cast those roles with real cowboy stunt performers. As I pointed out earlier in the book, many have acted in movies and television seamlessly. Just because they're not primarily employed as actors doesn't mean that they can't throw a few lines with conviction. The smart coordinator will try and cast those roles with pro riders to make sure they can control their animals for the camera as the director requires. If the scene calls for one of the minor characters to find themselves in a dangerous situation, that requires they be able to take a high leap into a river with his horse or be shot off a galloping steed; if the actor in those scenes is a pro cowboy, the stunt will look that much better because you didn't have to cut around and replace another actor who didn't have the riding skills. I'm particularly talking about roles that are not played by principal players.

> DALE GIBSON: *In* True Grit, *a few of the guys who made up the bad guy posse were stunt cowboys. When Jeff Bridges shoots them, there's no doubles, you really see the actors hit the ground all in one shot. I think that's a really smart way to go.*

However, there are numerous examples of cowboys such as the late Richard Farnsworth, who was one of the great stagecoach experts, who had significant acting roles in a few movies. He even starred in *The Straight Story*, which David Lynch directed. He also starred in *The Grey Fox* and had substantial parts in other features.

The other side of the coin that I've illustrated in the context of fights is when your principal talent is required to ride a horse or tame a steer. Most everyone would agree that the more the audience can verify that the person they've been investing in throughout the movie is the same person who is in the middle of a dangerous piece of action, the more authentic and, in turn, the more involving those moments are. As an audience we closely follow the characters. We get to know them and hopefully relate to their challenges. We therefore want to know what happens next. To the extent the audience is distanced from that character by using the wide or long shot or through editing around those moments that a stunt double would be revealed, there is a loss of connection to the story. The tight grip we are held by loosens just that much. It's not fatal, but it's not the standard storytellers aspire to. By creating the illusion that any character in a movie is experiencing each and every moment in the flow of the story, without stepping away, is the supreme objective. To create the illusion that there is no illusion is movie magic. So when your principal cast can be plainly seen in the middle of a dangerous on-screen moment, that clarity will grip us by the throat and won't let us go until we reach the perilous resolution. No angles on the backs of actors as they take a punch, no arms covering faces as they roll down a mountain, and no wide shots that obscure who is really driving the getaway car. That's the high bar to strive for, but of course it's not always achievable. When large animals are involved, the skill necessary to control those animals repeatedly and consistently is vital, as in any stunt. The safety issue needs no further mention; that's woven into the fabric of every stunt or special effect performed or executed. The living being aspect of this equation cannot be underestimated. The actor who overestimates their abilities has to be reckoned with. It looks easy, effortless even, when you see a cowboy ride up to the front of the saloon and, in one continuous motion, dismount and advance into the building just as Old Paint settles to a stop.

> DAN BRADLEY: *Every actor on earth will tell you they know how to run a horse. I'm telling you right now 99.9% of them have never seen a horse other than the one time they got on a rental. So, that for me, is a huge red flag. If you're doing horse stuff, get the actors in, get them with a wrangler, you get them training. I don't care if they grew up on a ranch. You have to see it before you put them in front of the camera. I've seen repeated problems with actors and horses. You need to rehearse.*

Whether it's ok or an honest misappraisal of one's talents or extent of abilities, it doesn't matter. The results may be the same, an awkward-looking moment or worse, a moment that ends with the actor face down in the dust as the paramedic runs to their aid. Time and money are wasted, results inferior, and important relationships strained when the star demands to do their own horse stunts. The coordinator or wrangler should be clearly designated and acknowledged as the de facto "chief safety officer": the one who decides who is qualified to do what with the animals. This is no different than on any other kind of production with any variety of stunts. The coordinator must be established as the professional authority on whose opinion everyone will rely and comply. Then of course there's always the 1st AD if the argument goes that far.

> DALE GIBSON: *I coordinated the IMAX version of the* Alamo. *Don Swayze was a mediocre rider. In the show, he would ride into the Alamo a few times. I would do his riding for him, including jumping and swimming a river with the horse. But when he would have to ride into the Alamo, they'd want him. He came in one time and we were using the English saddle which he was having a hard time with the stirrups. So said, "Okay Don, you're going to ride up here about 15 feet to Col. Travis. Just take your feet out of the stirrups when you ride in. You can ride in 10 feet with no stirrups and when you get there, just swing your leg over and step down." That's something I would do. He said okay. He rode in and the scene looked great. But the problem was that everyone was telling Don Swayze how great he looked and so he decided he knew how to ride. Halfway through the movie there's a scene where he comes riding in to the front of the Alamo and the guys have to swing the door open. They had the big IMAX camera*

set up in front behind a four-foot wall. They wanted me to double him and come riding in on my horse to jump over the wall and over the IMAX cameras and their operators. Don came to me about three days beforehand and said, "My wife and I have been talking and we think that I should do it." First of all, the shot was on his back. It didn't matter if it was him or me. Secondly, he would have killed everybody. He wasn't that good a rider. I just looked at him and said, "Don, no." He said, "Well I'm going to go talk to the director." The director came to me and looked at me and I shook my head "no." The director went to Don and said, "Dale said no, so no." As the stunt coordinator, I had the final say. A lot of times you get actors who really want the screen time and I applaud them for that, but it's not worth getting someone killed over: especially a crew person who's trying to operate the camera. It happens quite often.

There are some actors with long careers who have acquired pretty good riding skills having been cast in numerous movies or television shows that require horseback riding. So not every actor has blind ambition or is clueless about how far their abilities will take them.

DALE GIBSON: *Viggo Mortensen had been riding horses most of his life. He was also in* Young Guns II, *so it was an easy casting choice to put Viggo in Hidalgo.*

I suspect Clint Eastwood and John Wayne were pretty good riders in their day. Joel McCrea retired to a ranch and lived the cowboy life. But not one of them would be irresponsible enough to attempt dangerous stunts; they had too much knowledge and respect about how the business works to jeopardize their health or the investment made by the producers. If one of your stars gets hurt badly enough to stop production and send employees home, that's a pretty heavy consequence of either bad luck or, worse, unbridled ego or ignorance. Maybe people would be protected by an insurance policy, maybe not. If the leading man is suddenly given permission to do something on camera considered risky and he gets hurt falling off a horse, that mishap can have serious financial consequences. Having read the script, the insurers certainly identified that scene where the horse rears up frightened by a nasty rattler. They determine if the actor is qualified to execute that maneuver, and most everyone agrees, he is not. So it is agreed that a stunt double will be used when the horse rears up. The actor, by the way, may not be advised of this proviso until a later date. I say this because this is the way crises come to be, lack of communication. If the actor finds out he won't be allowed to be on the horse when it rears up, fully assuming he was going to be on that horse's back, time-wasting discussions or arguments will most certainly ensue. Producers and directors, take note: revealing these details on the day when the scene is about to be shot is not the time for that conversation to take place. Just imagine part of your budget draining down a rat hole every minute the production is held up as this dispute gets settled and ruffled feathers are smoothed. With that image in mind and being in possession of an unreasonable level of optimism, producers who attempt to smooth ruffled feathers by caving in to their star's demand to do a stunt are exposing their business to a major liability. If that plan changes and the insurers were not apprised of the change *and* something goes wrong, the production may very well be on the hook for damages both real and perceived. The lesson here is, be open with your talent when it comes to how scenes will be shot. No actor wants to hear that the director has decided that the heart-to-heart dialogue scene on the apartment building roof will be staged differently than in rehearsal. Rather than being staged on the roof's safe middle area on lawn chairs, the director thought it would be visually more interesting to stage it on the roof's ledge, five stories up from the ground. This is not welcome news to an actor afraid of heights. Some producers and directors go that route, hoping to put an actor in an impossible situation. The actor knows they can stop a day's work by refusing to work. Even if the actor is in the right legally and ethically, they may feel inclined to give in and sit on the ledge, their clear discomfort notwithstanding. If an actor was told they will be on the horse when it rears up in reaction to the rattler and is told at the last minute that they can't, that could be considered a cynical ploy by a producer to bait and switch an actor. After all, the producer figures, the star agreed to do the role because he was promised he could do the fun stuff on the horse and, by the way, add to the authenticity of the performance. That's the bait. But the producer knows fully well that this stunt would never be approved and, in fact, was not approved by the insurance company. He figures that he'll be able to deflect the actor's ire by placing the actor in a position of thinking "If I don't back off my demand ... my *right* to do this stunt, everybody will think I'm being the bad guy here; the spoiled, excessively paid star who fusses and fumes in their luxury trailer." Producer or director wins. Or do they? Maybe the actor calls that bluff. Costly delay ensues. If the actor gives in, you now have a mistrusting star who is not going to give you one minute's time without being compensated and will absolutely refuse to take a picture with your niece when she visits the set to see what a big shot you are.

Some actors have been taught by the best cowboys in the business. I described how one of the many functions of stunt performers is to train and instruct actors how to accomplish specific feats: how to throw a punch, how to do a 360-degree turn in a car, how to safely fall to the ground, or how to believably perform an infinite array of physical tasks. Horseback riders are often called on to teach actors the rudiments of riding. Given enough time and carefully shot, you might even be able to have an actor appear to be competent and comfortable on a horse.

> DALE GIBSON: *When we did* Young Guns, *I taught Lou Diamond Phillips how to ride. They gave us 2½ months before filming to teach him how to ride. I was also his double. That was my agreement. Most actors, especially your good actors, are fairly good athlete so they can learn. When it really came down to the fight stuff and coming off the horse, they used me to double Lou.*

Can an uninitiated actor be made to look like they've been in the saddle all their lives? Not likely, but if trained like Lou Diamond Phillips was and carefully covered by the director, their skills can look pretty good. But the factor that can never be forgotten is, no matter the level of competence an actor may display, accidents happen, and they happen more often with people who have less experience. This rule is no different than the rules that guide or daily lives when it comes to undertaking a risky activity, like driving a car to the market. The statistics are overwhelming regarding the percentage of very young, inexperienced drivers who get in accidents. Approximately nine out of ten kids get in fender benders before they turn twenty-one. We all know why. They haven't been "performing" this complicated task long enough to understand all its nuances and to learn from the vast array of experiences we accumulate and process into how we drive. But we also know that under the very best of circumstances, very experienced drivers also get into accidents. The root cause of accidents can be very difficult if not impossible to determine no matter how obvious the cause may appear to be. Sure someone ran a red light, but it happened at 1:00 A.M. when the percentage of drunk drivers is higher than at earlier hours of the evening or people are just tired at that hour, not performing to their peak standards. Had you decided to stay home because of the incremental increase in risk, you would've avoided the accident. So many factors go into this analysis. But the overriding active element here is that under almost any condition, accidents can happen. You will also be evaluating the levels of risk when deciding how to approach stunts and in particular when trying to decide whether or not to allow your talent to ride the horse or fall off it. Is it worth losing your actor for a day or a week because they twisted their ankle innocently getting off the horse between takes or cut their forehead falling out of the saddle when they inadvertently gave the horse the signal to run? These mishaps are mundane occurrences, hardly injuries that result from more daring activities. But they happen. It sounds like I'm steering you to the obvious conclusion that it's never worth the risk, but that's not the case. The value of having your actors in the heart of the action, and it's clear to the audience that there's been no sleight of hand, has huge dramatic value. That's worth some risk. Your experience and the experience of your team should form a consensus that will guide you to these kinds of decisions.

Another scenario is when the actor is afraid of animals. It may be hard to comprehend why an actor who's afraid of horses would agree to be in a Western, but it happens. Actors don't like to limit themselves or be perceived as being limited. That situation calls for a patient cowboy who will teach and reassure the reluctant cowboy actor how to appear to be a natural-born horseman. The word *appear* is the operative word here. That actor or any inexperienced actor cannot be transformed into an expert in a short period of time. But they may be taught just enough to do the essential things the script calls for in a convincing and safe way. They can be walked through most any risky activity to reduce their anxiety by patient, experienced professionals.

DALE GIBSON: *I get tons and tons of actors who ask me, "I have an audition next week, can I come out and you can teach me how to ride?" I look at them and say, "In a week? No. Can you teach me how to act in a week? Or teach me how to be a professional football player in a week?" I can take you for two months and teach you pretty well, but it's like playing a pro football player, they start playing in high school and college and work their way up through the ranks.*

Production Design

What do brutal "knock down/drag 'em out" brawls or blazing office buildings have to do with production design? Everything. The conversation that takes place between the art department and the stunt and special effects teams is persistent and fundamental to the successful execution of stunt and special effects. The art department, formally headed by the production designer, prepares the environment for the fight, crash, or inferno. I've already mentioned art department participation in the use of firearms and weapons with blades. Prop masters, who are part of the art department, are often in charge of weapons used on camera. They acquire, keep, and control rubber guns, swords, knives, and other replica weapons unless a firearm can be discharged. When a firearm can be discharged using blanks, armorers are the wisest choice to oversee and control those weapons. Prop masters, who are qualified in the traditional responsibilities of that department, not only acquire, catalog, house, and distribute weapons as needed, but they are craftsmen who can design and manufacture replica weapons (as well as other more common props).

I also mentioned the need for cooperation between the special effects team and the wardrobe and makeup departments to ensure safety for actors when fire is being used on set. Making sure that clothing and hair are not potential torches is a critical consideration that requires the art department to support a special effect. Flame-resistant treatments and careful use of hair sprays and other common makeup are as important a safety consideration as padding and descender cables. The collaboration of these departments goes beyond safety and mise-en-scène. In order to create the illusions of destruction and pain the story requires, wardrobe or hair may need to be designed to rip or erupt on cue.

> JOHN CHICHESTER: *There's a heavy level of collaboration between the art department and stunts and special effects teams. They're good at what they do and I'm good at what I do and when we put our heads together, we can make very convincing things happen.*

Who designs, makes, and implements those elements? Most often, it's the production designer, the art director, the set designer, the set decorator, props and wardrobe people, and their teams. But as with any production, a production designer is responsible for the overall look and design of a movie. It will be their job to create an authentic environment whether on a set or a practical location with the help of others in the art department such as the art director and the set decorator. The production designer will design a complete environment or enhance an existing one at a practical or real structure. What I've just described is the traditional definition of the production designer's role. I want to point out another facet of their efforts. Because of safety and physical requirements all stunts and special effects have, the art department are the people who will produce spaces that enable fights, explosions, or whatever. Production designers' pervasive influence on the look of a movie often requires them to either collaborate on or actually design stunts. If a set is designed in a particular way, how an action sequence is conceived may require that the production designer be intimately involved in designing an action sequence or event.

> JOHN CHICHESTER: *The stuntman showed me exactly how wide the car was. He showed me the path it needed to go through in the scene. Everything beyond that path didn't have to be breakaway, but everything that was inside that narrow channel had to basically fall apart. He made suggestions to me how to make things that would otherwise harm the car and will be convincing for the millisecond shot. He didn't want to break the windshield or have that many stunt performers involved. He wanted to make sure things didn't fly around and hurt someone. He was always filled with really good ideas. Safety is always their absolute primary concern.*

Layered into the designs, practical concerns must be designed into the aesthetic. When production-designing most romantic comedies, the production designer and their team can decorate a set or location with genuine articles. Glass tabletops, overstuffed chairs, original works of art can safely be utilized. Skew the tone away from romance and toward action such as was done in *The War of the Roses* or *Mr. and Mrs. Smith*, and, suddenly, some of those choices are no longer practical. So the art department must understand how a set will be used by breaking down the script and by communications with the director, stunt coordinator, and special effects supervisor. "Oh, you plan to set the couch on fire?" or "our star is going to crash into the house through that window and throw a knife that sticks in the wall over there?" Better be prepared to choose materials advisedly, and make sure enough space will exist in the set's floor plan to accommodate the action. That's the art department's responsibility.

An ornate set designed to replicate a Ming dynasty emperor's palace sounds expensive. It will be decorated with replicated furnishings and art that are accurate to the historical period. That stuff's not cheap, as it must be designed and made with detail almost as intricate as the authentic pieces possess. Clearly, replicas are going to be the right choice. They may be expensive in the context of your budget, but they're dirt cheap when compared to the real thing, not to mention concerns for breakage and theft. But even those replicas may not be appropriate for use in a scene where a fight takes place. Things break. Mirrors are cracked, tables splintered, chairs collapsed, lamps crash to the floor. As long as you have multiples of these items, what's the problem? Maybe nothing. But depending on the demands of the scene, you may need replicas that are not only authentic looking, but they must also be safe for the actors and performers who are either near them when they break or are the surface against which these things are broken. A bottle over the head, a face forcefully planted in a mirror, or even a window that shatters next to an actor because a bullet has supposedly passed through it, all require that the material used and the way the items are constructed pose little, if any, danger to the performers who potentially stand in harm's way.

When things break on a set as collateral damage to bodies being thrown or weapons slashing through the air, they lend a sense of realism to a scene. Of course stuff's going to break when a couple of full-grown men are trying to kill each other in close quarters. They also may very well use furniture and furnishings as weapons or means of defense. This is all great stuff because when things break, our imagination contributes a few pieces to the puzzle. First of all, our mind perceives that an action looks real. The assumption that what is happening on screen is really happening is an important assumption that all subsequent beats rely on, unless the tone of the story is larger than life or cartoonlike. In "slapstick" or over-the-top action stories, some degree of reality is still required in measured doses. In those kinds of stories, directors walk a fine line and must follow their instincts because they're guided less by what is realistic (their sense of realism is relative) and more by what may be entertaining.

No matter the tone, we imagine how painful it must feel when a vase is smashed against someone's head or when a character experiences a head-on collision in a fast-moving car. How we process that situation will be in the context of the tone. Should we laugh when someone falls down a flight of stairs or be afraid? When things break, we believe it breaks because the impact against a person plausibly causes it to break and we feel the pain. It sells the action. Even when things fall over or are kicked and they break, that's a logical result of that action. It supports the reality of that action. If bottles didn't break or skylights didn't obliterate when a body crashes through it, that would reveal the artifice: upset the suspension of disbelief that you have so carefully constructed. So in fight scenes or any action that could cause damage to anything, it's best to design the shot with some plausible damage. The more the better. Lots of smashed-up cars, broken windows, furniture turned into kindling increase the intensity of the action. When a car explodes, we want to see parts flying in the air to confirm our belief that what we are seeing on-screen is really happening. That the fireball is real and the force of an explosion apparently destructive is exciting to an audience. That's why John Hartigan and other special effects pros want to be certain that things will fly out from the explosion. They prep a car by loosening parts, scoring them, weakening the car's structural integrity, and add bits and pieces of things that can go flying. All of this is done in order to enhance and validate our sense that *that* car is really blowing apart, which, in turn, is dangerous to anyone in the vicinity or may serve to foreshadow jeopardy through this nerve-shattering event. In order to enhance or sell a violent on-screen event, things have to break and fly through the air.

That brings us back to how that is accomplished. Once the script is broken down scene by scene by members of the art department, specific notes are made that reflect the art director's, wardrobe's, prop's, and hair and makeup's thinking on what they will need to acquire or make in order to deliver what they believe the script calls for.

> JOHN CHICHESTER: *When I break down my script, I'm creating my set list every time there is an effect or a stunt. I'm making detailed notes using different colored highlighter pens.*

Those choices may or may not be informed by the director's vision, but solely by reading the script. In all likelihood, people in the art department have a decent idea of what the director wants, assuming they've paid attention in their many conversations and meetings where the vision has been examined or explained.

> JOHN CHICHESTER: *A good art director can second-guess a director. The director will be really grateful if someone has made a great choice that speaks to the intentions of the material. They can tell that you really thought through the scene as written in the script and came up with designs that supported the idea.*

The art department script breakdowns result in lists of props, set dressing, makeup supplies, cleanup materials, construction needs, and much more. The notes of the breakdown may contain creative thoughts to bring up at the next meeting with colleagues and/or the director. The breakdown may have questions written down to ask for clarification or confirm a perception. The breakdown is an organizational tool most departments use to inform their process of preparing and executing their jobs. It's also an important early step in order to flag any issues that are of immediate concern or is believed to pose a significant hurdle down the line. But the script or even conversations with director may not tell the whole story because some aspects of action sequences develop later on. Sometimes scripts describe action scenes in very general terms: "a chase ensues." When that's the case, the stunt coordinator or second unit director's input is elemental to art-designing a scene.

Stunt coordinators will approach the production designer as soon as they join the production and explain an action sequence that needs clarification or definition. The scenes may need special construction or placement of items on set that will facilitate the action. Since production designers and key art department personnel are almost always hired well before stunt coordinators, that speaks to how much productive planning or designing can be done by the art department before the stunt guys have explained their ideas: not much.

JOHN CHICHESTER: *Sometimes the description of a scene can be very vague. Unless the stunt coordinator is on the show at that point, it's a real waste of time. We can work on the environment, but until the second unit director and/or stunt coordinator are on board, storyboard artists really have to draw what those guys are thinking. When that starts happening, it really gets going.*

At this stage where most of the key creative players are on board and exchanging ideas, the production designer and their team have been noodling out sketches that suggest the environment as described in the script or as they imagine it if the script is not specific. Once the environment can be agreed on by and large, that's the best time to bring in a storyboard artist to the art department. The drawings they produce will show the action within the environment that is either being designed and built or has been locked down by the location manager. Obviously, not all of these stages are arrived at in harmony, all the time. But there is a point at which all the effort that goes into storyboards begins to make sense because some decisions have been made.

JOHN CHICHESTER: *Storyboards come from the art department designs and renderings. First you design the environment and the storyboards come from that and working with the second unit director and stunt people. I'm not saying the designers of the set are directing the movie; that's not the case. In order to adequately design an environment that action is going to take place in, your primary concern is going to be the action that takes place in the environment.*

And that's the purpose of storyboards and previz.　　.

Numerous meetings should take place to ensure everyone is pulling in the same direction: that everyone is preparing to execute the very same vision that must be specific, nailed down, and universally understood. A director who doesn't have a specific vision is then setting the stage for different collaborators moving ahead with different visions constructed partially from the director, others on the production, and their own. If the director has not specifically planned or approved a specific plan for an action sequence, that seems somehow even more irresponsible. Lots of people are waiting for that plan to move ahead and prepare their contribution. This is a recipe for wasted time and money, which will only serve to alter and cloud the vision, thereby diminishing the end product. The following story testifies to the efficiency and creative productivity that results from a stunt coordinator and director who know what they want.

JOHN CHICHESTER:　*There was a movie called* Monkey Bone *I worked on it and we were shooting the scene at a real museum. The scene took place at the entrance while there was a big party going inside the museum. The character was supposed to be a gymnast. Since he was a gymnast, he was going to do gymnast things. The second unit director wanted to place poles at the entrance for the stunt performer/ gymnast to work with. He's going to jump over again and do flips in the air and then land on his feet and go into the main room. It was a very quick sequence. He was also going to do somersaults on the steps outside the entrance to the museum. Starting on the steps, I decided to put down a red carpet with padding underneath. That's a lot of what you do in my department for the stunt team, find a way to place a lot of padding.*

　　So because the stuntman had worked out something where poles were required, I had to figure out a way to make it look like it belonged there. I had the dimensions of the poles and of the space and the stunt guys began to work out a way to go. I would talk to the stuntman and ask him if he thought this or that would work and he would say, "No, it really has to be right here." So we go back and forth and figure it out together. The distances between the poles were critical. That was a given I had to work with. I covered the poles with wrought iron because it was an older brick building. I introduced more wrought iron around the building so it looked like the wrought iron was always there. This was so much fun because I was given his absolute specifics to work with and then I had to make it feel like it was always there.

A very valuable planning tool is the image. Remember, words are often not sufficient. Pictures, images, physical models, or examples often are the foolproof way of communicating an idea. Models, sketches, storyboards, illustrations, plans, schematics, and previz, in its various forms, are all important tools used to make sure everyone has a common understanding and that no one is working on a different idea that doesn't support and perfectly integrate with everyone else's efforts. Not all forms of visual planning are always appropriate for every situation. A floor plan is a two-dimensional rendering of a three-dimensional space. That third dimension of depth or height may be all important to previsualizing a scene.

Let's say there's a scene that calls for a fight in a living room that leads to a fire. The art director will have numerous conversations with the production designer and discuss the scene's requirements. The production designer will have had numerous conversations with the director and/or stunt coordinator to hear directly from them how they see the details of that scene. Where is the path of the fight? Who will be performing the fight: principal cast or stunt doubles? What weapons are used? What will be damaged or destroyed? How does the fire get started? What burns, and how big are the flames? Once these and other questions are answered, the production designer will design the sets or locations. The various departments will meet regularly during the preproduction period, because it's likely that all the dramatic and visual elements the scene requires will be the responsibility of a number of departments and teams. The stunt and special effects coordinators or supervisors will also attend. Illustrations and storyboards will come out of these exchanges.

JOHN CHICHESTER: *On 47 Ronin we had all these Japanese castles working. The stunt coordinator who worked on James Bond movies was trying to figure out how to work out a fight sequence. After about a week, he came to me and asked if he could have a model. All of the previz he had didn't give him everything he needed to prepare. He wanted to see what the castle actually looked like so he could figure out the fights. He was concerned where the action was to take place and the previz didn't give him that perspective. He needed to know what the space really was.*

The set designer was very savvy about how he went about designing the set. The whole design of the castle directly reflected action that was scripted. They're very specific. Even before the set designer got into making a model for illustrators, he would draw different views of what the castle was going to look like. He copied the drawing and then with a red Sharpie, he wrote descriptions of where the action would take place using arrows and notes. He blocked out all the action on the plan itself. What's critical here is it wasn't indicating any camera angles. He's not telling anybody how to shoot the thing. He's just talking about architectural space and movement of the characters through the space. He's leaving a lot of room for development, but is showing how the staging can happen within his design.

They must agree on materials used and the placement of objects that may pose a danger or even a dramatic opportunity for the performers. Maybe pads can be placed on the floor under a carpet. Objets d'art can be made of foam or rubber. For a shot, objects hard to replace or that pose a risk can be pulled out for a quick shot. It's likely an audience won't notice because they're focused on someone getting their butts kicked.

JOHN CHICHESTER: *A good script takes your attention away from effects and stunts. You're into the story and less concerned with how realistic things look.*

Between subsequent setups, an art department person will replace the item so you can cut back to a wide shot of the aftermath, confirming subliminally or otherwise that the object never moved from its established position. The mind plays funny games on us, helping establish and maintain the illusions created in a movie. As a visual storyteller, you learn to work with that notion.

JOHN CHICHESTER: *We also figure out ways to take things out of the shot, off the set, and replace them with something soft. The audience only sees the shots for very short time. They're focused on the action and because everything is moving so fast, they don't notice if some item is missing in the shot or if it has been replaced with a soft version of that item. But you'd be surprised, by the time the art department gets through, it can look exactly like the original set. The only way you can tell is if you go over and touch something.*

A stuntman will crash though that skylight that is built on a stage. How much space on the hidden side of the skylight will be necessary to provide when the set construction people build it? The stunt coordinator will provide the answer, but he has to be asked. He may forget to say to the art director, "Oh by the way, we'll need at least ten feet of space above the skylight for the fall to look great and be safe." What if the art department creates the plans for that and discovers there isn't ten feet to give, that the ceiling only will allow six? What if the director says, "I want to see the city skyline in the background when the skylight is broken"? You'll need space to place a background that may be flat or have depth, but it'll need to be lit, requiring more space. Another conversation must be had to deal with these requirements. And, by the way, there's usually a solution that everyone can live with. But unless everyone communicates and understands the requirements of the scene on all its many levels, problems can't be solved, because someone may not know a problem even exists until it's too late or becomes very expensive to resolve. This is why there are many, many meetings in preproduction that take place in order to be ready to execute a stunt or special effect.

> JOHN CHICHESTER: *Stuntmen, visual effects, special effects, the art director, production designer, decorator or at least their lead man attend these meetings. The key grip and electricians could be there too. They all need to know what's going to happen, because it will concern their department. There's often a lot of give-and-take between departments for everybody to be satisfied and get what they need to do their jobs. But safety always trumps everything.*

If action sequences are designed by the stunt coordinator and accepted by the director, the art department can then come into the process and design and prepare for that sequence. There's little point in making designs without the input of the stunt coordinator or second unit director if the action is pretty specific or unique. However, as I've pointed out, movies sometimes require the production designer to be responsible for a part of designing stunts. So they can be right there on the ground floor of action sequence planning.

> JOHN CHICHESTER: *I love working with these guys. I've never had a bad experience. Ever. They always know their stuff. I've never worked with one [who] didn't know what he wanted to do. This makes it such a joy for a designer because this there so specific. They are actually dead on specific.*

Some scenes or actions, however, are pretty generic. Someone who gets punched in the nose in a bar or wrestles around in a living room may not require a specially designed set. And if for some reason you have sets you're committed to and must make the action work within them, so be it. It's done all the time. That requires creativity as well. It's often said that limitations serve to spur creative solutions that are better than the original idea. But an experienced art director or production designer will formulate a way of thinking and working that intuitively supports the stunt and special effects pros' process.

> JOHN CHICHESTER: *If there is a built set, the stuntman reacts to that. I kind of know how they work and I come up with ideas that I think they will appreciate.*

If a scene requires that a set be built for the specific demands of the story, it doesn't make much sense to require the action to work within the boundaries and limitations of the set. A boxing ring has specific and accepted dimensions as do football fields. You can't design a set that won't accommodate the realities of the event. The ring can't be too small or the football field too vast. Dining rooms in middle-class homes are pretty similar in scope. If a scene calls for a dinner party for twenty that erupts into a fight, the design of that set must support that action. Action on that scale won't fit into a standard-size dining room. The set will have to be designed to at once accommodate the production and story requirements. It must be large enough to fit the cast, crew, and equipment and also appear to be realistic as not to break our suspension of disbelief. You can see how it would be a waste of time to design a dining room without hearing from the stunt coordinator and director what they had in mind.

Why build a set anyhow? Isn't it easier to find a practical location and then figure out the action? Maybe. Location scouts are always looking for practical locations that support the requirements of the scene.

> JOHN CHICHESTER: *If it's a location, the art department has to design things they imagine stunt and effects people can work with. There's a real cooperation and collaboration going on between these departments.*

Sometimes, as I described above, the scenes require locations that aren't exactly true to life. They would suggest, for instance, that dining rooms are bigger than they normally are. Sometimes the real locations are suitable but need modifications to make specific story points work. That may call for minor construction, such as adding on to a structure like a garage add-on to a house. You never have to completely build it. It may be a two-sided façade with nothing behind it or at least very little. You only need to build what you will see. In the movie *Capote*, the production searched and searched for a house that reflected the austerity and honesty of the movie's setting. Furthermore, it was based on a true story, and the house's authenticity and location had to accurately reflect the real house and location. The scenes at that house were shot in Canada, and the location was a real challenge to find. They finally came upon an isolated house that was dilapidated. It was uninhabitable and looked it. The art department figured out exactly what needed to be upgraded and repaired. They didn't have to work on the whole house, but only on those portions the camera would see. In consultation with the director, who indicated what his compositions would look like, what the camera would see and not see, they rebuilt and renovated a wall here and a wall there inside and out and decorated those areas as if they were being lived in. Most likely, any surface or structure outside the boundaries of the frame remained in disrepair, and the audience only saw what appeared to be a perfectly maintained home.

You will not find a dining room big enough to accommodate an action scene with twenty or so people and the equipment necessary to shoot it in a middle-class house. You need to build it. Many things you may want to shoot cannot be shot on someone else's property. You can't set fire to someone's house or do structural damage in someone's place of business such as a restaurant. But if you own it, meaning rent a stage and build the location as a disposable asset, you have much more freedom and control. You don't have to placate property owners and neighbors. You don't have to speak in hushed tones after 10:00 P.M. to avoid disturbing the peace in the neighborhood. For that matter, you don't have to shoot at night at all if you're on a stage. Time doesn't exist there. So once an action scene has been designed, all manners of previz can be created. Sketches, illustrations, and storyboards can then be working from the same vision, reflecting the same reality. The art department is in some sense at the center of any action scene, because they create the environment in which the action takes place. All roads go through their department.

In a perfect world, as I've explained earlier when discussing second units, complicated shots that are a part of a stunt- or special effect-driven scene are left to the second unit. The time it takes to set up and shoot crashes, explosions, and destruction of all sorts can be time consuming due to degrees of difficulty and safety. The first unit will shoot everything they can with the cast and then vacate the set or location for the smaller second unit to step in and get the shots needed to complete the scene. On lower-budget productions, you have to allow for the extra time in your schedule. Plan ahead to have everything needed to shoot those connecting shots, inserts, or stunts, standing by to move in and shoot. From the following passage, you can get an idea of the concept behind a second unit and how dependent they are on a creative, efficient art department.

JOHN CHICHESTER: *Floods are another thing I deal with. When I was working on* Alien: Resurrection *with Sigourney Weaver, there was a scene where she goes into a room filled with glass containers filled with aliens in all different stages and conditions. The glass tubes were filled with liquid, of course it's always green, and the creatures were also inside. She freaks out and takes a flamethrower to the room. We built a set in a big plastic pool liner. The special effects people replaced all of the glass containers with candy glass. On these types of big scenes, the way it usually goes is the first unit will shoot everything except for the effect. The first unit will go on to shoot something else and the second unit will come on to shoot the effect: just those specific shots. Often the time it takes to shoot that stuff takes much longer than the time the first unit took to shoot the rest of the scene before moving on. The smaller crew will do very specific things. The pressure is off because there's no cast waiting around while everybody figures out how to do things.*

Interestingly, in a sequence that calls for a fire, the art director or production designer may be the person most responsible for placing the fire. Because they must provide not only a set that supports the story, but also a safe set. They might say, for instance, that fire bars must be placed in specific areas of the set or location in consideration of what can catch fire and what cannot, whether planned or not. The director, stunt coordinator, and special effects supervisor will do their jobs in compliance with those requirements. In other situations, where the fire has to be specifically placed, the art department will make sure nothing will catch fire or be inadvertently ruined.

JOHN CHICHESTER: *Burning buildings are a very common thing. That really involves the special effects people. They like to have everything on gas lines so nothing is actually burning. That way, they can turn it off right away for safety. They use gas bars that come in different sizes. When they're placed, I know I can't build anything out of certain materials that can catch on fire or melt around them. We often use real drywall which is resistant to flames. The amount of time that flames actually are touching walls or anything else is very brief, because the gas is turned off between takes. As a designer, I'll design the set with the script that calls for fire, in mind. When we're planning a set, we'll indicate where fires can be placed. That will get the conversation going. Everybody concerned will give their input. The director may have comments based on story. The producer may have comments based on cost. So as a designer, you do end up designing for where the fire goes. Of course, it's up to the special effects people to make the fire happen.*

The limitations or scale of the set also may dictate the action sometimes. If the construction budget or location budget only allows for a smaller or less complete version of what the script calls for, the director and, in turn, the stunt coordinator may have to alter their plans. Sometimes that's a painful compromise, but other times, the art director or production designer can make lemonade out of lemons. They can come up with a design solution that costs less or is more practical to deliver that actually made a scene better.

JOHN CHICHESTER: *On* The Book of Eli, *some scenes took place in what was a lobby of an old movie theater. We had these two circular staircases that were old and dilapidated. We were looking for ways to save money and we were asked to find places to cut. I suggested that one of the staircases should just be gone, busted and broken. In the back of my mind I was thinking that when they do the fight scene, somebody could just jump off this thing and make it a real interesting fight. When I was flying back to Los Angeles from the location and the stunt coordinator was sitting next to me, I told him I had this idea about how the set design could make for an interesting fight. He thought it was a great idea.*

We know that many movies that utilize stunts and special effects also employ visual effects when it comes to creating pyrotechnics or the illusion of a dangerous stunt. VFX are also a fundamental tool in set design and art direction in general, capable of making complete virtual environments as we've seen in so many movies such as *300*. The art department doesn't normally design or create VFX. That's another distinct department of visual effects. The cross-pollination is significant though. It makes a lot of sense for art department input to go into the designing of the VFX. Just as in the stunt or special effects themselves, it is often hard to distinguish between a scene that is fully practical and one that is a hybrid of practical and CGI. Space can be expanded, architecture can be transformed, and environments can be made up to accompany and enhance real images so that they become photoreal. This joint effort takes coordination and cooperation to not only organize the creative effort but also plan the funding of it.

In the extreme, production designers can now accomplish their jobs sitting in front of a computer creating virtual sets and designs and never buying, renting, or building a thing. That is the new, expanded definition of the production designer and of those who work in that department.

JOHN CHICHESTER: *Once you get your storyboards, I'll sit down with the visual effects coordinator. Using two different colored markers, usually yellow pink, we mark all of the storyboards in yellow that are live action and the VFX shots will be marked with pink. You'll go through every single board and we identify every part of those boards and plan how they're to be done, practical or using visual effects. By doing this, we make sure everybody understands their responsibilities. We also know how things are budgeted. If it's going to be physical, that's going to come out of the construction budget. If it's going to be shot on green screen, that will come out of the visual effects budget.*

So many movies provide vivid examples of the marriage of real and virtual to create a new and persuasive reality. The use of green and blue screen allows us to place characters or objects in another time and place in ways that defy detection. In pre-digital days, other methods that were "in-camera" were commonly used to create new environments. Rear and front screen projection placed actors in moving cars that were situated on a stage against a previously shot and projected image of a moving background. Hitchcock and countless others used that technique often. Even simple backdrops, back-lit or not, were used to create the illusion of an exterior environment. With the advent of digital technology and all it promised to do, and to a degree delivered on, those in-camera methods got replaced. As I've pointed out along with the professionals in this book, some degree of dissatisfaction or discomfort sometimes is felt by filmmakers and audiences. That's why there is the emphasis on starting with a real person or object that has been photographed on film or on a chip as a basis upon which a CGI-enhanced or -replaced version of the person or object ends up on screen. It looks more real.

Another old school method of mixing reality with illusion is the use of models. A great recent example in a great action sequence is in the James Bond movie *Skyfall*. A London Underground train crashes through walls and lands in the British secret services' new headquarters. That was accomplished using some very old school methods and most likely with a few CGI touches as well. But essentially, the train was a model that was inserted into a real set in a way we totally believed and were impressed by.

JOHN CHICHESTER: *Twenty years ago there were a lot of miniature effects houses in Hollywood. They made scale miniatures. The digital revolution so changed things and a lot of those places went out of business. People began doing those kinds of shots using the computer, but that technique never really went away in England. They kept doing it the old school way. In Harry Potter they made some really big miniature castles. My friend Dennis Gassner did the last two James Bond movies. When he did* Skyfall, *he used practical miniatures in that scene where the subway goes crashing inside the building. The helicopter's falling down into the farmhouse also was a miniature. Now when I say miniature, some of them are pretty big. That subway train might've been 12 or 15 feet long. You try to make them as big as you can, that way you have much more detail and they'll look much more realistic. I'm sure they used miniature-scale models of the set as well for certain quick shots. The combination is amazing and was also a result of incredible editing.*

Most action sequences that you ever look at, even if they involve a great amount of visual effects, will cut back and forth. One shot will be a practical shot, photographed on a real set with things really breaking. The next one will be a visual effects shot, and they'll go back and forth. Sequences are often done that way. As filmmakers, we're asking an audience to divine between what's real and what isn't. Our brains don't really want to play that game, and we give in to the inner reality of the story. We don't ask those questions of what's real and what's not if we're involved in the story. That integrity of the "fourth wall" or "curtain" is vital. For example, if you're doing an interior of the plane, which is on a gimbal, all the stuntmen fall to one side of the plane when it banks: very realistic. You got suitcases and things flying to sell it. Cut to outside the plane, which is a CGI (or miniature model) shot: it's on fire! One really supports the other as far as making it an engaging sequence.

JOHN CHICHESTER: *I think miniatures are on the rebound. Doing things practically is the way to go. Now you still may composite these things with green screen for instance. If you blow something up in the computer, it all has to be contrived from scratch. But if you actually physically blow something up, it has a certain amount of "gesture" to it, a certain amount of energy and unpredictability. It just looks better.*

These are choices of which tools to utilize. When choosing a tool, we consider the desired outcome. Then you assess what tools are available to me and will this tool help me realize my vision? Real or CGI … or both?

Often there's another advantage to old school, in-camera methods: it can cost less. CGI-generated bullet hits, $500. Real squibs, $35. This is not always the case, as the decision as to whether to go real or virtual can be a complex calculation weighing numerous factors of labor and materials. But it's an option always worth exploring. The results can often be more pleasing as well.

JOHN CHICHESTER: *Using old school methods of in-camera techniques, you can make your dollar stretch. Many experienced pros who know this stuff are happy [to] lend a hand to younger filmmakers and bring their experience to bear on a production, saving lots of money and giving more production value on the screen.*

Applying old school methods or concepts are often the key to lending a touch of reality to CGI-created visual components. It's an idea or approach that costs nothing and when utilized, can bring an otherwise inert VFX to life. These are the kinds of tips experienced pros bring to your production. This is why you should never be shy and should aggressively pursue experienced pros, in as many fields as possible, to bring on your show.

> JOHN CHICHESTER: *I've done a couple of Star Trek movies and early in my career, a few Star Trek television shows. Often times I found that creating a specialty prop, creating the thing that didn't exist, like a time portal or something like that, instead of having just a couple of buttons that people pushed, you could give them a physical action: something they had [to] do or grab onto and struggle with, before the visual effect happened. It's really so much better. Because the actor is really doing something physical, it really brings a reality to the rest of it. I always look for that in sequences when I'm designing specialty props. What can I do to make it physical? If the guy has to pick up something really heavy, then it feels real.*

I've explained numerous components that comprise the unit responsible to execute a stunt or special effect. There's the stunt team, the special effects team, the AD, the camera department, armorers, athletes … the list goes on. Each contribution to the stunt or effect impacts the budget by the addition of labor, rentals, and materials. When you need a stunt double to stand in for your star for a high fall, a specific gun from the 1860s, or a fight choreographer to design a martial arts-style encounter that takes place in an ornate, traditional Chinese home, it seems readily apparent that there are costs associated with those events. The stunt people, the location, the weapons' rental seem obvious. I wouldn't call these hidden costs, but it might not occur to you that there are costs that exist outside the vehicles, pads, pneumatic devices, and accelerants to spend money on. As in any other part of the filmmaking process, preparation is key. When it comes to the confluence of the art department and the execution of stunts, I think the stakes leap to a higher level. We understand how the core effort of shooting a stunt or effect can be costly, and preparation is critical to keep costs in check. The art department component of this dynamic presents huge challenges, in terms of organization and skill. As a filmmaker, your understanding of the interdependency and workings of a film are indispensable. Make sure your art department is capable of supporting stunts and special effects. Great portfolios are important. Set-building experience and good taste are what you're looking for. But if any department, especially the art department, is not capable of fully supporting the stunts and effects, you've got serious problems, potentially.

JOHN CHICHESTER: *You have to know what you're doing before you get there, there's a lot of money at stake. You really get into trouble on shows where they haven't figured things out. The ones that are rushed into production, where the script is really long, are terrible. If you've got all these kinds of elements involved, it can be really stressful and things can go south rather easily. People have been known to have heart attacks.*

Don't have a heart attack.

Sports

RON SHELTON: *Sports is a connective tissue now; it's everywhere. Everybody has a school team, Little League team, a professional team, everybody has a little girl who plays soccer. Sports connects us more than ever; sometimes ruthlessly and obnoxiously, but it connects us nonetheless.*

Sports are a part of virtually every culture in the world, most certainly the ones that go to the movies and watch TV. The passion and dedication fans everywhere demonstrate is truly universal. Love, war, … sports. What else is there in life that provides all the elements of drama so clearly, so visually? High stakes, committed objectives, and enormous obstacles are the foundations of those three narrative realms.

RON SHELTON: *I said this 25 years ago when I made* Bull Durham, *sports is the theatrical background which we share values and arguments. When I grew up, there were Westerns or war movies. There aren't any now, so sports movies are the new Western. And I hated sports movies when I was a kid, because I knew that sports were not about hitting a home run in the bottom of the ninth. It's not about the big play, it's about the moments between the big plays. It's not about when Hamlet actually thrusts his sword through Claudius, it's about everything up to that moment.*

Movies that portray the world of sports provide the perfect metaphors for life: the kind of struggles that we can all relate to, no matter our nationality or culture. There are goals, important goals individuals set for themselves in sporting events, just as we set out to achieve goals in our own lives; we have to get the girl, survive a dangerous mission, or validate our humanity. There's triumph and failure. Stories that live in the world of sports, vividly and dynamically, reflect those and, arguably, all our struggles.

RON SHELTON: *I thought television could do sports in a way movies never could; 20 cameras, high-speed, replay, a million angles. But*

I could take my one camera all the places their cameras can't: inside the locker room, in the shower, inside their head, home with the girl, to the nightclub, the phone call to mom … I just made sure I had to do it in a way that wasn't competing with TV. And, that they couldn't compete with me.

Sports stories lend themselves to serious and comedic treatments. *The Natural*, *Friday Night Lights*, *Rocky*, and *Brian's Song* occupy the more dramatic end of the sports movie hall of fame, while *Major League*, *Slap Shot*, and *Bull Durham* occupy the lighter side: all classics that so wonderfully examine the human condition, no matter the tone. Of course, they only represent a sampling of the memorable sports movies that have been produced over the span of motion picture history.

The principles and strategies of shooting action are much the same as when you're planning and shooting an action sequence. In many cases, sports sequences are more complex than fights or car chases because they often utilize many more players: lots more pieces on the game board. In every football play, you have twenty-two players on the field whose movements have to, at some point in the sequence, be carefully managed. Basketball has ten players on a court who must be choreographed in order to tell the story of that moment in time.

DAVID WARD: *You need someone to choreograph the plays. You need someone that instructs everyone, "here's the way the plays going to work, this guy is going to hit you, you're going to fall down. You're not going to be running into each other and really trying to resist the block. If somebody runs into you and you get blocked, you make it look good."*

Geography is a major component in any sports narrative. It's an indicator of the relative success or failure of characters' active journey to achieve an objective. If your central character crosses the goal line or hits a jump shot to win the big game in the final seconds or comes up short of that goal, those are two different stories that are told by utilizing geographical objectives as a means of expressing triumph or failure. The implications of those results are hopefully clear to an audience as you construct your narrative throughout the expanse of the story. Should we be happy or sad? Does this mean the hero gets the girl or realizes she's not the one for him? Is he now a hero who's redeemed himself or the "goat" who's getting his comeuppance? Achieving an objective is the point of almost every story. In Ron Shelton's great *Tin Cup*, Kevin Costner's character, a stubborn but talented golfer, Roy McAvoy refuses to take the safe path to the biggest win of his life: because that would not display his true talent. So he sacrifices the win to stay true to his moral code. His willingness to fail to achieve his objective allowed him to get something more valuable, the love and respect of his dream girl. That's where a loss was a win. It was played virtually without dialogue. Everyone's behavior, the physical and visual components of the final scene, told the whole story beautifully.

You must allow the audience to gain an understanding of what all these "actors" are doing and where they're doing it, because that is the narrative device you've chosen to tell the story.

RON SHELTON: *I think the mistake that some baseball movies make is, they shoot it too tight and they shoot it too cinematically. They're trying to make a cinematic statement. It's like trying to shoot a comedy too close. Loosen up. I don't need all the cutaways on a baseball play. It's large action; the field is big. It's hard to shoot that way because you're all over the place, but stay loose, go in tight only when you need to. Mr. 3000 was beautifully shot, but I had no idea what was going on because it was showing me the camera work. At the risk of not getting the cinematographer of the year award, relax; it plays in one big frame quite nicely. You can see the pitcher, the batter, the catcher, the ground ball hit to the shortstop, the close play at first base. It's much more satisfying than cut, cut, cut. Make sure you get the loose shots and don't be afraid to play them. But you need the players. Who knows, someday I may have to fake it.*

Allowing the audience to get an overview of the scene is so important. Once that wide perspective is established, you're then free to direct the audience's attention to all the visually dramatic and narrative elements in the scene. Kevin Costner's character, Roy, was on the final hole, across a water hazard from the green, the scoreboard in view and a huge breathless crowd as a backdrop to it all. A clear narrative tableau. So you must visually construct a pattern of images that will allow the audience to piece together the narrative flow and have an understanding of the possibilities that lie ahead as the story progresses. You need the wide shots to establish the geography of both the placement of players in relation to one another and their placement in relation to their environment. You can't just focus on a couple of central players; otherwise, the audience will be confused. But you also need closer shots to reveal the emotional values of the scene, detect the scene's flow through characters' reactions, and convey its physical energy.

There are other visual elements that help tell the story that must be portrayed in order to paint the complete picture, such as players and coaches on the sidelines and the fans in the venue or boundaries of a golf course. Their reactions to what's going on in the game are clear indicators of what you, the storyteller, want the audience to feel about what's happening on the field or court.

The amount of visual pieces to feature and move around can make your head swim (another sporting challenge). The only way to really manage all those visual elements is to break the scene down into smaller and smaller pieces: deconstruct the overall flow, and identify and mark every moving part of the complex dance you're constructing. When you identify all the moving parts and their exact patterns of action and location, you will then have the scene conceived and ready to execute. This is a painstaking process. Shortcuts or improvisation only increase the likelihood of mistakes or omissions. Few of us have the mental capacity to keep straight in their heads all the very small visual pieces that must be captured in a camera, in order for them to add up to a coherent narrative.

> DAVID WARD: *I think you have to approach the sports movie the way you have to approach an action movie. I always had every sports sequence completely storyboarded, every shot. It's very easy to forget a shot, because there are so many little pieces that you have to get. It's too easy to forget one or more shots if you're not storyboarded. It also helps the people who work with you choreographing the sequence to know what you, as the director, are doing at any given time. It's a shorthand that helps you save time because the problem with sports is, if you don't deal with it as action, it's going to take you much longer to do than you ever thought and you're going to be confused and frustrated. You just can't wing it.*

Storyboard or previz artists are an indispensable aid in designing sports action scenes. As in any action sequence, they help identify and, eventually, keep track of the specific pieces you need. The sport that your story exists in is very specific. The action that takes place in that narrative environment must observe the rules, boundaries, and numerous customs specific to that sport. Therefore, it makes sense that the person creating your previz in whatever form you choose understands the game.

> DAVID WARD: *When you're doing a sports movie and interviewing storyboard artists, you want to get a storyboard artist who understands the game. If someone doesn't understand baseball, you don't want them doing your storyboards. They don't know where to put people. They don't know what the distances really are or how people should act in certain circumstances.*

The previz phase of preproduction is the planning "on paper." Prep next graduates to practical, physical rehearsals in which you walk through the choreography of each shot. This isn't any different than a dance rehearsal, in which a choreographer leads their dancers move by move through the dance routine until they can do it effortlessly and at full speed. You know who the "dancers" are: they're your actors who are portraying the athletes. These actors obviously have to be athletic and skilled enough to pass for the athletes they're supposed to be portraying.

> DAVID WARD: *You pretty much need the actors and the players on the field when planning and choreographing a scene, particularly with football. People need to know where they're going to move, at what angle to hit someone, and what angles that person is going to fall away, so they don't actually, on the day, crash into somebody else coming from some other direction who's doing their thing. Players might not be aware of what's happening next to them and therefore they run into each other and there's collateral damage.*

Your choreographer should be a professional from that sport, preferably with experience in movie work. Their experience and skill in that sport are clearly a requisite, but if they also know how to best shoot the sport, know what angles and techniques can best capture the action, so much the better. There are numerous men and women who have the all-round experience of athletics and production. Once again, IMDb is one of the easiest sources of information with complete credits on each movie and TV show. With a little persistence, you can track down the person or people who consulted and guided the production through designing the action in the movie.

> DAVID WARD: *I happen to know about the sport. I know what looks authentic and what doesn't. So if it doesn't look authentic I say okay here's what we need to do. But if you don't know sports and you're doing a sports movie, you do need someone who knows what looks right. If you're doing a baseball film, for example, that person would be a professional or a minor league player who may be a former player, to come in and deal with the actors specifically on their baseball skills. They'll make sure they have a throwing motion that looks authentic. If they can't, then you, as a director, need to know that so you don't put those actors in situations where they obviously don't look like ballplayers. Then you know whether you need to cut around them or double them if possible. For example, Tom Berenger did not have a great throwing arm in* Major League. *But fortunately, he was playing*

catcher and so we put Steve Yeager from the Dodgers, back there with a mask on and no one knew it wasn't Tom.

A very present challenge in shooting any sports movie is the risk of injury. In most cases the severity of injuries suffered in sports is non-life threatening. A torn meniscus, a pulled hamstring, a cut forehead, or a concussion are, with time, common injuries that you recover from. These kinds of injuries are an everyday occurrence among amateurs and pros alike. We might miss a day of work or even a few if we have arthroscopic knee surgery. But for most of us, the world goes on without us temporarily. Someone covers for us, deadlines are extended, or our absence is absorbed or not even noticed. Maybe you can phone it in if need be. But actors can't phone it in. If an actor misses a day, a week, or a month due to injury, that can be a major financial setback for your production. Insurance reimbursement aside, principal actors who must miss scheduled days of shooting are a significant upset to a production. It unleashes a chain of events that throws an otherwise well-thought-out schedule into chaos or at least into a fallback position that doesn't allow you to run your show as efficiently as you could've before the accident or injury.

DAVID WARD: *On* Major League II, *David Keith had lost his contact lenses and he didn't tell me. So he's hitting at night without his contact lenses against Charlie Sheen and he's trying to hit it in the air with enough speed going out of the frame that we could believe that ball's going out of the park. 123 pitches! Charlie couldn't pitch again for six days because his arm was so tired.* Major League *pitchers don't throw that many pitches! They usually take the pitcher out after 100 pitches. Charlie had been building up his arm for a couple weeks before the shoot but to go out and throw 123 pitches was crazy. I considered shooting it another way, except Charlie and I had this thing. It was probably stupid, kind of a macho thing that we could play ball. We're not going to cheat this. And Charlie was into that whole mentality. I said, "Come on Charlie, we're at 65 pitches I don't want you to throw anymore." He said, "Naaah, come on, let's get it. I still feel good."*

A lead actor, lost for six days! As David Ward admits, he might've handled that situation differently by not risking injury to his star and lose his services for a week. But his star said he felt fine and he really, *really* wanted to do it. These are tough calls, and even when you have minimized risk, accidents happen and it's near impossible to hold your principal cast out of every shot that presents some level of risk. Many actors probably consider being able to throw a football or baseball to be a factor in taking the part. Take that away from them, and you can have a very unhappy actor on your hands.

DAVID WARD: *I remember also in* The Program, *there's a scene where the running back, Craig Sheffer, had to run up the middle and almost reach the goal line. Craig said to me, "Dave, I want to do it myself. I don't want the stunt double to do it." And I said, "Craig it only looks easy." And he said, "I played quarterback in high school. I've been tackled." I said okay that I would let him do it as long we choreographed how it's going to happen. I took the two safeties who had to tackle him and said in order to make it look authentic you guys have got to run together and hit each other and he'll go down between you. You don't hit him, you hit each other. And so we practiced it in slow motion. Everybody knew what they were supposed to do. Craig ran the ball. And the two guys really sold the hit beautifully. As a matter of fact, one of the guys knocked the other guy out! They barely grazed Craig. But… Craig was out for three days with a neck injury. You have to realize there is a huge gulf between what an actor thinks he can handle and what he can actually handle when they're playing with people who actually played this game professionally. So even when an actor has the skills, it just goes to prove that bad things can happen.*

   So you don't risk your actors unless you absolutely have to and can find no way to double them. And then you've got to be incredibly careful. You have to really choreograph it. You have to choreograph every movement, people have to know where they're supposed to be and when they're supposed to move out of the way. It's an action sequence is what it is. So you have to choreograph how everything's going to happen. There's a lot of planning. The big thing that saves you time and money is planning in preproduction or whatever rehearsal you can get in so you can make sure that everyone knows what everyone is supposed to do. One of the things you do in the boot camp is you practice doing fake hits and tackles and falling down. You teach actors how to fall down. And not break their elbow or something. You just have to give them the training. If something can go wrong it will. You've got to plan for every possible situation and even then there's things you can't control.

As we all know, even pros get injured. If you think of it that way, it should inform every decision made about exposing your valuable, nonpro cast to unnecessary or even necessary risk. But even the small stuff, the bruise or twisted ankle, can put a sizable dent in your schedule and budget.

DAVID WARD: *You get a lot of "charley horses" and hamstring pulls*
and stuff like that. Or you'll have a guy who hits a foul ball off his ankle
and hurts himself. Not expecting that to happen, but it does happen.
Major League hitters do it all the time. They're in pain, so you always
have the basic trainer there all the time to take care of the minor stuff
that can hold you up. You don't want to be down for a half-hour so
your actor can recover enough to shoot again. So you should have a
basic trainer there to attend to injuries as best as they can. You don't
have that kind of time on a movie set to wait around and let the pain
subside on its own.

You should have someone there with the sprays, bandages, splints, and balms. It's a specialized first aid kit and a specialized medic. Injuries are not just freak occurrences either. The factor that distinguishes recreating sports action in a movie and the real thing is the element of repetition. Numerous takes can cause injuries and discomfort that come from an accumulation of actions rather than a solidary incident. One hundred and twenty-three pitches and dozens of slides or tackles can take their toll.

DAVID WARD: *There are comfort issues you have to deal with too.*
Wesley Snipes had to steal a lot of bases in Major League. *We had*
to pad his hips so he didn't get raspberries from sliding so much.
Sometimes you have to do multiple takes because you want the play
to appear to be close. You want to make it look like he gets to the base
just before the tag and you don't want it to look like the fielder is sitting
there waiting to tag him. That looks phony. By the end of the movie,
Wesley's hips were pretty torn up. You try not to do too many takes
of physical things, because the more you do, the more you're risking
injury. That's why you have to choreograph these things and get the
timing down before you make somebody actually do it. People get tired
and then get hurt.

If you have some flexibility in the shooting schedule, you should always try and schedule stunts of any kind early in the day. Everyone is awake, alert, and near capacity in their level of energy. Everyone needs to be firing on all cylinders when a stunt or physically challenging work is being done.

DAVID WARD: *Usually if you're requiring someone to do something*
slightly skillful you want to shoot it earlier rather than later when
they're tired. It's going to take them longer to do it well. If they're tired,

you're going to end up doing more takes and the more takes you do, the more risk you're incurring.

It looks very funny at times, because there's people running in slow motion or just walking through the choreography of the scene. It's like a dance. You move to a specific spot and do a specific thing. And then you get it to the point where you do it with pads on and move faster. It progresses. But everybody knows to the inch, where they're supposed to go. If you say, okay here's the play, let's run it, everybody better know their role.

And then you've got to know where to put the camera so that you can get inside the action and make a space for the camera to be able to move in and get what you want so that people aren't falling into the camera. So it's all about planning and choreography. As a director you know the sport you're choreographing it in concert with whoever is your consultant and who's taught everyone who plays, so you say to him, "look, this guy's going to run around the end here and I want to see him tackled as he comes through this space here. So run the play so I have room to get my camera in here." We have to accommodate the camera by reworking the play sometimes. So you're working with a consultant to choreograph this.

The consultant takes the first pass at the choreography. What they do is set up the play and tell everybody where they have to move. Then, I'll look at it as the director and say, "okay I like the way the play looks. Can you move the end out a little more, have this guard come back this way so I can move between them with a camera and catch the action right there in the backfield?" And they'll say, "Yeah, I can do that." Then we'll rework it with the camera and rehearse with the camera at the same time the play is going on to make sure there isn't something we didn't think about that's somehow in the way or somebody who is not aware of the camera gets blocked or something like that. Because if you don't plan for that it, will happen.

Casting a sports movie

When looking for actors to cast in a movie that requires authentic athletic ability and ability in a particular sport, you have some very big challenges. Normally, you're looking for the best actor available to play the role. Sometimes physical appearance is important; sometimes it's not. In a perfect world, your charge is to find the best actor for the role, and that actor will make that role their own. Certainly, not every famous actor fits the common perception or ideal of beauty. However, when casting a movie in which the actor will be required to convincingly play an athlete, you have the very difficult task of finding the right actor who is both superior in their acting talent and superb in their athletic ability: not a combination easy to find, although many actors will tell you it's not so hard to find, that they look great on a field or court.

> RON SHELTON: *Actors think they can go up there and hit a Roger Clemens fastball. "Do you really want me to film that? You want that to get out? You want to guard Kobe Bryant? Really? It will be committed to the digital world forever."*

Before the advent of the ubiquitous cable sports channel, movies were pretty free to try and disguise an actor's lack of ability in a sport and few people objected. Our standards are so high now; our understanding of what an athlete at the top of their game looks like in action has become more sophisticated. The modern audience is not likely to accept a forty-year-old actor like William Bendix playing a teenaged Babe Ruth as he did in 1948 in *The Babe Ruth Story*. He didn't swing a bat like the Bambino did either.

> RON SHELTON: *I thought that actor athletes were terrible: Gary Cooper and Tony Perkins being the great examples. But they were all terrible athletes. Terrible. And when they cut to the double, it's even more obvious how bad they were. So if I was ever going to make a sports movie and I've made a number of them, I'll use guys who can actually play. I've never used a stunt double.*
>
> *I rely on real ability. It takes me out of the movie when I see a movie that doesn't do it that way. It may not take other people out, but it takes me out. Cutting to the ball going through the basket… I do that too, but half the time, there's no cutaway. You don't have to see the springboard Woody uses when he dunks or how high the basket really is. But he's really doing it. We just make sure we train them on the little stuff, the behind-the-back dribbles, the rosin bag, how you step into the batter's box: the little details that are so telling.*

Times have changed…

> RON SHELTON: *I understand why Gary Cooper worked, baseball wasn't on TV. My mother loved Gary Cooper and loved* Pride of the Yankees. *But I could never get past how bad the baseball was. Or Babe Ruth, William Bendix is 40 playing an orphan: a 40-year-old guy playing the*

15-year-old Babe Ruth! But television now is so relentless with ESPN and all the coverage, it's unforgivable to have bad sports. I think I was a little ahead of the curve on that one. You're competing with television, SportsCenter or Fox Sports.

I made a fundamental mistake on my first directing effort, *Jake Speed*. The role of the sidekick called for the character to play catch, with a baseball and glove, with the lead character, when they would have heart-to-heart talks. It was a more visual way to stage pretty straightforward dialogue. I knew the lead could throw a ball and look good doing it. The sidekick assured me that he could throw a baseball with the best of them. I had no reason to doubt him as he had made his name in a movie that required athletic ability. The scene was designed very carefully. Two heroes, contemplating life, playing catch as the warm, red sun went down over a shimmering African lake, elephants frolicking at the water's edge. Not only was the timing critical to make this shot, but the entire film company had to travel by boat along with our equipment to this remote, pristine location. As I said, lots of planning went into this one. So everything was going according to plan. The crew was setting up the shot, so I decided to rehearse the scene with my two actors. They put on their baseball gloves, I threw out the ball and they proceeded to play catch and run lines. But wait a second! Something was very wrong. The sidekick threw like, let's say, many girls do: awkwardly. My eye started to twitch. My stomach began to do somersaults. The star looked at me strangely. I stopped the rehearsal and asked the sidekick as politely as I could, why he was throwing that way, like he never played baseball in his life? His response was, "Why? Is there a problem?" He played that one about as well as any less-than-truthful actor could. Hours from civilization, no roads out of there, thousands of miles from Hollywood, my choices were limited. So I shot the scene in a way I knew I could cut around his obvious inability to throw a baseball like someone who could actually play baseball well. The lesson here is, try not to take the word of an actor as to his or her physical abilities and skills. That goes for ball games, horseback riding, surfing, bowling … whatever. If you haven't seen footage of them performing the task, you need to ask them to demonstrate the skill they must possess for the role. Watch them throw, kick, swim, or jump. Only then, should you offer them the job, if they meet your standards.

DAVID WARD: *You have to be very careful in casting. Every actor will tell you that they are experienced at the game that they played at some serious level. They will tell you that just like every actor they can ride a horse, because they want the part. So if you don't test*

*them and actually see if they can do what the script requires, then
you may get a bad surprise. You actually take them out and see if they
can throw a football. See if they can catch a football, play catch with
them and you can tell.*

You have to be sure…

RON SHELTON: *On* White Men Can't Jump, *we had basketball trials
before an actor could read. We started with the gym. I threw a ball out
there and I could quickly eliminate 90% of the guys. There were some
stars that came in and they were just humiliated. It was insulting to me
that they would come in. It's like saying you can play flamenco guitar.
Ok. There's a guitar, show me. So I went through all of that and then
brought in guys to actually read.*

DAVID WARD: *You have to make sure they can at least look like they can
play the sport. If you get them out there and they can't, then you got
a big problem. You can't teach people how to play a sport, particularly
in a sport like baseball where you're asking them to throw accurately
or to catch a baseball. If you've never done it, you can't just suddenly
start doing it and make it look real. I have to say except for Wesley
Snipes. Wesley had not played much baseball, but he was a dancer
and a fantastic athlete. The thing that impressed me so much about
him in* Major League *was, he learned not only how to hit, but to hit
under the baseball to get pop-ups, which we needed to get on camera.
Today they would do that all CGI to do something that specific. He has
amazing hand-eye coordination.*

I don't think there's anything you can do to test an actor's athletic ability and
skills that's too much. This is such a critical factor, one that will make or break
your production. Take no shortcuts and assume nothing. It's too important.

RON SHELTON: *When I got Kevin Costner involved in* Bull Durham, *he
was about to break as a star but he wasn't yet. In Hollywood you say
you have Kevin Costner, they knew what you meant. In Peoria, they
didn't. Kevin liked the script but he said, "Before you hire me, I have
to audition for you." And I was desperate to have him. So we drove
out to a batting cage, video arcade, and miniature golf course with
a pocket full of quarters. We played catch in the parking lot. And the
truth is, you see a guy catch a ball once, you know if he can play. I
don't need to see anything more. Then we went to the batting cages,
nobody recognized him. He looked beautiful from the right side, he*

switch-hit … great. I thought to myself I'll never find an athlete this good who was also right for the part.

Every actor you cast, in any kind of movie, is a vital choice. One bad actor or one that performs below the standard set by the rest of your cast can take an audience out of the story. It will make them suddenly aware of the fact that the world on screen is fictional. The same goes for the actors surrounding your principal actors, who, we'll agree for the sake of argument, are totally persuasive in their role as athletes. You will have to find other athletes who may have no lines in the movie, but have roles to be the players who comprise the rest of the team your stars play on. They have to look right. They too are a challenge to find.

RON SHELTON: *What's really interesting and difficult and I have not shot, but I could someday, is football. I've talked to the producers, the directors, the first ADs, and the stunt coordinators. It's really a bitch. The part that's forgiving is that everyone's got a helmet. But how many hits can you take and who are those guys? Because stuntmen aren't necessarily athletes. You need to get real football players who are going to take stunt bumps, but they can't be professional because of the risk and their contracts won't allow it. So where do you find those guys? It's really tough.*

  On Friday Night Lights, *the movie, I think NFL Films' guys shot the action. But it was only like five plays a night, only. It takes hours to set that stuff up and shoot. And the hits had to look better than real. There were lots of takes to get it right, night lighting, and there's a ton of action in that movie. But I remember the big problem was, who can actually do it? He can't use college players because they can't take money because of the NCAA. And you can't go around it by giving money to the school's program. They can't take $100 or even $50! On a shoot I was doing for Liberty Mutual, I was shooting a story about a woman's softball team. We couldn't even contribute a few thousand dollars to the college whose field I was using and that had a team that could have provided players. So I had to find a girls' club team and that was a nightmare. I finally found them at USC because they don't have a regular team, they have a club team. It was finals week and I had to let the pitcher go to take her final exam in one of our trailers. But again, I had real players surrounding my three actors. And the three actors could play.*

There's a more sublime test of an actor's appropriateness for the part of an athlete. Yes, they have to play the game like the person they're portraying would've. If they're playing a champion, they must play like a champion. But the moments in between, the behavior and attitude they display between their moments of action, are critical. How do they stand in the on-deck circle and swing the fungo bat or how do they line up a tough putt on a green or even just stand there and wait their turn to bowl? Elite athletes have a way of doing it we can all recognize.

> RON SHELTON: *You must teach a guy to walk right, wear his uniform right, and swagger right. We had more trouble teaching Kevin how to stand up, lean against his putter on the green, and tee up a ball, than how to hit one. There's a way the pros do it; there's a way you get into the batter's box, there's a way you pick up the rosin bag. Learn those details.*

When casting, behavior reveals a lot, both in front of the camera and before you even get to that point.

> RON SHELTON: *When I cast the rest of the movie, I would put a baseball on the table in the audition room, because a ballplayer couldn't help but pick it up. I could tell how someone picked it up and rubbed it. Later I put a bat out. The athletes had to touch it and the nonathletes were afraid of it. That was sort of my audition.*
>
> *And where Tim Robbins may not be a totally convincing pitcher, he was big, goofy, and gawky enough and he was perfect in every other way: that was my area of forgiveness. Costner did every stunt, he hit for himself, he caught, he hit two balls out of the park even though you can't tell on camera, but he did. He played high school ball and a little bit at Cal State Fullerton.*

Special techniques

> DAVID WARD: *The problem with that is if you're trying to speed up how fast a pitch looks, if you do that you're also speeding up the pitcher's motion to an extent that starts to look Charlie Chaplinesque. What I used to do was if I was shooting behind home plate toward the pitcher, I would actually move the plate up 10 feet and use a slightly wider lens that emphasizes speed. Because you're (the audience) isn't looking down at where the plate is. I would use a slightly wider-angle lens so the guy is pitching 60'6" is throwing 50'6." So Charlie Sheen, who could throw in the low 80s, could use that 10 feet to throw the ball in*

the mid-90s. It looks like the same distance, but man, especially the last half, the ball really comes in like it's on fire. When you're shooting behind the pitcher, it's a little more difficult because he's on the mound and it's harder to cheat the distance because of the way baseball fields are constructed. So you can move it up a little bit, but not very far. What you tend to do then, is you go on a longer lens and stack it up. It can make it look like the ball is getting there a little quicker.

DAVID WARD: *When I did* Major League, *we did everything live. But I had ballplayers who could really play ball. But in baseball movies now, you'll see a shot on a guy pitching and then you do a reverse on the hitter hitting the ball. I never like that. First of all, the speed of the ball coming out of the pitcher's hand and the speed of the ball going to the batter looked phony to me. So I always try to have the pitcher and the hitter in the same shot. I could do that because I was using real ballplayers, mostly minor league guys who could really hit. It just looks better and Charlie could really pitch. But sometimes you can waste a lot of time.*

DAVID WARD: *Today with technology, you would just have them go into his motion with the ball, David Keith swings and you put the ball in digitally and you would never know the difference. The only problem with that is timing the swing to the delivery of the pitch. If there's an imaginary ball and the batter waits too long to swing, it looks like the ball went in there at 25 miles an hour. So you have to have the pitcher throw a few real balls so that the batter can figure out how long after the ball is released does he have to swing to make it look real.*

RON SHELTON: *Woody was a good basketball player but not a particularly great athlete but knew the game. Wesley was a great athlete, but knew nothing about basketball. So Wesley we just taught skills to; behind the back dribbling, he could jump. He wasn't that tall but could jump above the rim. So we had an okay athlete and a great athlete and we had to train them just to do certain things. And then I mixed in real players with the actors.*

How I'd make it look real was I made scripts. All the players and all the games had scripts of plays. There were like 20 basic plays. We run it from the left then we'd run it from the right. They were numbered one through twenty. You ran one through twenty left, then one through twenty, left. They were basically "backdoor" plays and "pick and rolls": basic fundamental basketball. I could call in a play any time and say, let's do number 12 from the right side. So they run all the plays until I had all the stuff I needed, then I'd let them play a pickup game so that I could get the fumbles and the sweat, all the stuff you can't stage, I got and I would cut the two together. So I was cutting between the real game in the staged game. The ball is fumbled and kicked around all the time, but try to stage it and it looks that way. That's how I did it.

I would just say play and I would shoot all of the magazine on a few cameras, shooting different sizes. If there is some little bit I didn't get, I just go back and shoot. I'd say to one of my better players, run a "backdoor" on Wesley and Wesley didn't know what that meant, so I'd get real reactions.

Actor safety

Stars want to do their own stunts all the time. I say to them, "If you do that and get hurt, it's not on you, it's on me."

Ron Shelton

When it comes to sports movies, there are special things you have to think about that you don't for regular movies, because your actors are doing a lot of physical activity they aren't used to doing and they can get hurt. And if they get hurt then you can't use them. An actor may tell you they play pickup basketball every weekend. That's good, but a couple of hours a week is not that much when compared to the hours it takes to shoot a pickup game. An actor will tell you they're in a baseball league made up of Screen Actors Guild (SAG) members. Fine, at least you know they enjoy and probably understand the game. But the role you're offering will require hour after hour, take after take, angle after angle to capture the action. That's a lot of wear and tear on most people's bodies, and so the greatest caution and care must be exercised to preserve your cast's health.

A very useful role professional athletes/coaches can bring to your production is to train and condition everyone who will be playing an athlete. On larger-budget pictures, the cost of this form of rehearsal is readily accepted. They lead the cast in an exercise regime that resembles the exercise programs of professional and college sports departments. The camp will condition your actors in order to improve their stamina. Tired actors are more prone to injury. The training is to prevent injuries that occur due to a number of factors and can be a significant setback for your production. You have to go in assuming someone will be injured. With that pessimistic view in mind, the less physically prepared an actor is, the more you're risking disasters large and small.

DAVID WARD: *Whoever choreographs the action may be the same professional person that is running what we call the sports boot camp. This includes improving everyone's physical abilities and also getting them in shape and physical condition so that they're not breaking down physically.*

You have to pay everyone who participates in training before a production begins. Even though it's for your cast's benefit, it's really for the benefit of the production by trying to limit delays due to injury. So if your production is more modestly budgeted, you may have to figure out a way for your actors to condition themselves on their own time, unsupervised. Maybe a day or two of instruction would be a meaningful way to begin that process and less expensive than a two-week boot camp. You just have to hope they don't injure themselves getting into shape without supervision. Something's better than nothing, maybe.

Even though most actors try and stay in relatively good shape to be ready to take on physically demanding roles (and to look their best), the physical demands of shooting take after take of a strenuous action can cause even the fittest actor to become vulnerable to injury.

RON SHELTON: *I had a former NBA scout and an assistant coach running a camp, it was like a boot camp. It ran the whole show. We had to scatter the basketball throughout the schedule because guys would get injured, movie stars would get shin splints, because you're playing all day on asphalt. That's why we booked all the players for the whole show, because I didn't know how their bodies would hold up. We set up the schedule not knowing whether after six or eight hours of playing, their bodies would go or if it would be after two or three days. In fact, we realized about three days into shooting* White Men Can't Jump, *shooting at Venice Beach, from about 7 o'clock in the morning till 6 o'clock at night on asphalt, we needed masseuses. We didn't have any special medics, but we really needed someone to deal with the soreness.*

We also had a baseball camp in Bull Durham. *We were in Durham in September to shoot October 1. The minor league season had just finished. We discovered that the guy who had just managed the real Durham Bulls was looking for a job. His name was Grady Little. He ended up managing the Red Sox and the Dodgers. He was kind of like Crash Davis looking for the next thing to do, so we hired him. He put together a bunch of players from junior college or whoever he could find and fill it out.*

As is the case with stunts and special effects, there's a larger consideration looming over any production where there's risk to an actor or a crew member's health and safety. You have to see the big picture: what's really important. It can't just be about the shot or about the movie. Those very important considerations, which are key, must take a backseat to safety.

> DAVID WARD: *There's something the director always has to be aware of. It's really part of the larger comprehension of the safety issue. As a director, you're always pressing for the best possible shot, but you always have to make sure it's safe. There is that ethical aspect to the job. Too many directors just don't think about it. There's both a production and a moral issue here. You can worry about your actors from the point of view of the production by not having them available if something happens, but you should be worrying about the moral point of view. It's not worth anybody getting hurt. It's just not. There's always another way to do it.*

An interesting aspect to this world of sports and jocks concerns a cultural or psychological component to putting together teams that will exist only on-screen. The egos on display in competitive arenas or virtual competitive arenas such as a sports movie set can create a special situation. There can be a lot of pride at stake, just like there is in a real competitive environment. Pro players or very accomplished athletes who are working in a movie have been known from time to time to feel the need to prove how tough or talented they are in their sport. Watch out for the extra hard or late hit. It's not unheard of for a signal to be sent to the actors to make them acutely aware that they're not the real deal, only pretenders. This behavior can make these athletes, turned actors, feel as important as or superior to the star. If you sense that kind of tension, you owe it to the show you're on and to the cast and crew to ensure safety by addressing any potentially dangerous behavior right away.

> DAVID WARD: *I had a situation in* The Program *with Andrew Bryniarski, who played a football player on steroids. The first play that we ran on the first day of shooting, there's a play where a guard pulls and blocks him and he sheds the block and he makes the tackle. And I told the guard who is an ex-professional football player, I said "look don't hit Andrew hard. Let him overpower you and shed you so he can get in the backfield and tackle the running back." And this guy, everyone was looking at Andrew who was a bodybuilder, not a football player, and thought "oh so this guy thinks he's tough. So in this first practice play, I'm going to pancake him. Welcome to real football Mr. Muscleman."*

So he hit Andrew. Andrew went down and broke his hand. I fired the guy immediately who did it. But here's my actor Andrew on the first shot of the movie and he breaks his hand. You have to make sure when your real actors are in any kind of physical scene and this tends to happen in sports movies, that everyone is aware of how it has to go for them to safely make the play.

Now we put a cast on Andrew's hand and wrapped it, which for a defensive end is something you're used to seeing in football. So no one really knew his hand was broken. And after that, all the football guys accepted him because he never complained about it. We were lucky in that instance. The thing you really have to think about in any sports movie is that the actors are going to be doing their own stunts. So you have to get them in shape, you have to choreograph things very carefully so that it not only looks good but they don't get hurt.

Of course the crew needs to take special precautions when shooting sports. Hard balls, buzzing through the air from all angles, can catch someone looking through a lens or connecting a cable unaware. Wooden bats and metal clubs are being swung in the air. The crew person who's focused on their task could walk right into a backswing. So everyone needs to be on high alert, which will certainly be discussed in a safety meeting. When shooting the action, not only could bats and clubs be swinging, but big, heavy, and, sometimes, well-padded men are running around focused on their task. How do crew members trying to capture the action stay safe?

DAVID WARD: *If a guy on the crew [is] going to get hit, they're probably going to get hit in the legs by someone falling into them. That's also why we rehearse so much. We also make the players incredibly aware of where the camera is at all times.*

In baseball you have to protect your camera sometimes from batted balls. If the pitchers [are] pitching to a hitter, we usually shoot with a big piece of Plexiglas, which we either just shoot through or have a hole cut out for the lens to fit into.

The chances of the ball hitting the lens is pretty small, but the pro players we often use can hit a line drive pretty hard and if your crew is standing there and they're not looking at the ball because they're concentrating on doing their job, then all of the sudden, bam! Somebody gets hit and you have a bad injury. So I have everyone wear a batting helmet when they're out on the field, because you never know when a ball is going to ricochet off something and hit you in the head. You always take safety precautions. But mostly, you try to anticipate by saying let's build something safe around the camera, so if the ball is hit in the direction of the camera, the crew is protected. You've gotta be heads-up. The camera crew's not just looking at the action, they're looking at the camera.

Crowds

One of the elemental pieces to the narrative puzzle of creating stories in the world of sports is the crowd: the fans. It's through their reaction to the action on the field or court that an audience can perceive the storyteller's point of view on the action. The triumph, disappointment, tension, or relief that fans so clearly reflect is a hugely effective storytelling device. The cheers, the fists raised in the air, the snarling, or joyful tears are all effective visual and aural storytelling tools. How to go about assembling a large sports crowd figures into the calculation of how to shoot the scene. Cost and plausibility are major factors that combine with storytelling value to suggest a path.

DAVID WARD: *You always want the crowd to react to what's happening in front of the camera. If there's a close play, somebody misses a ball, you want the crowd to be able to specifically react to that. You cannot do that with a crowd that's been digitally inserted into your movie. If you did try to insert a digital crowd that does some specific action, I'm not sure that would be less expensive than if you had the real thing, as long as you're not paying the real people or at least most of them. So there is the calculation of how many extras are we going to be able to get, how many of them are we going to have to pay versus the cost of creating the same result digitally. That's now the big question when you're doing a sports movie.*

Those images, whether portrayed as background to the principal action or as featured shots that cut away from the main action, are akin to the reaction shot in drama and comedy. It's through reaction shots that we take in as an indicator of how to feel about what we're watching on screen. It's not that reaction shots or crowd cutaways will necessarily reveal a mystery (although they might), but they will either confirm or further illustrate what we suspect we should feel. Crowd shots in sports movies or scenes are a character. The crowd plays an important role in the telling of any story that uses sports. But the challenges of shooting a crowd are huge. The most obvious problem is the sheer numbers that normally attend a game. On the professional and college level, a stadium can hold from 20,000 to 100,000 fans. Minor league baseball games can require a few hundred or a few thousand people. The logistics of bringing in and managing a large crowd are enormous.

> RON SHELTON: *Having a real crowd is a disadvantage because they're slow to wrangle with their bathroom breaks and coffee breaks and they're always moving around … I'd rather have 400 extras that I control and the digital world. It's just a waste of time and it's expensive. You have to have the extra crew to bring them in, process them, and feed them. But you need that detail from shooting a crowd.*

Depending on the type of sport, level of game, and special circumstances, the numbers vary widely. But just know that extras are expensive. If your production is a SAG signatory, there are minimum amounts of union extras or "background actors" you must hire at certain rates, plus fringe benefits. And you have to feed them. Often the pay structure is tiered when compensating extras. So the more you hire, there can be one or more price breaks that help mitigate the cost. That cost still is usually unacceptable.

The most obvious way around paying thousands of extras is to shoot your story during, before, or after a real game where a crowd is already gathered. This certainly saves a lot of money, but has its challenges as well. Since anyone and everyone who is recognizable on the screen in any movie must sign a release, giving their consent to have their image on screen, this poses an interesting question for large crowds at real games that are difficult, if not impossible to control; you post signs at every entrance that notifies everyone entering that there is a movie being shot during the game they're attending. The sign will state that if they enter into the stadium or beyond a certain point, they are giving their permission to be in the movie by going past that line. You can't have thousands of people sign releases. That will never happen.

Since your crowd is a character, you have to be able to control their behavior to support the story. If you have a real crowd, you have a chance to direct their reactions. You can't use digital technology to show great detail without incurring a gigantic expense.

> DAVID WARD: *The biggest thing, the biggest variable, in shooting sports is the extras, the crowds. People used to use paper cutouts for fans in the seats. Now we can place crowds in a shot digitally. But the thing is, if you need a crowd to do something specific, like in my movie* Major League, *the crowd was singing the song "Wild Thing." That, you cannot do digitally. You have to have real people singing "Wild Thing." And they danced around! You need a real crowd for that. Now how do you get a*

real crowd? That's something else you have to plan for. You have to plan for one big night or day that you can fill a large part of the stadium and do all your big shots for all the games on that one day or night. You're just not going to get people to come out a second night.

When trying to attract big crowds, figuring out ways to get their butts in the seats is challenging. The more resources you have, of course the easier it can be. You need a very special plan, one that springs from the specific set of circumstances you're working with. You have to offer value for the fan's time and effort.

DAVID WARD: *You can usually only promote a crowd for one night. Milwaukee had not had a movie shot there in 15 years. They were primed for something exciting. In places like Atlanta where they shoot movies all the time, you're not going to get that many people. We got very lucky in Milwaukee, where we shot* Major League. *We promoted a night where we gave away a car, a free trip to London, and we advertised the fact that we were going to have five or six cameras roaming through the stands, so that if you came to the game, you had a chance to be in the movie. We got 27,000 people! When they're standing, you place them in every other row, because you can't see the empty row between them. So you can actually make 27,000 look like 50,000. We also had a group of comedians to entertain the crowd between shots. We did not want them to get bored. We told the crowd in advance they were going to get to sing the song "Wild Thing" in the movie.*

   We also had in Milwaukee a hard-core group of extras, maybe 150, 200 people who came out every night. They would bring cookies! They got to know the actors and they were indispensable, because I would move them around and put them in every shot. They're far enough back that you never see that they're the same people.

There's so many things to think about, that if you haven't experienced it, you may never even think about. When you haven't anticipated the worst, the worst or something approaching that will happen. Planning and logistics are especially critical here due to the volume of people you're depending on to be in the stands, fairways, or sidelines.

DAVID WARD: *That night, we started shooting as soon as it got dark, which was around 7:30. Most people are going to bring their kids, so they're going to leave earlier. So you really have to get most of your stuff by midnight. A lot of people start to leave around 10:00. That means you have to get your biggest stuff right away. But I really think the singing of "Wild Thing" really got [the] crowd into it. We had the words up on the scoreboard. There were girls that came out of the crowd and jumped on top of the dugout and started to dance! I didn't ask them to do that. As a matter of fact, I was scared to death. I thought, what if one of them falls off? What's our liability here? I mean I loved it and I asked if we had a camera on that. Are we getting this? They said we got it.*

There's nothing like the real thing. Real people, in a crowd, behaving in natural and believable ways cannot be imitated without it appearing to be just that, an imitation. True behavior is critical to the telling of any story. When a crowd spontaneously erupts in pure joy or crushing disappointment, it's movie magic. That energy is an important element to the overall story you're telling.

DAVID WARD: *It was probably the most thrilling night of shooting I've ever had. And the actors got caught up in it too. When Dennis Haysbert is rounding the bases after he hit the home run and everybody's going crazy in the stands, he said, "I've never had a rush like that as an actor." You're acting in front of the crew all the time. All of the sudden you're acting in front of 27,000 people! He said he finally understood what it's like to be a professional ballplayer. Anybody who says they can't hear it... How can they not hear? It's deafening. It was so fantastic!*

Real fans can also present challenges. It can be difficult to control the behavior of thousands of people, particularly when they're in an excited or, even, bored state. You have to be sure that you're setting the table for them to enjoy their meal. Have you created an environment that they will delight in, remain engaged in, and, as a result, deliver the performance you need? That's a tall order that will keep you up at nights.

DAVID WARD: *On the one hand, if you're doing something great, it's fantastic, but it made me think, what if you're bombing out there and the 27,000 people are booing you? That's got to be tough.*
RON SHELTON: *I had a $2 million extra budget in* Tin Cup. *You would never get that now. We had hundreds and hundreds of extras every day and the second unit shooting a lot of it. And then there is one big shot based on a famous Ben Hogan shot on the last hole of the tournament, the whole fairway and green is lined with extras. You would do that digitally now, very easily. Crowds are easier to shoot*

these days. The first time I could digitally fill stadiums, it was great. I had 500 extras in a pilot [that] was shot a couple of years ago about AAA baseball. I could shoot batters with nobody behind them in the stands and that was hugely helpful. Big money saver.

But there is the other scenario I alluded to. If you need a big crowd to react in stereotypical ways, the cheer, the groans, the silent disbelief, or the tense anticipation, by all means, shoot at a real event. What this entails is getting permission from the authorities connected with a game you've identified for its location and the sport being played. See if they'll allow you a brief window in which you can insert your actor/players onto the field or court to shoot whatever it is you have to capture. That could be before the game or at halftime, for example. The fans will be alerted as to what you're going to do, so they'll cooperate and act their part as opposed to seeming confused. You have to be very prepared, to say the least. You can't hold up a game for thousands of fans.

DAVID WARD: *We shot much of* The Program *in South Carolina. We actually shot at a real game we had 11 minutes at halftime to get 14 shots we had six cameras. We had the camera crew move from camera to camera. The cameras were all set up so they do a shot and they rotate onto the next camera for the next shot. Sometimes after a shot the camera team would wrap the camera and reset it up in another position for the next shot. It was very well orchestrated. In so we actually didn't have six cameras, we had three cameras, but we used them in a way that gave us the advantage as if we had six cameras. So we did get 14 shots in 11 minutes.*

RON SHELTON: *The only time I ever shot at a real event was for my boxing movie* Play It to the Bone *with Antonio Banderas and Woody Harrelson. That's a real crowd. It was a fight in Las Vegas where we put our extras to fill the first 10 rows. I think if I were to have to do that today, it would be done digitally.*

Special qualifications for crew

Different strokes for different folks or boats, whichever you ascribe to. Some directors value specific and long experience in the sport certain of their team may possess. The DP has to know the game. Makes sense. But not everyone feels that way. The camera operator should have experiences following the game, understanding the trajectory, speed, and acceleration of the ball, puck, or whatever. Also makes sense. The AD is another important role in which experience is highly preferable. Here's what two very accomplished directors, who are widely considered among the top directors of sports movies ever, have to say. Their styles are different as are their methods and preferences.

> DAVID WARD: *It helps to have a cinematographer who knows the sport. I always asked the question do you understand baseball or do you understand football? They all say they do. They're like actors in that sense. Ray Villalobos shot* Major League. *He's a terrific cameraman and I wasn't going to quiz him, put his feet to the fire to see if he really knows sports. It turns out he did know baseball. He was great. It's not really necessary for other crew positions to have an understanding of sports although once again it always helps. Art direction and wardrobe always can do the research. In* The Program, *having a camera operator who could follow a football flying through the air is really hard. If a camera operator has seen something done 1000 times, then of course it should help them to be able to follow the action much better, probably because they can anticipate the arc of the ball or the path the runner takes. I guess any camera operator who's used to following things at a fairly rapid pace would be good shooting a sports movie.*

Be insistent that your camera team has taken into account the finer points of a game. Like anything else, unless there's someone on the team that does understand the game, then saying you're prepared is not the same as being prepared. Take that advice from someone who knows the game of golf intimately and understands that understanding a game's dynamics isn't the same as knowing how to shoot it. It helps, but there's another dimension to it.

Shelton agrees; camera operators should have the experience of following a ball hit off the end of a bat or a football spiraling over defenders' outstretched arms.

> RON SHELTON: *Before I shot* Tin Cup, *I brought in two camera operators to go to the Riviera Open golf tournament in Los Angeles to watch in the control booth and go around with the handheld TV camera guys. I couldn't have done* Tin Cup *without that. "You talk about being able to anticipate," the TV camera guys said, "try catching a golf ball coming off the head of a club, it's like catching a bullet. The camera can't move that fast." So you stay loose and there's a subtle move, you can hardly see it, it's actually anticipating the flight and its opening up wider. Otherwise it'll be herky-jerky. The camera guys know the players with slow swings and the ones who are quick on the downswing; the*

tv guys know everybody's moves. They tend to know the low ball flight guys and the high ball flight guys and that, really saved us. The hardest sport I ever shot was golf, by far. The golf world is so critical of a bad golf swing. We had two PGA guys, CBS announcers who were former players who were top golf teachers. Every time we shot golf, we flew them in. They were there looking at the monitor and they would go print it or don't print it. But, I generally like my cinematographer to not know the difference. Robert Leighton, who cut Bull Durham, *is British and had never been to a baseball game. My editor, Paul Seydor, knows football because he played it, but he really didn't know the other sports. I like that they're approaching it fresh.*

The consensus is that the people behind the camera, the operators, must have experience shooting sports. Knowing how balls react when hit, the arc of a basketball shot from thirty-three feet, is all the more reliably captured by someone who's done it a lot.

JEFF TUFANO: *I think you just have it or you don't. It's a very physical job, very demanding. You have to be flexible, you have to be coordinated. I think you can learn some of the skills, certainly composition is something you can learn. You can look at a book and learn all kinds of things about composition. But the actual ability to frame things in lifetime and be accurate, that is a natural ability. When I was a camera assistant, I had to work really, really hard to be a good assistant and in the end I did. I never took it for granted though. When it became time for me to become a camera operator, not only was I an athlete, right out of the University of Miami, I got a job on something called "cable television." It was brand new. This company shot many different sporting events like University of Miami baseball and football. I also worked for NFL Films. I also shot tennis, jai alai, a little bit of winter league baseball, lots of different sports. So right out of school, I never had the chance to stop and be afraid and say oh my God what if I can't do this? All of the sudden, I was just doing it. And since I played sports, I had a sense of what was happening, where the ball was going. I had a feel for it. Later on this experience helped me professionally when I shot a movie called* Eddie *with Whoopi Goldberg. I could follow the basketball all over the place because I played and understood the game.*

The thing in live sports is if you don't get the shot and they have to cut to your camera and…uh oh…nothing's there, because you didn't get the shot: you don't come back the next day. So I underwent a lot

of really valuable training for shooting fast moving action. I can't say
enough how blessed I was to have the opportunities I had early in my
career that prepared me for shooting sports in stunts.

Your AD's is also a position that demands experience and familiarity with the
sport you're shooting.

RON SHELTON: *My AD has got to be a sports guy. I lean on him heavily.*
If he says we're set up at first base, I know we're set up at first base.
If I say set up the double play because I have to go set up something
over here, it'll look real. My AD happens to be a former baseball player
and a golfer and a jock. But I like the other guys to be fresh.

On the subject of the importance of your AD knowing the sport you're
shooting, both directors agree: it's a must.

DAVID WARD: *It really is helpful when your AD knows the sport you're*
shooting. You just don't have to explain so much. If someone doesn't
understand the game for instance, they don't know how to have extras
react in certain situations. I don't want to crowd reactions to be too
big, like every play's at a World Series. That is one of the things you
really have to look for and pay attention to in sports movies: what the
extras are doing what they look like. Sometimes they can do things
even way in the background that calls attention to them that will drive
you crazy. It has to be consistent with what's really going on with the
stakes or the story and the AD should understand this. So you really
have to have someone watch them who knows what's appropriate.

Even when you have the experienced guys in key crew positions, you may
need to call in other experts, people who have specific experience filming
a specific sport. They will bring with them a bag of tricks that addresses
challenges even the more sports-experienced filmmakers may not have.
Cameramen in network or cable television, for example, may know not only
about camera placement or camera moves to catch a ball in flight as it leaves
a bat or club, which is huge, but also the specific tendencies of many players.
This can be a big help if you can put your camera team together with those
TV pros who can share their experience and insight for a much better result
in your movie.

Final Words

Experience, collaboration, sound judgment, respect for the safety of your coworkers: stunts and special effects bring excitement to the stories we tell. The underlying themes I've detailed are common to all forms of stunts, special effects, and, in some ways, filmmaking in general; only the stakes are higher if something goes wrong. Be safe, be smart, have fun, be wildly creative. Go out there and work with great, experienced pros who will make you look good. Learn from them, benefit from your collaboration with them. They love what they do and they will go to the ends of the earth to help you make the very best movie possible.

List of Authorities Quoted in the Book

John Badham—Director, Producer
60 directing credits—features and TV
17 producing credits

Notable works
Saturday Night Fever
War Games
Blue Thunder
Bird on a Wire
Nick of Time
The Bingo Long Traveling All-Stars & Motor Kings

Martin Campbell—Director
30 credits: features and television

Notable works
Two James Bond movies: *Casino Royale* and *GoldenEye*
The Mask of Zorro
The Legend of Zorro
Vertical Limit
Killer Women (Executive Producer, new television series, 2014)

David Ward—Director, Writer
Academy Award-winning writer and successful director of many feature films

Notable works

Writer—14 features:
The Sting (Academy Award winner)
Sleepless in Seattle
Major League
Major League II
The Program

Director—7 features:
Major League
Major League II
The Program
Cannery Row
King Ralph
Down Periscope

Ron Shelton—Director, Writer
Known for his outstanding movies about people in the world of sports

Notable works
Bull Durham
White Men Can't Jump
Tin Cup
Cobb
Play It to the Bone

Buddy Joe Hooker—Stuntman, Expert Driver, Stunt Coordinator
Hundreds of movies as a stuntman and coordinator; a true living legend

Notable works
Grindhouse
To Live and Die in L.A.
Close Encounters of the Third Kind
The 40-Year-Old Virgin
One of the most honored stuntmen in the history of motion pictures. Cofounder
    of Stunts Unlimited.

Gayle Hooker—Stunt Performer
Stunt coordinator, stunt performer

Dan Bradley—Stunt Coordinator, Second Unit Director
One of the very top stunt coordinators and second unit directors currently
    working in the world

Notable works
The Bourne Supremacy
The Bourne Ultimatum
The Bourne Legacy
Spider-Man 2
Spider-Man 3

Dan Lebental—ACE Editor
A leading editor and innovator

Notable works
Iron Man
Iron Man 2
Thor: The Dark World
Cowboys & Aliens
Elf
Couples Retreat
From Hell

Dan Speaker—Sword Master, Stunt Coordinator
A leading authority and expert in the field of swordsmanship and scholar in the
    field of historical weaponry

Notable works
Master and Commander: The Far Side of the World
Hook

The New World
Hidalgo
The Three Musketeers

Jan Bryant—Movement Expert, Stunt Coordinator
A leading authority and educator in the field of stage combat and movement

Notable works
Master and Commander: The Far Side of the World
Hook
The New World
Hidalgo
The Three Musketeers

James Lew—Martial Arts Choreographer, Fight and Stunt Coordinator
One of the most respected experts and practitioners in Hollywood, with dozens
and dozens of credits in features, television, and online

Notable works
Inception
Pirates of the Caribbean: At World's End
Traffic
Get Smart

Dale Gibson—Cowboy, Stunt Rider, Stunt Coordinator

Notable works
3:10 to Yuma
The Assassination of Jesse James by the Coward Robert Ford
Deadwood
Pirates of the Caribbean: The Curse of the Black Pearl
Behind Enemy Lines
The Mask of Zorro

Roy Wagner ASC—Director of Photography
Noted cinematographer of dozens of TV shows and features

Notable works
CSI: Crime Scene Investigation
Burn Notice
Elementary
Nick of Time
Drop Zone

Jeff Tufano—Camera Operator
Dozens of feature and TV credits

Notable works
Oblivion
The Fast and the Furious
The Twilight Saga: Breaking Dawn—Part 2

G.I. Joe: Retaliation
Lee Daniels' The Butler

Linda Montanti—First Assistant Director
Dozens of credits in features and TV

Notable works
L.A. Confidential
The Time Machine
Righteous Kill
American Horror Story
Turbulence
White Mile

Mike Tristano—Armorer, Weapons Expert, Special Effects Makeup Artist
Master armorer for 500 movies and TV shows

Notable works
The Purge
Vanished
God Bless America
Top Shot (TV series—seasons 1–5)
Harsh Times

John Hartigan—Special Effects Coordinator and Supervisor
Dozens of credits in movies and TV

Notable works
Hawaii Five-0
Kill Bill: Vol. 1
Kill Bill: Vol. 2
American Beauty
Catch Me If You Can
Charlie Wilson's War
Dexter
Hung
Enlightened

John Chichester—Art Director
Dozens of credits in movies and TV

Notable works
Pirates of the Caribbean: On Stranger Tides
47 Ronin
Alien: Resurrection
The Book of Eli

Paul Holehouse—Entertainment Risk Consultant for Fireman's Fund Insurance Co.

German Guttierez—Director of Production Safety, Gallagher Insurance

Sources

Dale Gibson interviewed by phone at his ranch, Sunland, CA, December 11, 2013.

Dan Bradley interviewed at the Academy of Motion Pictures Arts and Sciences, Beverly Hills, CA, May 7, 2012.

Dan Lebental interviewed at his office, Universal City, CA, September 21, 2013.

Dan Speaker and Jan Bryant interviewed by phone at their studio, Los Angeles, CA, November 23, 2013.

David Ward interviewed at his home, Los Angeles, CA, November 8, 2013.

Gayle and Buddy Joe Hooker interviewed at their home, Los Angeles, CA, June 21, 2013.

German Guttierez interviewed by phone at his office, Los Angeles, CA, October 8, 2013.

James Lew interviewed by phone on location, San Juan, PR, January 27, 2014.

Jeff Tufano interviewed by phone on location, New Orleans, LA, December 19, 2013.

John Badham interviewed at Chapman University, Orange, CA, October 1, 2013.

John Chichester interviewed at Chapman University, Orange, CA, January 22, 2014.

John Hartigan interviewed by phone on location, Hawaii, January 12, 2014.

Linda Montanti interviewed at her home, Beverly Hills, CA, September 25, 2013.

Martin Campbell interviewed by phone at his office, Burbank, CA, January 17, 2014.

Mike Tristano interviewed by phone at his workshop, Los Angeles, CA, December 14, 2013.

Paul Holehouse interviewed by phone at his office, Burbank, CA, October 1, 2013.

Ron Shelton interviewed at his office, Los Angeles, CA, January 16, 2013. Roy Wagner interviewed by phone, Los Angeles, CA, January 16, 2014.

Publications

ATF Federal Explosives Law and Regulations 2012 http://www.atf.gov/files/publications/download/p/atf-p-5400-7.pdf.

California Workers Compensation and Safety Guide January 2013 https://www.capspayroll.com/live/upload/CAPS_California_Safety_Guide-Jan2013.pdf_2cd99.pdf.

Directors Guild of America contracts http://www.dga.org/Contracts/Rates-2013-to-2014.aspx.

IATSE contracts http://www.iatse728.org/contracts/2012_BasicAgreement_728.pdf.

Industry-Wide Labor-Management Safety Committee bulletins http://www.csatf.org/bulletintro.shtml.

Alliance of Motion Picture and Television Producers (AMPTP) Injury and Illness Prevention Program http://domesticproduction.com/amptp.htm.

Office of the State Fire Marshal, California (2013) http://osfm.fire.ca.gov/ strucfireengineer/strucfireengineer_motionpicture.php.

OSHA for Motion Picture Safety https://www.osha.gov/pls/imis/sic_manual. display?id=65&tab=group/.

Screen Actors Guild contracts (2014) http://www.sagaftra.org/production-center/ documents.

Screen Actors Guild Safety bulletins (2009) http://www.sagaftra.org/files/sag/ Safety_Bulletins_AMPTP_Part_1_9_3.pdf.

Index